Private Lives of Public Servants

Private Lives of Public Servants

Kenneth Lasson

INDIANA UNIVERSITY PRESS

Bloomington & London

Portions of chapters 1, 2, 3, and 6 have appeared in *The Washingtonian Magazine.*

Manufactured in the United States of America

Library of Congress Cataloging in Publication Data
Lasson, Kenneth.
  Private lives of public servants.
    1. Civil service—United States—Biography.
  2. United States—Officials and employees—Bio-
graphy. I. Title.
JK693.A2L37   1978   353'.00092'2   77-15758
ISBN 0-253-34606-1   1 2 3 4 5 82 81 80 79 78

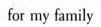

for my family

Contents

Preface

Public servants are those chosen by the People to
distribute the graft.

                                        Mark Twain

SCOUNDRELS, scallywags, scapegraces. Even when America is not being distressed by inflation or tormented by unpopular
laws or revelations of scandal in high office, many of the
people persist in their feeling that the government is made up of
elected thieves and appointed incompetents. Such cynicism may
be little more than a universal human impulse—but the fact
is our federal bureaucracy is so immense, its operation so
unwieldy, its impact often so impersonal, that a large part of
the citizenry, even those on the government payroll, would tend
to agree with Mark Twain.

We should know better. Most public servants labor under
handicaps that, taken together, are unique to the bureaucracy.
There is the absence of a tangible work product: an end to which
they could aspire or that others might admire. There is the sheer
size of the power structure. And there is the inhibiting notion that

policies are being handed down from above, running from the main trunk of the executive through its various branches to the twigs in the federal hinterlands, policies promulgated by an essentially political administration always subject to attack from the party out of office, policies that must be implemented by the career civil servant—often against his will, conscience, and common sense.

Just who are the public servants, and why are they a breed apart? A lot more goes into running the country than the activities of the relatively few elected officials. Probably no more than two percent of all government workers are in policy-setting positions; the lower echelons are seldom called upon to make a decision, and even more rarely do they have access to cash or purse strings. In fact the average bureaucrat has little to gain from dishonesty.

What the nongovernment public often overlooks is that the bureaucracy is too multifaceted to be completely bad, and that public servants are too ubiquitous to be very different from the rest of us. One's neighbor down the street is likely to be on some government payroll and will complain as loudly as anyone else about being ripped off. He is too minuscule a part of the whole to perceive himself culpable. And indeed he alone is not. While much about government may be necessarily and inherently ineffective, it is equally clear that the bureaucracy is not ridden with evil people. Incompetence and lethargy are born more of the impossible complexities generated by sheer size than by an individual's inability or his laziness.

Yet the public servant in America remains as misunderstood as the blue-collar worker or the owner of a small business. Each, of course, has a distinct personality and prejudice. Though there are innumerable plodders, many others are genuinely diligent and efficient, some even heroic, in bucking the bureaucracy.

Above all, the public servants portrayed in these pages (like most government workers) are very individual human beings who happen to share similar frustrations in their work. Thus the physician views the Food and Drug Administration as noble in its mission but evil in its means; although he is outspoken in his criticism he is strikingly accurate in his charges of malfeasance—and nothing whatever is done either to satisfy his conscience or to correct the abuses he has exposed. The meat inspector has worked diligently and competently for two decades at the Department of Agriculture, and is wrongfully charged with having accepted a bribe. The management analyst is smothered by the weight of his bureaucracy, trapped into doing a job for which he sees no value, contributing minimal input and delivering minimal output—but reluctant to sacrifice his salary and fringe benefits for something more satisfying.

Others have different concerns. The programmer is not certain whether her full-time effort promoting bicycles for the Department of Transportation is more bemusement with a current vogue than an important part of urban planning. The procurement officer at the Pentagon finds deliberate or negligent cost overruns and receives sympathy for his efforts at exposing and correcting them and assurances against future abuses—only to see more and more cost overruns. The diplomat works hard to implement foreign-policy decisions spun out from chameleonic administrations, a new one elected every four years by an unknowing populace.

The individuals from whose lives the portraits have been drawn were chosen at random, but all serve to penetrate the stereotype most commonly applied to government employees—anonymous bureaucrats shuffling paper and tangling red tape behind massive marble walls. Perhaps they reflect even more clearly than others the strengths and frailties of American society.

Appreciation is due for the assistance and encouragement of Pat Allen, Edgar and Phoebe Berman, Howard Cohn, Lisa Davidson, Julie Portnoy, Genevieve Rafferty, Richard Rubin, the Brookings Institution, the Center for Study of Responsive Law, Indiana University Press, and Loyola College; for the time given and lives shared by various public servants (particularly John Nestor, whose name and story, unlike those of the other subjects, have not been disguised); and for the support and inspiration of Barbara and Tammy.

Private Lives of
Public Servants

1

The Inspector

One man's meat is another man's poison.
Old English proverb

IS BIG OLD green car isn't what it used to be, but Thornton Daniel won't set it out to pasture. He's satisfied. His cuss words when the ignition misses exactly four times every morning before the engine finally fires carry little more thought than love taps on a steer's muzzle.

Daniel tastes the fetid air outside his white wood-frame house in Catonsville, Maryland and knows that it's going to be another hot day. Only six-fifteen, and already the heavy tattered looseleaf notebook he is carrying under one arm—the federal regulations he studies and regards as the most important book in his life, after the Bible—is beginning to pick up sweat. He opens the trunk of the car and places the book carefully between a spare tire and a large corrugated box containing tools and equipment, then slams the lid shut. That's another thing he likes about the old car: the trunk is big and cluttered, but it is like an important file cabinet. Daniel knows where to look for what he wants.

He catches a quick glance of himself in the rear-view mirror as he backs out of the driveway. His skin is tough, a bittersweet chocolate that turns darker in the summer and nearly black in the shadow cast by a hard yellow plastic helmet. The wrinkles and folds on his face are hard and sinewy. His countenance, like the rest of his body, is small. He is a well-built, wiry man. When talking he looks hard and tough, though there is no bluster in his manner, nothing of the longshoreman—only a strange, resigned kind of satisfaction. What is life if not a good day's work? Daniel likes to think that he is responsible, a totally honest person, and who of those who know him would disagree? He measures his words with his eyes, dark brown against the black, and his smile, too, is almost calculated. When it unfolds teeth glisten and a gold spot glares against the white. He shakes hands briskly and firmly, much the way he grips the steering wheel now. His hands are dry and very calloused.

I first started working in the packinghouses when I was about twelve. Ever since I was big enough I was around meat plants. I doubt if the packing house I was born near was more than fifteen hundred feet from my back door. In those days all kids worked—there was a job waiting.

I lived in that area for 28 years. When we were kids we would ride across to the old picnic grove where people used to raise hogs during the summer. In November, when the moon got right, everybody carried the hogs over to Old Man Green's place and killed them and hung them up in the trees, and the women cleaned the intestines out and the men did the scraping. In those days they killed them with a bang in the head.

Daniel steers his green sedan into a narrow alley behind an old office building, one floor of which is leased by the United States Department of Agriculture. It is a small, dreary structure, situated at angles to the Inner Harbor and The Block—Baltimore's notorious show–bar district. With one hand he reaches into the side pocket of his coat for an opened five-pack of panatelas, pulls one out, and lights up. He puts the package in an initialed briefcase resting on the seat next to him, the sort with cardboard dividers for papers and file folders. The case is lying open; Daniel places another, larger cigar and a fountain pen in his shirt pocket and checks his supply of report forms and replacement request vouchers. He is not in very much of a hurry this morning; he will be the first in the office anyway, since Beall is on temporary assignment outside the district. If he were leaving the office early, he could park just in front of the building and be off again before violating the time zone. This morning, though, he will be inside until at least eight o'clock.

I was born in Baltimore in 1911, a neighborhood called Carroll Stations, the eighth of fourteen children. Nine brothers and four sisters. Five of us are living now, all around here.

My father was a horse trader. My mother was a housewife, taking care of all the kids. We lived in an eight-room house. I had to ride horses for my father, to show them. The girls worked around the home—we had a small garden and they worked there. When most of the boys were big enough they went to work in the packinghouses.

In that area you went to public schools, all black. I went to Douglass. I guess I did as well as could be expected in school. You either learned or got whipped. When I first started school, there were two portable buildings and eight grades. There were only about five kids in the class. There weren't many people in that section of town—it was in the city limits, but there were a lot of farms, small one-man, two-man operations. If you didn't get good marks, a note went home to your parents and the old strap came off the wall. I made a couple of bad marks and I remember to this day my father made some bad marks too. With the strap.

In the summers we worked in the fields. We didn't have any need to go to camp. We had everything we wanted—swimming pools, baseball diamonds. When we were finished working in the fields, we'd play ball from sunup to sundown. Baseball.

On weekends we'd go visit my grandparents in Prince Georges County. It would take us about a day and part of the night to get down there by buggy. The whole family, sixteen people, went down in a couple buggies.

My grandfather used to tell us how he was hooked up with the underground that would steal slaves and get them to their freedom. His family was free-born itself. We never thought anything about discrimination. We were left alone. We played baseball and the team was just about fifty–fifty. Whoever could play—the best players. We stayed too busy to ever think about anything like racism.

My father was king in his house and everybody abided by his rules. I didn't have nerve enough to question anything he said. His rules were fair—you just had to work, mind your business and treat the other fellow the same as you wished him to treat you. If you didn't, you got the strap.

Up until about '29 we lived pretty good, but when the Depression hit my father lost his money. That was it. I never recall going hungry, because we had a garden and we had chickens and turkeys—we always had something to eat. It was kind of like a farmhouse—we were self-sustaining. But we didn't have money to buy clothes.

My father's business suffered even before the Depression. Automobile trade started coming along, and there wasn't many sales for horses. Then he died, in '29. Several older brothers and sisters were left to take care of the family. They didn't go into any business. They went to work. Wasn't any use going into business during the Depression— you couldn't get any money to start.

Daniel takes an old freight elevator up to his office on the fifth floor. He has been a federal meat inspector for 32 years now, and he has fashioned and refashioned his work days according to the many different schedules that he has been assigned over the years. Each has had its personal routine. He tries hard to make things fall into place the way he wants them to, showing just as much of his private side as he cares to hold up to view. Even-tempered and circumspect, he does not readily tip his hand.

In fact he cannot afford to: as both monitor and adversary he must maintain distance from the plant owners, butchers, and packers he sees every day on his rounds. His overt camaraderie is genuine, but it passes through a filter of measured aloofness. Whether that is inevitable from his particular role and circumstance—on the one hand a government official with sub-

They weren't that active in the civil rights movement. During the '60s I said to one of my sons, I don't hear much about your school with the hippie movement and battling with the policemen. He said, "Daddy, we don't have time."

They had scholarships good all the way through college. I tried to clothe them as well as I could, give them spending money when they wanted to make a trip to see a school. They all attended music school.

The thing that can make me maddest of all is to see some grown-up say about a kid that the kid is no good. Somehow or another, that burns me up. I don't think any kid I've ever met is no good. I've had other people say to me that my kids are something special, but I fail to see it, because I always live on the theory whatever you want to be you can be if you go at it. I taught my kids that—whatever you want to be, go at it. And my wife always said to them, whatever you're going to be, you have to know more than the garbage man; be a good one. If I got a job to do, I go ahead and do it, that's it.

Five minutes later Daniel is in his car and heading east on Baltimore Street. There is little activity on The Block this early in the morning save what small business is transacted in the coffee shops and at the newsstands separating the nightclubs from the movie houses and hard-core bookstores. Wisps of steam spill from subterranean sluices. A marquee reads INEEDA MANN AND THE PERSIAN PUSSYCATS. Across the street a large woman wearing red patent-leather high heels, black tights, and an open white-on-white blouse walks with her pocketbook under one arm and a toy poodle under the other. Daniel recognizes her, and his street-wise eyes narrow in disapproval. He tightens his grip on the steering wheel, chomps on his cigar, and drives through three more green traffic signals. He knows the lights by heart, but even though they are synchronized he cannot make more than five of them at a clip. At seven-thirty, having passed through the early-morning bustle of fresh vegetable and fish wholesale centers, he arrives at Castle Brothers—processors, picklers, and purveyors of kosher-style corned beef, frankfurters, wursts, and salamis.

I get paid by the government eleven cents a mile. How much mileage I put on during an average week depends on what assignment I'm on. It varies from one to another. When I worked at Hyattsville, it was around 67, 69 miles round trip.

There are roughly about 60 federal inspectors in the Baltimore area. You have to be an expert on both meat and poultry inspection. I was trained in Omaha at the stockyards, and last summer I was out to Ohio State University for a training course. Maryland has an agricultural department and meat inspection of their own. We try to work together. So far it's going along pretty good.

I'm in the GS-9 category and in the seventh step of that grade. If I was a young fellow right now, I'd be shooting for some of those 12 and 14 jobs. The young fellows start out as a 5 and within two or three years, they could be anywhere between an 8 and a 9. They are looking for qualified people.

If all the civil servants worked as hard as the meat inspectors and grading service in the USDA, things would be a lot different compared to a place like the Post Office, where you see those people going through the motions. Because these people work. They keep active. Of course, a lot of it depends on the inspector in charge, whether he's on the ball or not. If he's on the ball, the men are on the ball. If he's not on the ball, the men tend to get lax. We have round-the-clock inspection.

In the chilly receiving room at Castle Brothers, three men who seem to be blood relatives stand to one side talking. The tan-tiled chamber is shut off from the street by large steel double doors. Daniel, wearing his helmet, enters through a smaller opening within the large left-hand door. There is a strong smell of brine in the cool room's air. An open newspaper lies on a maple butcher-block counter top running the length of the rear wall, and the group standing there is engaged in a rather animated conversation about a local story. One of them, a short heavy man wearing a white apron, the edges of his paper hat accentuating his large hairy ears, waves to Daniel and offers him a cup of coffee. Daniel declines. The man's apron is already stained with red-brown juice from the day's first cutting. Two briny vats of pickled tongue, the large hunks floating in dark liquid, stand to one side. One of the men squeezes between them and passes through a glass door to the kitchen.

The majority of hot dogs are all-meat, especially the kosher ones. It's perfectly good meat, but if you are going to the market to buy a cheap hot dog, the only way you are going to get it cheap is to get cereal. Now to me, a cereal hot dog in many cases is much healthier than all-meat hot dogs. Cereal has a lot more food value.

There's no difference in the taste of kosher meat—it's just a religious way of killing the animal. But kosher meat has fewer blemishes in it because there are certain things that at the killing stage they call *kosher* and the other things they call *trayf*. On kosher meats there are certain blemishes on the lung that the slaughterer or rabbi won't take, but the gentiles will eat. Several of the rabbis and slaughterers, they call them *shochets*, are pretty good friends of mine. Kosher style, though, is just the flavor, not really kosher.

I like mostly to inspect fresh meat. When I get on fresh meat, the first thing I try to look for is a cyst or a worm and once in a while I will find one. They are right tough to find. Most of the time it just looks like a grain of rice.

In the regulations themselves there's not very many loopholes. The law is pretty tight now but it wasn't always that way. The biggest thing that changed in meat inspection was caused by health hazards. I read Upton Sinclair's book. A lot of it was truth, because back in the '20s, when I was just a kid, things that would happen around the packing-houses, if they happen now, they'd have the jailhouse full.

Daniel begins his rounds casually, passing in front of two large cooking ovens. It is very warm here, but he will remain fully suited throughout. Over the years he has found little ways to preserve his clothing through wide fluctuations in temperature and atmosphere; by the end of the day his shirt and pants and sports coat are nearly stain-free—only his boots pick up the blood and muck of the cutting-house floors.

Five ovens face the entranceway. One of the men in aprons leads Daniel to a side desk where a small stack of thin blue packing slips await. The inspector spends about fifteen minutes reviewing these carbon vouchers, then returns to the cutting area near the ovens to examine the sides of beef hung there. The time that has passed between the raw butchering of the animal and the final packaging of the meat as sandwich slices is relatively short. The tying, trimming, stamping, and processing into regular and uniform shapes, as if fashioned by a master hand, are largely automated. There is little red blood left in the meat by this time, so the cooks' aprons are almost clean as the men stack their heavy-laden trays in the stainless steel stoves.

The ovens are over six feet high. They appear to have been recently scrubbed: by regulation, the gauge clusters and door fronts must be washed several times a day. There is a corresponding rule for most of the cooks' and cutters' activities. Thornton Daniel watches casually as the men move from oven to meat table and back again.

Contrary to the general impression, none of the meat inspector's time is spent stamping an animal. We may stamp canned goods, but not freshly slaughtered meat. We have control of the brands and we lock them up and we release them for use—but company employees use the stamps on the animals. Most people think that all a meat inspector does is stamp animals. What we're interested in is what's thrown away; we have to keep track of that. What's good the packer will take care of.

There would be a great change if inspectors weren't around all the time. If one would be away even just for a day or so, or if you go on vacation, or if you change inspectors, or something happens, it would just deteriorate overnight. You're really being a watchdog here. You simply have to be. There is a certain adversary process.

The only thing we look out for at state plants is their labels. Once in a while the supervisor goes around inspecting for sanitation. We really don't have any authority or any duties in a state plant, not unless they get out of line. The circuit supervisor and the director both make periodic checks of these plants.

In the last 20 to 25 years they've made a lot of big changes. At one time you could take 'most any building material to put up a wall in the packinghouse, but now it all has to be a hard surface that is readily washable and that the water won't penetrate. When I was a kid I remember the walls used to be filthy, but not now. You can make it any color you want to. Some of them are brown, some are white. Most of them are a light color. The floor, too, has to be a hard surface that can be easily washed. All the utensils have to be rust resistant and easily washed. And the detergents that are used have to be approved by the Department of Agriculture. They can't just use any kind of detergent. Even hard soap has to be approved.

About ten years ago things were a lot worse. Now, though you always have loopholes somewhere, just about everything that you can regulate is covered. They used to put meats in tubs and they used to have it loose. We used to have salted bellies come in from one of the big meat companies and they would be open, have no cover on them. But since the government a couple of years ago passed a new law, the Clean Meat Act, everything has to be in a container now. It makes it work out a lot better.

And it used to be that it was easier for meat to get contaminated because the cartons weren't of very good material. In the '50s you could pack the meat hot and by the time it was frozen, blood had caused the carton to fall apart. A certain percentage would come loose. Then the packers found out *they* were losing money too. Not only were they losing the stuff that broke through and got contaminated, but the inspectors would throw a lot away. By putting out a few cents more and buying a better carton and chilling it before they package it, they're now getting a better product all around—and saving themselves money.

Most of the cartons now are waxed on the inside. That wax throws off the juices. You have some products that even have to be put into paraffin bags, into plastic bags, and then put into cartons.

Swinging open the thick heavy door on oversized hinges, a white-frocked worker at Castle Brothers escorts Daniel into the walk-in freezer. The inspector carries with him a bunch of blue carbon receipts. He must check their dates against those stamped on the sides of beef just put into cold storage. What is important in the meat business is the time sequence from truck to freezer to oven. Daniel and the foreman peer closely at a line of shanks. After five minutes the inspector returns to the outer room.

A young man with a sallow complexion and a pock-marked face, his straggly long hair covered by a paper hat, is squatting on his haunches, pulling out a lower oven shelf. The odor of tallow wafts from within. Thornton Daniel, seeing the boy's tattooed forearm and black boots, is reminded of an Army cook he once knew. Protruding from the boy's back pocket is a tattered paperback potboiler, *Seven Angels in Hell*.

Relighting his panatela, Daniel goes back into the receiving room. The double doors are now wide open, and a flatbed trailer loaded with steel tubs can be seen backing noisily into a nearby yard. The three men in aprons and overalls have gone into their small paneled office; Daniel enters as they are pouring and drinking coffee. The company's delivery trucks are dispatched from this office. The hairy-eared man is giving instructions to a driver, who is also sipping coffee, decorating the top of his styrofoam cup with thumbnail prints while checking the day's appointments: four dozen tongues to the Pimlico Hotel, corned beef for the commissary of a sandwich shop chain, three large barrels of pickles and a carton of hams to the Stadium.

The driver leaves for the loading dock as the others busy themselves with their assignments. One eases himself into a swivel chair, making conversation with Daniel, while the other disappears through swinging doors into the kitchen. The inspector talks for five minutes about last night's Oriole game, mentions what he found on the floor today (no violations, two minor discrepancies on forms), makes a procedural suggestion ("Why don't you leave the ham cartons out front?"), and bids adieu.

Eight-forty-five. On the street, the mercantile life of the city appears to be in full gear, trucks of various sizes already rolling up and down the avenue. Carling Black Label Beer, Greenbaum's Furniture and Carpet, Jed Hardware (A Tool for Every Job),

Ryder Rent-a-Van,...The nation's most asked-for mustard, Baltimore Gas & Electric (NO Home Is Complete Without Natural Gas Heat). Daniel heads north on Wolfe Street.

Now it all depends on who the butcher is. A lot of these meat cutters, the old-timers, always did like to find those cysts. I know I did when I was a butcher. Now a lot of the meat-packers or butchers or processors try to put something over, to hide things. I don't say all of them, but the majority.

I get cussed out just about five days a week for condemning a bunch of meat. I never go ask my boss what I'm supposed to condemn. I condemn it and then call him and tell him that I have condemned it. This happens more than once a week. I'd say most inspectors on this Baltimore station condemn something every day.

Sometimes it's just caused by a mistake. A guy will be in a hurry to get something done so he can go and loaf. He'll pull a tub of meat out of that corner and drop some on the floor. Instead of picking it up and washing it or trimming it, he'll put it back in the cart. The cart probably has water in it. And if that cart has water I'll condemn the whole works. Water is a carrier—it'll carry the dirt that was in there. But if it was dry meat, I'll let him trim it up.

There are some very good companies. When I was a packer their first instructions to me were, "We want nothing bad put into our products. If you have any doubt about it, call an inspector or call the foreman. We'd rather throw it away than put it out on the public and lose business."

It's not necessary always to call in the inspector. But the butcher should call him in if he sees any blemishes, the minute he finds anything wrong. There are some conscientious fellows in the business and then there's others who are just in for the dollar they get. If they do find blemishes and they do call the inspector, they can get reimbursed by their suppliers—most of the time, that is, if they buy it on a legitimate market.

But a lot of these guys will go and buy meat they know is in danger of spoiling, and they will try to get it cleaned up before the inspector has a chance to see it. You try to catch the fellows that bring the stuff in like that. In some way or other you sort of punish them. Maybe you catch them with some of the meat they brought in. You know it's not bad, but from a sanitary point it would need a certain amount of cleaning up. I have caught them taking it and sticking it down under some fresh meat. It might or it might not hurt anybody. We can hold it up and make them go over it piece by piece sometimes, in some way to teach them a lesson. The way I do it is to try to make it expensive to them. By and by, if you do that enough times, that man is not going to do it any more, because he knows it's going to cost him. It's going to cost him in labor and so forth and so on.

If they repeat their violations, there's a process we go through. The inspector very seldom does any prosecuting; he turns it over to the law boys. Years ago I caught a fellow bringing stuff in from a city house and reprocessing it and selling it back to federal houses. Well, I turned that over to the law department and he was fined for it. I turn in maybe fifteen or twenty a year.

There's no certain way of catching them—it's by chance. Say I have two places, I try to make it a point that they don't know when I'm coming in. A lot of times if they have a back door or a side door open, I'll go in there and start looking around. I don't have a key to the places, but there's a rule that there's certain doors that are supposed to be kept open, so the inspector can get through. I have access. Some of them will put a lock on certain different doors and you can't get in unless they let you in. I have a badge and an ID card. But after 25 years, everyone knows me. Quite often they try to get rid of you or challenge your authority—that happens so many times I can't even count them. I've had a few people just about threaten me.

Eight-fifty in the morning. Daniel follows a meandering route to Metropolitan Storage. It is a big, old, four-story building of dark brick, with iron grates over all the windows. Daniel takes a clipboard and a small wooden box from his trunk, pauses for a second to throw the moist succulent stump of his cigar into a bucket of dirty water near the loading dock, and goes inside. A clerk waves to him through the wire-reinforced glass window of the company office.

Climbing the steel treads of a narrow stairwell one at a time, Daniel reaches the first-floor landing, walks to a huge freight elevator, lifts the heavy steel grating that shields the open car, steps inside, and rides to the third tier. Outside the elevator he unlatches a heavy gray fire door and pushes it open, waiting to be met by a slow rush of frigid air. Inside, a porcine black man wearing soiled coveralls, a fur-lined checkered wool jacket, and a peaked leather cap with fleece earmuffs is maneuvering a yellow forklift between an aisle of large wooden crates. He pulls up in front of the inspector.

"What you lookin' for today, Doc?" Many inspectors are called "Doc" by the meat cutters and packers, but Thornton Daniel thinks it took him a bit longer, as a black man, to earn the title.

"Let's do them hams," says Daniel.

Two hundred and fifty cartons of smoked hams, imported from Portugal, are stacked to one side waiting to be stamped. Except for the man on the forklift, Daniel will be virtually alone for the next 45 minutes, checking and stamping; the few hirelings who inhabit the third floor of the cold-storage plant have little cause to deal with him on an official level.

Daniel surveys the mass of boxes before him, six rows high in the dimly lit room. Refrigeration pipes crisscross the ceiling, jutting here and connecting there with large flat thumbscrews and levers and other protuberances, all winding around thin fluorescent bulbs. Stray hand trucks are barely silhouetted against the walls and the barred windows. As if endowed with some foreknowledge of a soon-to-be-discovered secret, perhaps like a sergeant reviewing barracks, Daniel stares at the ceiling while the lift operator separates a dozen crates from the rest and deposits them on the floor in front of the inspector.

The cartons are ready. Clipboard in hand, Daniel pulls the small wooden box from his back pocket and takes from it a bulky round rubber stamp and a purple ink pad. He begins to work, carefully and deliberately, oblivious to the near-freezing cold. His routine is one of well-practiced random selection. He pries the lids off several cases, checks them against some vouchers that have been supplied by the U.S. Customs Office, examines the cans, and opens one of them to look at the grayish-pink meat flecked with the white of marrow. Nodding approval, he stamps all twelve crates on each of their four sides, and waits for the next dozen to be pulled off by the forklift. Another case, another nod, the only sound the hollow flack-flack-flack of the rubber stamp.

You look for everything. In hams the first thing is the color in the ham before you cut it, and then you cut it and look to the center and if it has the appearance of being cooked through. If the center of it has any grayish or other color, right away we turn it down until we get a laboratory analysis. It is supposed to have been heated to at least 156 degrees through the center.

You look for irregularities, to see if it's free of hair or any foreign matter. If I'm inspecting meat and I find any rodent material, I condemn everything. I once found rodent waste and I condemned every bit of it. After that the only thing they can do is make it into fertilizer.

Some companies, they hire people and don't instruct them. When a fellow's put on his own on a killing floor, he has to take an awful lot of instructions from a veterinarian. I spent close to twelve years on a killing floor. I couldn't even begin to name some of the diseases you have to look out for today. I haven't been on the floor for close to fifteen, twenty years now, but it used to be the most you had to look out for was TB and signs of cancer.

On a lot of chickens, if they don't use them this year they'll use them next year. They wait for the price of the market, if they can get the right price for them at the right time. A chicken can last indefinitely if it's frozen, even past a few years. In Russia, they have found animals that have been frozen in Siberia, and they have been there for three or four hundred years. They could have been eaten if anyone ate that kind of meat. I think fresh chicken tastes a little bit better. The longer it's been frozen the more it will dehydrate. But we've had vegetables frozen for five, six, seven years, and still good.

Meats can't stay that long. All smoked meat like pork and bacon will be bad if you put it back in the freezer. It can only be frozen one time. It's not really a disease problem but a flavor problem. Freezer burn will set in. There's practically no disease you can't kill by cooking, and you kill the same germ by freezing. Once you freeze meat and thaw it out, though, you break down the tissues and lose your flavor.

Nine-forty. Daniel finishes stamping the imported hams, then moves across the warehouse floor to inspect a much smaller array of cartons stenciled CANADIAN BACON.

Twenty minutes later he takes the freight elevator to the first landing, walks down the steel stairway to the ground floor, and enters the clerk's office. Here he will check some receipts against the papers on his clipboard. The man at the desk makes an observation about the weather; Daniel grunts acknowledgment and offers a cigar. The two of them light up and go about their business.

A short time later Daniel goes out into the first-floor storage area, a contrasting bustle of people and activity involved in the commerce of meat: receiving, lifting, inspecting, categorizing, stamping, hanging up and taking down tons of beef and poultry. The warehouse contains room after room, floor after floor of foodstuffs: the remains of pig, lamb, steer, and fowl, stocked in crowded bountifulness, stacked here as insurance against the propitious windswells of the market. Nice, pink, and trim, the meats are assigned to various parts of the building, each after its kind and according to different storage temperatures. From the cold here many will be trucked to shops and supermarkets for further butchering and dressing, cutting to size, slicing, and labeling.

There is a lot of traffic in the cold-storage rooms on the first floor, but the business is purposeful and is accomplished with a noticeable quiet, at least as compared to the clatter emanating from the large rear office, where teletypes and other business machines mix with raised voices quoting prices, investigating deliveries, talking by phone with warehousemen and dispatchers... "Food-Fair truck the second shift..." "Not without prior approval..." "Seventy-five five the pound..." "Chesapeake Restaurant and Haussner's..." "Hot veal on the floor..." "Poultry sales for the second quarter..." "No later than the thirteenth...." The bright fluorescent light from the office dimly illuminates the dark storage area outside.

I worked for a time in a poultry dressing plant. The average poultry inspector would get out of bed about five o'clock in the morning, and commute along country roads, since most of the poultry processing plants are in small cities or rural areas. I would drive some six or seven miles.

All inspectors have to wear some sort of protective devices like boots, a smock or butcher coat over an outer street garment, in some cases a uniform of white or some washable material. Inspectors are not allowed to wear gloves, so they can feel with their fingers, except we could use surgical gloves when we had cuts or bruises on our hands. A third of the inspection is done by feel, smell, and sight. An inspector who is on a routine pre-operational sanitation check comes in an hour and a half earlier than the processors. He checks the facilities: the receiving dock, the killing area, the picking room, the pickers, the scalders, the equipment, the conveying lines. Then he goes through the eviscerating room. He'll check the floors, the troughs, the lights, the walls, the ceilings. This is everyday routine. If equipment or something is found unacceptable, it may be tagged; sometimes it can be cleaned on the spot, on some occasions it can't.

This is the beginning of the warfare between the poultry industry and the grass-roots inspector. All inspectors are required to prepare a daily tally of the condemnation, and it can be rough.

The birds can either be killed mechanically or they can be slaughtered by the slice of the jugular vein with a knife. They bleed to death. They come into the picking room either fluttering, or dying, or dead. Then they go into the scalder, which first wets them real good before they're picked mechanically and by hand. This department is divided by a partition and they'll come into the eviscerating department with the unfeathered or yellow part of the leg removed. The blood's gone, the yellow part of the foot, and the chicken's dead. In some cases the head is cut off, but everything else is intact.

You don't hear the chickens clucking as they're killed because that's too far away and there's too much mechanical noise from the conveyors and pickers and other machinery: it ranges 90 decibels and higher. There are areas in the picking department and the eviscerating department where the safety act of 1970 has required the industry to post warning signs of a high noise level. (But it's still not as bad as with hogs.)

The eviscerating room has the gizzard splitters. You have one plant employee who assists, usually a woman called a trim girl. She will do the trimming and the removing of the unwholesome carcass, after the birds have come through the picking room. In my particular area nearly all the trimmers were white females. We had some experiences with men trimmers, but they seemed not to be as cooperative as the women.

The birds come to you on a metal shackle with their drumsticks suspended. They used to pull them through with a little fork which would wedge the head up. You would reach for the bird with either the right or the left hand, catch the drumstick with the ring finger and the little finger next to it and you palpate. Then you would catch it at the bottom of the breast going into the abdominal cavity, what we call the rump or the vent area, and you would press inwardly and push the skin and the fat back. This way you would get an inside look at the chicken: the lungs, the rib cage, the kidney area. In the female bird you would look at what would be the ovary, in the male the testicles. Then with the other hand you would palpate and catch the viscera which had just been laid out. You would have there the edible giblets: the heart, the liver, and the gizzard. You check all these for abnormal color, for lesions which would be compared to cancer in humans. Sometimes these things are pinpoint small; sometimes the whole lobe of a liver will be infested with a hard lesion or a growth.

We did a bird-by-bird inspection. In a young chicken we'd inspect up to 25 birds a minute, which is a whole lot of chickens. There are different standards, and they never really say or tell a company how fast they can operate as long as they operate efficiently. But you could nearly always find something wrong. So a maximum speed would be 25 or 26 birds a minute. This would be on a single conveyor.

Now say if they wanted to double their production, they would put little green or re- tags on every other shackle to identify them, and they would put two inspectors on that line. Some of the plants had four inspection stations, and they had a mechanical clicker which would throw two birds each way so if inspectors were getting errors or sick chickens on one side of the line the other side could continue in production. These were called quad lines. Now in the past few years they have increased these to eight-man lines.

Some plants will have seasons when there is not a great demand for the product and they'll work as short as maybe three or four hours a day. In other plants in other areas, especially in the prime picnic season or in the fall of the year when there is a great demand for turkey, they will run as many as twelve or fourteen hours a day. Up until we as a group of government employees organized and collectively bargained, we had inspectors who were working sixteen even seventeen hours a day. It's nothing uncommon to work in the eviscerating department ten hours' line time. That's where the poultry inspector spends 95 percent of his time.

We did have a break for lunch, and this varied from plant to plant. Some would only allow a 30-minute lunch break, some 45 minutes, some an hour. (Yes, there were times when I ate chicken for lunch. I like it spiced up, though.)

Our day's work actually would end about two-thirty or quarter of three in the afternoon, but very seldom did we ever get home this early, because of mass production and the demand for the product. It was nothing unusual to work until five-thirty in the afternoon.

Both mentally and physically it was a very demanding job. You just had to experience it. We had trimmers, both men and women, who stood right by the side and assisted the inspector, and who at a later date would be employed as inspectors. Now they say, "You know, I stood by the side of the meat inspector for years and I didn't really realize how tired and mentally depressing this job is." There is no way to describe it unless you personally experience it.

Near the loading dock Thornton Daniel intercepts a shipment of fresh meat to be stored at Metropolitan until summoned by a large packing company in East Baltimore. He walks around a steer's carcass rotating on its rope, his practiced eye scanning a shank. Blood and juice drip slowly onto the concrete floor. White-coated workmen, their shoulders stained brown and red

the noontime run: 200 hogs to be killed. But first they must be sorted, weighed, inspected, and dyed to identify the lot in process. This batch will be done up in blue, the next red, the next yellow.

Soon the staging area fills with hogs—some a natural tawny color, others mottled—and they all become part of an undulating mass, the animal noises rising from deep within, the whole bulk swaying and lapping wavelike at the sides of the huge pen. White-coated men with clipboards move casually around the pens. The animal sounds increase as the trains and trailers empty, the last bleating stragglers poked and yelled into motion by workers in overalls.

Once into the staging area the hogs are moved along quickly: motorized bay doors are closed, nozzles aimed, valves turned, dye-spewed hides coated, tallies made. The men with clipboards count carefully. Within an hour these 200 pigs will have completed the next-to-last stage of their journey to a final enumeration: 800 feet and all that can be processed above them into knuckles, bacon, ribs, hams, butts, snouts, maws, hocks. At this point, though, neither Daniel nor any of the other men working in the slaughterhouse perceives the ultimate goodness—the baked, glazed, cloved, and sliced ham wrapped in a full-color package, sweet potatoes and black-eyed peas and cranberry sauce on the side, a tasty morsel of life's bounty. All of that is still far away, as it must be, from the business at hand.

Daniel knows the sounds and smells here—the constant whine, the moist and pungent air of the abbatoir—far removed from the dining-room table. He is at home on the killing floor.

When I was a kid working at the slaughterhouse I used to have trouble going out and eating meat, but after a while I got used to it. I just about always worked in a packinghouse—was born right in sight of one and grew up in one—and it never worried me.

When I worked on the killing floor they used to knock animals over the head with a hammer. There was a lot of pain. Sometimes the animal laid there four or five minutes just suffering. At some plants they have a gun that they hold to the head, and that gun shoots a rod right through the brain that instantly renders them unconscious. Then they cut the throat and let them bleed out. An animal that doesn't bleed out, you can't examine him very well: a lot of times he'll be condemned. The animal doesn't make a lot of noise when he's shot. None at all. He just drops. Some plants now use a shocker and some still use a gun. Chickens are often shock-killed nowadays. When they kill kosher cattle, they just hush him up and slit his throat. That is much more humane than knocking him with a hammer.

I never did like killing, but had to go along with it. It's a necessary job. You just have to get used to it and take your mind away from it.

I remember a lot of fellows who used to like it, killing animals with sledge hammers. Years back they just ran them into a pen one on top of another, knocked them in the head and then dumped them on the floor. The animals would try and run away. They would get back up after they had been hit in the head. You just had to go and hit them again. I've seen men hit them and knock their brains right out. There was many a day when I had to go wash the hammer which still had the brain of the animal on the end of it.

Daniel's smoky eyes follow the preparations at the slaughtering area. He stands with two other inspectors and a veterinarian on a grated upper tier, their voices raised in volume and pitch above the unremitting noise below. They must make sure that all the animals are properly alive; indeed, even small signs of ambulatory disease will be magnified by their trained eyes. This is but a cursory inspection, however; their work will not begin in earnest until after the carcasses are skinned and trimmed.

The mid-morning run is now in progress. Hogs with splotches of green dye on their flanks are ushered into a small inner chamber and then forward down a long channel; steel pipes on either side prevent any movement save in one direction. The closer the animals get to the front of the line, the louder their squeals seem to become. Two men with shocking rods stand poised on either side of the chute as the hogs are forced to present themselves. The men are protected from the high-voltage tools of their trade by rubber grips and heavy rubber boots. The floor beneath them is damp from sprayed dyes and water and blood, and the current from the rods, though relatively small, can generate a powerful shock.

The slaughterers alternate in applying the rods behind the hogs' ears, shocking them senseless. With a final squeal each is laid to rest on a conveyor belt that passes at right angles just beyond the steel-piped channel. Meanwhile the live animals in the large pen outside continue their last walk toward entrapment in the small inner chamber and then down the chute—oblivious, according to the veterinarians, to what's ahead.

Yet for all the mechanization of the modern slaughterhouse, the killing itself is still done manually. A man in stained coveralls and black gloves stands a few feet down the conveyor, now carrying toward him its cargo of limp, haphazardly spaced animals. He has in his hand a long thin knife, and with a quick, almost graceful, sliding motion, he reaches around the neck of each hog as it passes before him and slits its throat from ear to ear.

Some animals die before they get here. But we have regulations. Dead animals cannot be slaughtered, cannot be brought into the plant. They have to be alive before they lose consciousness from the shocking. I was just down to see seven of them that had died from the heat in the truck. We put a condemned tag in their ears and inject a solution that makes the meat inedible. Then we release them for fertilizer. In the summer months I think I would die in the truck, too, if I was hauled that many miles. It also depends on the size of the animals and of the trucks. In a three-tier truck, they can haul 200 hogs.

It takes just about ten seconds to shock them. They're rendered unconscious, then hung up. The noise from the animals doesn't bother me—after a while you get used to it. Sometimes it's pain, sometimes it isn't—it's simply the animals' desire to get out, and their fear. They don't feel anything. If you put all the hogs in a pen and turned cold water on them they would yell the same way. With the shock they're knocked out: they are completely unconscious. It takes about three seconds for the eyes to quit blinking, and they can't feel anything when their throats are slit—that's what kills them. The shock itself will cause them to lose consciousness. It's almost instantaneous.

A veterinarian inspector once told me, the way he looked at it, if you're eating them you're just as guilty as the man drawing the knife. It's a moral question. He said, all religions are based on excusing ourselves for our moral actions, but we are animals ourselves, aspiring to be gods. But he guessed he did find it difficult to be an animal lover and involved in this kind of thing. In his case economics probably put him where he was—a meat inspector. He was taught in school not to destroy life. That was his purpose when he went into veterinary medicine. He had practiced for 21 years as a veterinarian, saving animals. But then he thought, what was he saving most of them for? For food purposes, of course. As the farms got larger and the economic conditions changed, he decided to come into this kind of work.

The killing floor is probably the most humane part of the meat processing business. The way some of these animals are treated before they get here, that's where the government really ought to do something. Every now and then I run into sadism, where, for example, someone has rammed a broom handle up the rectum of a hog. That is cruelty. And they are beat with clubs. Some of these animals we have to trim off an inch of the outer surface of the carcass because they're beat so hard. There's no necessity for that. I've lived and worked with animals all my life, and if you talk to them and are gentle with them they'll follow along. These guys get in there and get them excited with clubs and they work against themselves. They don't do themselves any good.

Breeding practices have changed a great deal, now that they are trying to get them fat faster, and I think for the worse. I mean just the handling of the animals. When you get big corporate farms, then you get some cruel laborers. And you have some cruel farmers, too. I remember a neighbor we had who used to whip his horses and make them run with a big load of corn on them. No sense in it at all. He would just whip them until they dropped.

I've been able to divorce my love for animals from this slaughter of them. I mean, this is a necessity. I still like them. I guess the purpose of a good animal is to produce food. The beauty of everything is in its purpose. I've seen 4-H kids who have loved their animals follow them through the packinghouse, and stand there and cry while they are being killed. They just can't afford to let that animal live to old age and die. It's too expensive. So it finally comes down to economics, to the dollar.

Some plants specialize in processing alone—they don't kill anything. They just buy the parts to make bologna and ham. Others just do slaughtering. The modern trend is to go out and build plants in the beef-producing areas; they kill two or three hundred cattle an hour there, probably on two shifts, and then ship them. It's cheaper to send beef carcasses than live animals. The freight weight is lower.

Here we have the capacity to supervise the killing of 287 an hour. That is what we permit, and what the blueprints call for. There are some men who work down there who do nothing but kill hogs.

Not everybody can take this kind of thing, though. About four or five years ago my doctor son took his brother to see him perform a post-mortem on a body. The one boy came back home before the other, so I asked him, "What did you do, leave your brother?" He says, "Yeah, I left him." He couldn't take it. He was the lawyer son.

Eleven-forty-five. At the end of the conveyor belt the now lifeless hogs are hung up with large hooks to be bled out. In fact, the carcasses never stop moving; from here they are carried through various rooms and buildings for gutting and hair removal, beheading, and finally butchering. Now all of the screeching comes from the machinery, as the belt moves from the ground-level killing floor diagonally upstairs and across the open yard to the cutting rooms.

Thornton Daniel leaves the ramp and walks back toward Hazar's administrative offices, which are in a large brick building near the parking lot. On the top floor a small full-time staff of Department of Agriculture employees has its headquarters. The rooms here are more like plain square cubicles than offices. The walls are half-tiled, half-painted a dull shade of salmon pink. In the largest room are four old wooden desks, some painted metal cabinets, file cases, and charts tacked on a bulletin board.

Daniel climbs five flights of steep, narrow, steel steps—the only access to USDA at Hazar. It is much quieter here than in any other part of the plant, and the inspectors come in when they can to do their paper work and eat their lunches. From one wall the windows overlook the supply house and the gray asphalt entrance yard. Daniel says hello to the three inspectors seated at their desks, and mentions to one of them the pigs' feet he condemned at Metropolitan Storage. Then he goes into an adjacent lavatory, where he puts out his cigar and washes his hands. It is warm in here, despite the air conditioner in the outside office. Daniel is tired. As he looks at himself in the mirror he begins to hum, then slowly sings the words to a tune he's known all his life:

> Beneath the steel wool of his blackamoor head
> and above the thick lips and his flattened-out nose,
> a pair of yellow'd eyes with their sadness boiled in
> and a pallid resignation in his colored-man's skin. . . .

Outside the washroom, Daniel passes through a small hallway and the refrigerated storage area that separate the USDA offices from Hazar's cutting rooms. Here the gutted carcasses of animals slaughtered less than an hour ago are already being conveyed by hooks to various way stations around the floor. At one of them an inspector stands hunched over half-empty hogs' heads. Daniel nods to him and moves on.

The inspector who cuts the glands in the hogs' heads, I think he has a punishing job. He has to stand still there, when a lot of times they run around 400 an hour. He has to cut those and watch for the dirt on the hog's head eight to ten hours a day. He can't move. And he's got to keep his eyes open. He gets around $9,000 a year. And he earns it, every nickel. That's the one job that most inspectors shun and try to get out of.

The noisiest job on the slaughter floor is the sawyer. An old hog, a sow that they are going to use for sausage, has got a lot of calcium in it and all the bones are hard. You've heard a rip saw, a chain saw when it hits a knot—it's a very similar thing: umm, umm, umm, and a whining noise. The sawyers do that all day long. They get accustomed to it, but their backs hurt them after a while. In the old days, they used to do it with a cleaver. That's when they had to do the chopping all day long. The fellows became muscle-bound. Now it's on a pulley, and done with saws.

Two of the main things of the slaughterhouse are arthritis and bow-leggedness. You see a guy who is bowlegged and there's a good chance he works in the slaughterhouse lugging beef. You get arthritis in your hand from clutching a knife and working in cold temperatures. It's a disease of the slaughterhouse.

People ask why I've stuck with it for so long. Well, they got a saying, once you get blood on your shoes, you can never get it off. Like a printer—once he gets ink in his veins, that's it. You throw a penny in the fountain over in Rome that one time and you shall return.

I wouldn't be here if I didn't like it. There's something new everyday. And the butcher people are different: they are a bunch of kidders and they are a rough bunch, but they are nice guys. They are an odd lot from the ordinary Johnny-with-the-brown-bag laborer who runs to the office every day with his two peanut butter sandwiches.

Back in the office, Daniel opens a small refrigerator and takes out the other half of yesterday's lunch, a chicken salad sandwich on whole wheat bread. The conversation around the room is about a bribery and conflict-of-interest charge brought against Thornton Daniel and several other federal inspectors and local packers. All of them understand, even if they do not appreciate, the patently double standard: conflict-of-interest regulations are applied very strictly to low-level public servants like meat inspec-tors, while the Secretary of Agriculture himself may admit to

accepting free vacations and other gratuities from farming interests and escape without punishment.

The only way I'll ever be able to answer the charges brought against
us is for someone to ask me questions, or tell me point-blank what I did.
I don't know what I did. If my lawyer knows, he knows more about it
than I do. I first heard about it in the summer of '70. I had just finished
building a garage in my back yard and was putting the trim on, when
my wife called me and said my supervisor was on the phone. He told me
he had just heard on the radio that I had been indicted for bribery.

I tried to get all the information I could, but I didn't have any idea at
all where it could stem from, and still don't. They said I was given
meat—no, carried packages out of Sandler's Packing Company. I said
sure, I carried packages out of Sandler's. I often carried samples, and
once I had one of the other packers from around town deliver some
freezer meat to me at Sandler's. As far as I know it was perfectly okay for
me to buy from that outfit, because they sold to the general public. I
have bought stuff and cut it up at work just about ever since I've been
married. I'd buy a carcass, or a piece of a carcass, and cut it up. We
have a freezer at home. It's cheaper that way. A lot of the old fellows,
the meat inspectors, used to do that—buy some meat somewhere and
cut it up and freeze it.

I've never in my life been in trouble with the law, never been in jail. I
never got close enough to any packer for him to offer me any bribes. I've
never been taken out to lunch or given a turkey for Thanksgiving or
Christmas. I've never been given anything. Except once, a cup of
tea—and I bought him a cup of coffee.

But when I heard I was indicted for something like that, I couldn't
believe it. And from that time on I suffered until I went down before the
judge about six months later. I tried to figure out what I did and where I
did it and how I could ever do anything. It was just like somebody
stabbing me, because I always thought I did a good job, an honest and a
good job.

Anyway, the judge said I was indicted because at the time I was in
charge of inspection at the plant, and in order for the government to
bring a case against the packers they had to indict the inspector, because
he was on the job. The packers were found guilty of shipping unin-
spected meat, but we had no way in the world of knowing about it. The

judge read a resumé of the trial to us in his chambers, and he said, "Nobody's bringing any charges against you." He said, "You fellows had nothing at all to do with this."

I wouldn't be a meat inspector again, if I had to do it over, for fear of being blasphemed like I was. I really think I do a good and an honest job. Everything I make out of meat inspection I make with an honest salary. But I'd be afraid that I could be hooked into something I have no control over.

I don't think we are really a respected people. In the early years of civil service employees, I guess probably the postal people made the deepest impression on society. The average citizen thought that if you worked for the government you had it made. A few years ago I was having a discussion with the pastor of our church and we got to talking about work and occupations and things of this nature and he said, "You've got it made." I said, "You know this is far from the truth. We fight harder for a lot of things than the average citizen would."

I've been accused of being too particular as an inspector. I think most good inspectors have, at one time or another. Although it's never hurt my feelings to be honest, truthful, outspoken, I think this has been the basis of some adverse action that has been brought against me. I am not really bitter at anyone, but I blame the Department of Agriculture more than anyone else.

At one time the packer could just go to the head inspector and say, "I don't want that guy in my place any more," and the head inspector would take that man and send him to another place. It seemed they would back the packer more than the inspector.

Of course, vice versa, some of the inspectors had very little respect for the packer and they could almost bring him right to his knees. They would go into a place of business and with the least scraping find a little grease or something left over from the day before, and they'd stop him right there.

Nowadays, though, they have investigators who try to keep a balance between the packer and the inspector, so one can't run roughshod over the other.

Daniel finishes his half-sandwich, passes a few more minutes of small talk with the other inspectors in the office, then gets up to leave.

I vote all the time, but not necessarily Democratic or Republican. I vote the one that I think is going to benefit me and my neighbors and the community. A couple of times I had a chance to talk to Vice President Agnew. Tell the truth, when I first heard about Agnew convicted it was a worse shock than later on, when the President got it. To this day I really don't believe the things they say he did. Some way or another they framed the man. It was a worse shock to me because I had known Agnew much longer. I first met him when he was still going to school, and then when I was president of the neighborhood association here. I don't know whether he remembers me, but I did talk to him when he was Baltimore County Executive. We went out and had an audience with him on some of the sewage problems we had, and he seemed to be a pretty fair man. He kept some of these businesses from invading our neighborhood.

I voted Democratic in the last election. The Nixon affair made me lose all confidence I ever had in the Republicans. I voted Republican when I first started voting. You vote one way all the time for a certain party and they get to think they're kings of America. I like to see a change every now and then.

I like simple things. If I get off in time to go watch a few innings of sandlot baseball, I'm satisfied. In 1945 I saw every home game that the Orioles played, and even now I go out to the Stadium every time I can. The whole family goes sometimes. I had season tickets a few years, but now I can't afford to lay out that much money at one time. I played baseball last summer. I guess I played all summer long, eight full innings. I still love to play. After I retire, maybe I'll just go around somewhere where kids are, boys, and play ball with them, teach them.

I like to garden in my spare time. Mostly shrubbery and flowers. In my back yard, out in the country, the suburbs. I was the last house up in the woods until a few years ago. I built it myself. Shingles and block. It took me eighteen months. I still do the same things I did when I was nineteen. No special diet. I don't eat a whole lot of meat.

At twelve-thirty Thornton Daniel moves on from the packing plant and drives south toward the wharves, where he will check one more shipment of imported meats before returning to the office and a backlog of paper work. He lights another cigar. The temperature has climbed to 90 degrees, and it won't start to get cool again until three hours later, when Daniel leaves for his home in Catonsville.

2

The Bureaucrat

Labor omnia vincit.

Virgil, *Georgics* I

NIGEL VASSAR, now deep in the lotus position, will whistle the same tune every morning at seven-fifteen when he leaves his house in Rockville. Sometimes when the weather's nice he'll look at the green-brown lawn in front and think how lucky he is for what he's got and say quietly to the world, "You ain't just whistlin' Dixie."

Punctual levity is the pith of your psyche, he muses—this is but one flash of an eternal reverie with himself, one fed at first by his fascination with words and since nurtured by a kind of docile cynicism he has come both to need and to enjoy. He knows such fun will end abruptly, as soon as he hits the rush-hour traffic speeding toward and around the Capitol Beltway and the three lanes south on Sixteenth Street. Competing to get to work is serious business for one who tries hard not to take himself too seriously.

Vassar never did appreciate car pools or trains. When he can he likes to drive through Rock Creek Park because he wants to look at the trees and, recently at least, because he resents the idea of rushing to work every day, almost as if he were eager to reach his carpeted cubbyhole at Customs. But he is aware that it would be hard to receive the same salary and benefits elsewhere, and, now, coming out of his morning meditation, Vassar finds it rather pleasant to think ahead a few hours to the time when he will ease himself into his swivel chair with his third cup of coffee and take a second look at the *Washington Post*.

The first coffee and reading of the *Post* came earlier this morning, at six-forty-five. By then Vassar had been awake for nearly half an hour, and even before the paper had been delivered to the kitchen door he had showered and dressed, put the kettle on, and done his quick version—little more than a short bow to the East and semi-silent reflection—of Hatha yoga. Although he sometimes regrets not spending more time each day in the lotus, he knows he does not have the patience to be more orthodox. Besides, he couldn't get up earlier if he tried. Six-fifteen is Nigel Vassar's absolute dawn.

If he is not perfectly true to yoga as a science of relaxation, Vassar does appreciate it as the art of elongation, an ideal time filler. He is thankful that at the point he became interested in meditation he had already begun to grow a beard, so he was able to do something better with the ten minutes he used to spend shaving. And the brevity does not bother him. Interrupted composure is eminently appropriate to your life and times, he tells himself.

He is five-feet-seven, a tall leprechaun with a small ruddy face and a full, whitening beard. A few years ago his hair would have been too long for a man nearing fifty but now it is the vogue: black and gray, combed straight back and all the way down to his neck, where it begins to curl. Despite a liberally administered hair cream it flaps at the slightest movement. Vassar's only concession to old-style government respectability is a pair of heavy black horn-rimmed glasses. His brown eyes are deceptively passive, belying the cynicism that becomes less gentle as the day, and his career, wear on.

There is something curiously incongruous about his attire. He seems to aim for what in conservative Customs Service circles would be called *avant-garde*. Today he is wearing a bright red shirt, a wide black tie with red polka dots, light-brown flared slacks, and, perhaps as a final gesture of mocking, subdued defiance, white patent leather boots.

My beard cost me a promotion a year ago, and I think it was a damn shame. It may well be that without the beard I still wouldn't have gotten the promotion, but I've had criticism from a lot of people. Not as much now as when I first started growing it four years ago, after I came here. It grew on me—I mean that literally. I started to lengthen my sideburns and they came down gradually until they closed. Most of the people I care anything about like the beard. Those who don't like it don't give me any trouble anymore. Even if they did I'd keep it because it's become a part of me. I think I have it for life now. If somebody would come in to me and say, I'm going to fire you if you don't shave that beard off, I'd say go to hell.

When his morning yoga is concluded, Vassar collects the paper and returns to the kitchen. He is meticulous in his ministrations over an hour-glass pot as he makes more coffee, the brew dripping slowly through a cone of filter paper and collecting at the bottom. He makes three cups, one for himself and two for his wife, Vera. Two slices of bread singe in the toaster oven next to the stove.

Religion has played a very important part in my life. I was born and reared a Catholic and was active in church. Sent my kids to parochial schools. Then I got involved a couple of years ago with the dissenting priests in the Washington archdiocese. I wrote two articles about them, neither of which was published. I met with the priests, defended their interests, and gave them all kinds of support. Looking back, much of my religious interest seemed to have been wrapped up in institutionalism, dependent upon a dominant individual—cardinal, bishop, priest. I did a lot of reading and had discussions with many people on the subject. As a result of all this I just about completely dropped my formal church affiliation, although I still consider myself a religious person, a liberated Catholic.

Vassar spreads one slice of toast with a thin film of butter and the other with orange marmalade. He eats them methodically, sipping coffee and reading as much of the *Post* as he will be able to absorb in the next twenty-five minutes. He is very quiet. Vassar values this last half hour of morning solitude, when he can gain a comfortable intellectual grasp of the world one day farther along. Another few minutes and the children will be up, frenetically preparing for school.

Vassar spends the time it takes his youngest daughter and son—Jane, fourteen, and Zachary, eleven—to move from bed to bathroom to school bus by helping with their breakfasts. Children, especially, he feels, reveal their true dispositions most readily when they are not fully conscious, and so he watches for the subtleties in their morning behavior. By evening their ordeals with friends, teachers, dentists, and cello lessons will have made them a touch more cynical and impenetrable; but in the morning they are still his children, still innocent from sleep.

Vassar has yet to share this theory with Vera, who is now padding to her own coffee in housecoat and slippers. Such introspection is too rigorous this early in the day. He superintends the pouring of juice and the choice of cereals from a large and ever-growing stock. The children appreciate their father's attentiveness, now that they are old enough to indulge him in it. It is at these rare moments that he is master of his kingdom, comforting and uncanny, with the same magical air, he tells himself, that used to be limited to nighttime storytelling.

This morning there is no crisis, no need to ferret out hurt

feelings or lost footwear. Vassar learns that at school Zach will present his discoveries about local rocks and that Janie will be taking a field trip to the Smithsonian.

Vera smiles sweetly, just waking. It is her custom to use this somnolent half hour to pack the children's lunches in brown bags, while she sips coffee and tunes in on the chatter.

Vassar is thankful when his wife and kids are more cooperative than irritable. He reminds Vera to have snow tires put on the station wagon and to be at home when the plumber comes to caulk the tub in the children's bathroom, and she tells him to pick up the wine she needs for a dinner party the coming weekend. She specifies a case of St. Veran 1973. They both know that later today she will call him at the office and they will go over the same details. Such inefficiency is not the kind that bothers Vassar; the sense of a household dependent is reassuring, and he appreciates the subsequent temporary distraction from forms, reports, conferences, and memoranda.

I had an ordinary childhood, nothing special. I can't say I was un-happy and I can't say that I was extremely happy. I was drifting along. I guess maybe that's the best way to characterize it. I wasn't taking any initiative at doing things for myself but I was letting things happen as they did.

The most strenuous sport I ever enjoyed was chess. I have never enjoyed competitive sports. One of the reasons for this, I rationalize, is that I'm a little guy and I can't compete against big guys, so the kinds of things that I have enjoyed have been the intellectual things rather than the physical.

I have a hell of a lot of fun out in the woods, though. I spent an awful lot of time by myself in the woods as a kid, hiking long distances, seven miles, ten miles. I admired nature, listened to the birds, whittled a stick, or just walked along and thought. I couldn't get people to do that with me. They weren't interested in hiking.

Vassar says goodbye to his wife and children, gathers up his briefcase and a few file folders that would not fit in, and goes out to the car, a four-year-old sedan that is too large to be economical and too small to impress anyone. It will take him a little over an hour to travel the eighteen miles from Rockville to Constitution Avenue and Fourteenth Street.

For the past two years he has usually listened to WTOP, an all-news station, while driving to work. Occasionally, when he feels industrious, he flips on a small tape recorder containing the previous few days' conferences or speeches, some of which he was unable or chose not to attend. He would rather waste the time on the way to the office, he has often thought, than sitting around listening to endless bureaucratic orations. He prefers the radio: somewhere deep down, Vassar's conscience expects him to be primed on public affairs before facing the day's work.

He makes his way along the nearly empty stretch of highway that leads to Viers Mill Road, his mind lazily emitting caricatures of his neighbors as he passes their houses. By the time he reaches the main road he has heard the day's headlines reinforced by radio. News of the Carters, down home. He will need all the cynicism he can muster to penetrate the defenses of his office-hardened colleagues.

In a city like Washington, littered as it is with intelligent and well-educated but politically impotent functionaries, there is an overwhelming temptation to ponder all the implications of every event, announcement, or impending press conference. Vassar prides himself on having overcome this middle-brow form of neurosis, though he remembers all too well when his pulse raced with every minor crisis. Those were the Kennedy years. In an important sense the country was much younger. Civil servants and others who pretended to responsible citizenship were still under the impression that something depended on them.

Like the news, the highway is punctuated by commercials and human-interest stories, all of which serve to relieve the ponderous repetition of look-alike turnpikes. Gas stations, rapid-service restaurants, and groups of stores cluster around broad intersections. Wheaton, Silver Spring, D.C. When Vassar stops for a red light near Wheaton, he turns to watch the storekeepers opening up for another day's business, and envies for a moment their sturdy, physical presence—the earthiness and usefulness of Zaftig's Hardware, Mechaya's Bake Shoppe, Tammy's Toy Box, and the other small stores and shopping malls that saturate once-open space.

As the light changes to green an impatient horn from behind honks him into moving (*toward the long lamented labors of public service*, Vassar says to himself). Now it is the back side of a suburban development that crowds the edge of the highway. As Alaska Avenue merges with Sixteenth Street a mild bottleneck slows the traffic briefly (*impeding our deskward progress*).

At eight-twenty he arrives at Customs and pulls into one of the dwindling number of empty spaces in the parking lot behind the building. Higher-level workers from Commerce and the Post Office share the choice spots, while the lesser bureaucrats, secretarial and clerical staff, and service employees must make use of more distant lots and garages. What little street parking that exists in the vicinity of Customs is reserved for short-term meter locations that would require more daily dime-feeding trips than even the government's most ubiquitous employees can afford to make. Vassar fought hard for his space.

We never went hungry although I think we came pretty close to it during the Depression when we lived on relief. Many of my friends' families were also on relief. What I remember mainly about the Depression is that we were better off than most people.

In school, I never put forth the effort that I should have and my grades were mediocre. I felt my parents couldn't afford to send me to college, so I didn't think about it. I had no ambitions. I took a couple of courses in night school—typing, shorthand, that kind of stuff. I never caught on to shorthand, but I can still type pretty damned well.

Vassar squeezes out of his car. The headquarters of the U.S. Customs Service is in the old Department of Labor Building, eight stories of gray-brown concrete ribs and slabs situated across from the sleek marble-and-glass Museum of History and Technology on Constitution Avenue. It seems to cover more territory than its official dimensions of 350 by 220 feet, probably because of the adjacent Interstate Commerce Commission. An auditorium connects the two buildings. The overriding external drabness disappears on close inspection of the elaborate Roman bas-reliefs molded into the concrete and the decorative balconies outside the windows of the third and seventh floors. Four columns at each end of the building reach from the third floor to the roof.

Despite an interior treated in the lighter style of the French Empire, with paneled walls and ceilings and more detailed bas-reliefs of Roman symbols and trophies, the drummed-in feeling of bigness and impersonality remains. There are four small elevators across the main lobby and a still smaller one past more columns and up three marble steps. On the back wall is a photograph of the President, hung between the American flag and that of the Customs Service, a red-and-white banner with an insignia at the center depicting an eagle, sheaves, and olives.

Beyond the flags is a large double glass door leading to an interior courtyard, around whose fountain, benches, trees, bushes, and flowers rise 279,675 square feet of Net Assignable Office Space.

Vassar presses the button outside one of the elevators in the lobby. Its burnished brass doors open to show a rich, wood-paneled cab with gold trim and gray-blue carpeting; Vassar enters and pushes the fourth-floor button. There is no one else in the cab.

The elevator is slow in ascending. It finally opens onto a long, wide corridor, painted light beige and lit by large fluorescent globes. The ceiling is domed, and the floor, tiled with octangles of brown marble, tends to magnify the sounds of typewriters and office voices. Nigel Vassar, management analyst, walks past the public telephone, the white marble water fountain, the rest rooms that he has seen every working day for the past nineteen years, and enters his office through a frosted glass door numbered 4112.

> When I got out of migh school I was kind of lazy, I guess. I was not ambitious enough to go out and find work.
>
> After several years of working at jobs my father had gotten for me, I finally started to do things for myself. I applied to the federal government. The war had already started, and I got a telegram from somebody in the Department of Agriculture offering me a job—$1,140 a year. Oh my god, I thought, am I going to make that much money? Wow! I'm very proud of what I did at that point: I took that goddamn telegram and I walked down to my boss and asked for a raise, and when he refused I quit.
>
> I came down to Washington and after three months I got an increase to $1,260. I came in as a mimeograph operator and then transferred to a $1,260 job as a tabulating machine operator—which I knew not a damn thing about, but they hired me anyway. They needed all kinds of help in Washington, even inexperienced people like me. Six months later I was drafted into the Army.

Within a few minutes Vassar is at his desk, coffee cup in hand, a fresh copy of the *Post* spread out on the desk so that his appointment calendar is concealed from view. He knows it is there, however, and that in fifteen minutes or so one of the secretaries will breeze in to remind him of the day's meetings and deadlines.

Usually it is Maggie Cragg. It would be an exaggeration to say that he could not function without Maggie's help, but she has worked for Vassar for nearly ten years; she understands and humors him, permits him to pretend to be absentminded, and tolerates his predilection for looking out the window. Vassar respects Maggie; he thinks of their relationship as professional and friendly—were he more serious or optimistic about his work he would consider her his collaborator, but as it is she is more nearly his alter ego.

The office is small, a recently renovated cubicle distinguished only by faintly sculptured walls covered in a new shade of yellow; the gray carpet dates from before the redecorating. A desk, a table, two chairs, and a portable blackboard are all that fill the space. The table sits in the corner near a bare window with the venetian blind raised halfway. Immediately outside is a reception room with three secretaries.

Vassar swirls his nearly empty cup to bring up the sugar, empties it in a single gulp, and then puts it on a low counter that runs along the window behind his desk. He sits down and props up his feet.

I never cared for the military style of life, the discipline, the unthinking way of going about things, and the fact that you don't question the orders given. I have an aversion to violence of any kind. I spent two years and ten months in the Army, most of the time in a communications unit, six months in the desert out in California and the rest of the time overseas. I spent a year in England. We were there for quite a long time, inland from the coast. Winter in southern England is beautiful; you can't go very far and be away from the ocean or the Channel. But after a while it got so damned boring, I just couldn't enjoy it at all. Then I got a three-day pass, and another guy and I went off to Somerset. We got mixed in with a whole bunch of soldiers in this resort—they were going to school there. My buddy said: "Hey, Vassar, we could mix in with this group and nobody would ever find us wearing the same uniform they're wearing." So we did. We found a little rooming house and we stayed away for about a week. Then we decided maybe it's time to go back, maybe they're going over to Germany. They were going over to France soon and we wanted to go along. This was before the invasion. So we went back. This stern old colonel who could hardly see—right away he wanted to give us a general court-martial for desertion. We did get a court-martial. The other guy was just a private, so they couldn't take anything away from him, but I was a Tech 5 and they took my stripes away from me and said six months on hard labor.

So we were both in the city jail in this little one-street town and both of us wrote letters to our parents about the boring conditions. They would take the gun crews out every day to a little meadow, allegedly to go through maneuvers, but they would loaf all day long and do nothing and our group would stay back at the barracks all day long because we were the communications crew—and we could do anything that we wanted. Of course, our letters were censored; any mail was censored.

I got called in to this colonel's office, and he said, "You both wrote letters to your parents here. It doesn't sound very good, what you have to say about this unit. Are you sure you want to say this?"

"Sure we want to say this; it's the situation."

"Well, we were thinking of reducing your sentence and we might want to throw these letters in the fireplace here." As it wound up, the letters were in the fireplace before we left that room, and we got suspended sentences.

I think I can see an evolution of myself in this whole process. I was probably still pretty much inner-directed, as I had been in my youth, but certainly much more of an extrovert and becoming more aggressive in things and asserting myself more. I had reached a point where I just didn't give a damn.

I got five battle stars in the European campaign from the Normandy beachhead on through to the end of the war in Europe in '45. How the hell did I get five battle stars? I was there, that's all. I didn't do a damn thing worthwhile during all that time.

Vassar takes his feet off his desk, turns to the editorial page, glances briefly at Art Buchwald, and refolds the paper in preparation for Nicholas von Hoffman. But he gets up and walks to the window and looks out at the Museum of History and Technology across Constitution Avenue. The Smithsonian began to occupy this marble hall, built at a cost of $36 million, in 1964, just before Vassar himself came to work at Customs. Gazing out at the building, Vassar often imagines that he and it are growing old together. The museum is currently exhibiting all manner of Americana—"A Nation of Nations—more than 5,000 prints, photos, and original objects which record people who immigrated to North America, what they did here, and how America changed them"—and it is to these that Vassar's imagination is drawn. He has thought of this accumulation as a history of the struggle and collaboration between men and machines, and he once romanticized his own work into an aspect of that history.

Now his mind wanders to other things. These reveries never last long, but when he falls into one Vassar usually awakes to find himself gazing far beyond the Museum—past the space occupied by the Department of Agriculture, beyond the Potomac—and his phone ringing or his desk buzzer sounding or Maggie Cragg standing at the door patiently but insistently calling his name.

This morning it is the phone; he takes a few deep breaths before lifting the receiver. At the other end of the line is Grafton, across the building in labor–management relations. Vassar collapses into his chair while Grafton asks about the personnel memo. He hears himself composing the beginnings of a statement strewn with words like *interface, maximize,* and *infrastructure.* The last, Vassar thinks, must have wafted over from the Pentagon, on the other side of the Potomac, but it reminds him, as he tunes back in on Grafton, to consult his calendar first. There is nothing big on tap for this afternoon. He tells Grafton he will try to have it ready soon and will call him back.

Vassar rings for Maggie. When she comes into the office she finds him in the far corner of the room, hunched over several of the charts that have survived a project he finished months earlier on "The Spatial Relations of Chain of Command in Bureaucratized Environments." Will she have time to help him with the memo for Grafton? Maggie says she will make the time, and reminds him that in half an hour, at nine-fifteen, he is to participate in a conference within the department on "The Inefficiency of Efficiency." Vassar looks up like one struck, rapidly opens his briefcase, pokes through it, throws it down next to his desk, then suddenly smiles, and picks up a folder next to the phone. He remembered after all to bring his own report, and it is a funny one. He thanks Maggie, and she retreats to the outer office.

Vassar complains to himself that he never has any fun at the

office any more. He knows that he will soon be playing the
Yahoo at the inefficiency conference, but it is a role he has
already mastered and exhausted. Long ago he found a maxim he
enjoys refuting: *Solemnity is as inescapable a refuge for the
bureaucrat as patriotism is for a scoundrel.*

Vassar fingers his tie, picks up the folder holding his report on
inefficiency, retrieves his suit coat from the small closet next to
the door, and, winking at Maggie, steps through the outer office
and into the corridor that leads to the conference room.

The years I spent in the military permitted me to develop my own
way of thinking, my outlook on things, my willingness to take some
initiative. But my only personal goal was to get out of the Army as soon
as I could, although I was patriotic all during my military career. I was
very idealistic: we're going to do something to change things and the
American Army is going to do it. Nobody else is able to do this but the
American Army. I was very patriotic.

Vassar walks down the wide hall, built to the scale of an earlier
age and now a bit seedy, less functional though perhaps more
aesthetic than the newer government buildings. He enters the
elevator.

The conference room, a dull gray chamber with one large
window, is on the other side of the building. By the time Vassar
arrives most of the chairs around the long oval table are occupied.
Vassar finds an empty seat and places his folder in front of it, but
then he goes over toward the window to exchange commonplaces
with Ron Flurry, an industrial engineer whom he respects, and
Fred Schlockhaus, another management analyst.

The meeting begins. The format is a familiar one for Vassar:
Each member of the study group presents a brief report on an
aspect of the topic, and there is a discussion after each presentation and again at the end, when the participants try to achieve a
consensus on policy. But the atmosphere is decidedly informal.

Vassar knows today's seminar will be deadly, because ultimately nearly everyone in the room, even Schlockhaus and Flurry, will come out strongly in favor of centralized, coordinated administration of sophisticated bureaucracies. Only Vassar will argue for individual prerogative and decentralization, as much to try to open up the discussion as to affirm his point of view. His real opinion is that a bureaucracy tends to achieve a ponderous identity and direction of its own, impervious to anything but the grossest stimuli, so that it hardly matters what sort of administration one chooses. But he has finally learned that it would not do to promulgate those theories before such traditionalists, so Vassar instead confines himself to playing devil's advocate.

He is aware that he is by no means unpopular in the role. The other analysts in Customs may think him a little weird, and he is sometimes characterized as the "house hippie," but most of them enjoy the wit if not the occasional insights he brings to their conferences. One of the exceptions is Tom Ogre, an assistant director in the Division of Management Analysis, the first speaker today. In the past, Vassar, with mock solemnity, always made a point of taking copious notes when Ogre spoke. But for some reason his heart is not in the masquerade today, and he finds himself doodling, gazing out the window to his right, or trying to conceal his restlessness by pretending to stare reflectively at the elaborate chandelier hanging over the table. From time to time his glance meets Flurry's, and Vassar realizes that he is fooling no one. He hopes that Ogre, a well-meaning man toward whom Vassar has no personal animosity, is not offended. But his topic this morning—a defense of standardized forms, with a brief excursion into the virtues of the special treatment that permits the making of multiple records without carbon paper—is hopeless.

Getting out of the Army was a drawn-out affair, but I finally did and stayed in Paris working as an American personnel officer. I met my wife at a dance, at the Red Cross Club in Paris. We were married six months later. When we came back to the States, I decided I was going to go to college. So I started school in my home town. I moved with my wife and two kids into my parents' home.

We got an apartment nearby shortly thereafter. I was getting a couple of bucks from the GI bill and expenses weren't then what they are today so we made out all right. I studied for two calendar years and I finished my junior year. By that time I was working a couple of jobs keying answers to tests into a three-key tabulating machine, the old-fashioned kind—clang, clang, clang, bam, bam, bam, bang. You had to get the right key each time. It was boring, but I made my living that way while I was going to school.

As soon as Ogre has finished speaking, Vassar gets up and walks over to a table next to the door where there are glasses and several pitchers of ice water. He stands with his body only half-turned toward the others in the room, as the discussion begins. The participants seem to agree that standardized forms are a good thing, although one or two of them suggest that perhaps their uniformity encourages overuse. Vassar comes back to his seat and interjects a quote by a friend, asking whether everyone agrees that a bureaucrat has "an inherent right to shuffle." There are a few laughs. Even Ogre seems amused.

Several other presentations follow, and then it is Vassar's turn. He ceremoniously opens his folder to reveal a pile of sheets of various shapes and sizes. He has intentionally written his report on several kinds and colors of paper, cut, folded, and torn into different sizes and typed and written with various pens and type-writers. There is even a page in yellow crayon written on a sheet of construction paper that Vassar begged from one of his children. His tone is wry. Enumerating the variety of materials and writing tools, he asks whether anyone thinks his paper suffers for it.

Then he delivers a strong but comic attack on bureaucracy as a megasystem for stifling human ingenuity and denying freedom or creativity. He talks about the nature of bureaucracy and the kind of work a bureaucrat usually does, and compares the alienation of this work to that experienced by assembly line workers.

When he finishes, there is at first silence, broken only by the sound of Vassar tearing up his report into more or less uniform strips each about the size of two postage meter stamps. Amid the snickers, Flurry asks him whether he thinks his theory of anarchism itself could be expressed without the very controlled structure of modern bureaucracy to mitigate its effect. Vassar offers to paste his dismembered paper back together in a different order and read it again. Flurry and Schlockhaus laugh, but Ogre and the four others in the room merely squirm in their seats as if they believe he might do it, although they are used to indulging his excursions into alienation. Vassar smiles benignly and remains perfectly silent until the consensus period is nearly over.

The talk has turned to the technological sophistication of bureaucracy. Vassar suggests that when thoughts can be typed into data banks, speeches taped in, and gestures and actions filmed in, very few bureaucrats will have anything to do. Relatively few people will be needed to program the computers and even fewer to figure out what information is needed and devise ways of retrieving it. But by then even the computer card will probably be obsolete. A few of the people in the room think that this is an interesting notion. Vassar suggests they meet to talk about futuristic ideas of bureaucratic operation, and the meeting breaks up.

In his more serious moments, Vassar has expounded his view that there are people both within and outside the system who see little good coming from it. A few years ago a disgruntled colleague circulated a bitter memoir entitled "The Compleat Bureaucrat," in which he wrote that bureaucratic types do not abound in private industry, where the results of their work would have to show a profit (or at least could be calculated in measurable units); that they are too often in positions where they can waste huge amounts of public money; that no prestigious high-level personnel are ever fired (but always promoted); that as each government function grows and grows less actual labor is performed; and that an intelligent bureaucrat watcher will observe what his subjects *do* rather than listen to what they *say*, especially because most good bureaucrats eventually assume an intellectual arrogance that causes them to believe their own double-talk. "If you are ever maneuvered into a position where you have to shake hands with a bureaucrat, go lightly," the man wrote. "Some of them are so filled with corruption that they ooze pus."

Most critics are less vitriolic, but many persist in claiming that instead of serving the public, today's average bureaucrat behaves like its master, exercising authority before establishing it, spending a few decades on a gilded treadmill headed for early retirement, earning a higher salary than is paid for a comparable position in industry, and enjoying excellent vacations and other benefits.

Although at least once a week now he tells himself he is no different, Nigel Vassar still does not identify with the stereotypical bureaucrat. He likes the acronym he has devised for a lot of his office mates: *sedentary, inspirationless, torpid* (SIT). His mind's eye still fashions the classic bureaucrat after an old fellow he once met in the Internal Revenue Service next door: a nearly perfect dud, who had come to the Civil Service after having achieved medium rank in the military and who exhibited that familiar schizophrenia which flaunts power and quakes with paranoia. His bailiwick was his castle, and he would permit no entry from below or above. His hands shook, his chair creaked, he wrote down everything anyone ever asked him, he granted no interviews. And he drank. Surely a perfect fit, thought Vassar, for IRS.

But then there are those who declare that *bureaucracy* is not a dirty word, that the system can be and is increasingly efficient. They point to an elaborate study recently completed by three government agencies, which yielded the surprising conclusion that federal employees are actually *more* productive now than five years ago, and in some cases may be outpacing their counterparts in the private sector. In 1967, for example, it took 3,800 employees of the Pentagon's Defense Supply Agency—one of 114 bureaucracies measured—to process 19 million requisitions; five years later, only 2,800 were needed to process 18 million. And that, said the government, amounts to a gain in productivity of 28 percent. Self-serving or not, the study was the first attempt ever made by the government to measure its own general efficiency. And now President Carter claims that too many bureaucrats are "underworked and overpaid" and wants to revamp the entire system.

A friend once complained to Vassar that the essential difference between blue-collar workers and civil servants is less one of productivity than of availability. Vassar's friend had been trying to reach him, of course, and on successive phone calls over a three-day period had been told by a secretary that Mr. Vassar was in a meeting, on a long-distance call, at a conference, out to lunch, out of the office, and, finally, out of town. At least, the man said, he had not been subjected to the infernal hold button—he had learned a long time back never to say yes when asked "Can you hold?" But he fully expects one day to receive the coup de grâce of the runaround: "I'm sorry, Mr. Vassar is no longer with us."

Vassar himself has a Kay-Eye (his acronym for *Keen Insight*) into the problem: All these things happen because the government is just too damn big.

While in school, at Penn State, I got a job in the architecture library. I mingled with the architecture students, the professors, and the guy in charge of the program, and I really enjoyed it. It was a good diversion from my studies and other problems.

I had spent my three years overseas in personnel work and I wanted to get into personnel. But these people at Penn State had a hell of a lot of trouble trying to figure me out. I could go into business administration, they said, but there isn't much in personnel there. And industrial engineering has a heavy engineering emphasis, they said. As stupid as I was, I said, "Well, it looks like psychology." I didn't realize the heavy emphasis on physical aspects at that time in the psychology program at Penn State.

After about a year and a half in that work, I learned of a new curriculum they were just starting in labor–management relations. I said, "By God, this is what I want." It was an interdisciplinary thing, involving industrial engineering, psychology, and business administration. I wasn't able to transfer all my credits. At that point I had applied to the Pennsylvania Civil Service Commission for a job as an employment interviewer. They came through with two job offers, and I accepted one, which was only a few miles from where I was living. It was close to the end of my junior year when I left and I did manage to get all my credits for the year, so I had three years of college behind me. I figured on going on in night school, but I was stupid and hadn't even looked into it. They had no night school in this little town back in 1950. When I came to Washington years later, I started back to college. I took two or three courses a year until I was able to complete my bachelor's. Since then I have taken a few graduate courses. I've been thinking about getting set in an organized program, but I haven't yet.

On the way back to his office, Vassar walks a short distance with Flurry and promises he will continue to do anything he can to prevent people from droning on about carbon paper.

A few minutes later he is behind his desk, going through the morning mail. It is ten-thirty-five, and Maggie Cragg has already opened and sorted a small pile of letters into rough order according to subject and importance. Vassar scribbles an occasional note in the margin as he skims through the batch of papers. At the end he comes to an interoffice note about a memorandum from the office of the assistant commissioner, calling for a response in four days. Vassar sighs. He glances quickly at three pink phone-message slips on his blotter. One is from Vera, who will call back. Vassar's mind returns to the assistant commissioner's memo, and he rustles through some documents on his desk before locating it.

Subject: Management and Training Plan for FY '77

Management Plan

This is a critical plan since it is our current "implied contract" on what we are to accomplish in FY '77. A comprehensive critique should be made of past year accomplishments and imaginative planning is necessary for FY '77. We have talked about ideas and the directions to pursue. I welcome further detailed analyses and projections. The innovations are to be fully reflected in FY '77 plans. If you believe you need additional resources beyond those available to you in FY '76 to carry out the plan, we must document the needs including specifically what would *not* be accomplished if the additional resources were not made available.

Training Plans

The policy in OMP is that each employee shall have the opportunity to discuss career development interests and needs with his supervisor. The results of these discussions should be in terms of the needs and education and training for each employee. An individual development plan should then be prepared with a copy to the employee.

You should cast out your total training plan and if our '77 budget is not adequate to provide necessary training to the employees, we will request additional funds.

I view FY '77 as a threshold opportunity to make significant progress in many areas of Divisional leadership and responsiveness to the needs of Divisional staff at all levels.

Despite the current vogue that makes Gobbledygook an outwardly unpopular language, it is increasingly difficult for the layman to translate government documents. What does it mean for the commonweal, Vassar wonders; on the other hand, what would happen if when each civil servant faced a day's work he asked himself the simple question: How am I contributing to the public good? That's it, he thinks. It is *too* simple. Even management analysts are too caught in the morass of bureaucracy to discern an answer. The bulk of three million civil servants, Nigel Vassar suspects, feel a vague uneasiness about true personal responsibilities and contributions, but few see the forest for the trees.

Will any amount of internecine reorganization, congressional investigation, or journalistic outrage ever overcome the bureaucracy of government? On those increasingly rare occasions when the weather or an office joke moves him to a Kay-Eye, Vassar tells himself again that it is just too damn big, and that's all there is to it. In the normal course of events, budgets will increase, agencies will be established, committees will be named, and individuals will become entrenched, bored, and ultimately ineffective. But all those critical labels—Disneyland East, the Marbled Jungle, the Citadel of Creative Non-Responsiveness, Fat City, the Fuddle Factory—somehow mask the point, that the little men and women who people the federal bureaucracy have no control over its massive machinery. If not for the fact that the cure would often mean the dissolution of their jobs, they would be every bit as appalled as the public at the monumental boondoggles being perpetrated around them every day.

Vassar has made a study of them and feels that the Department of Defense generally beats all others for outright overspending, the Postal Service for sheer bumbling. As part of its two hundredth anniversary celebration for the armed services, he remembers, the Pentagon decided to publish a book depicting the military's humanitarian achievements; when the planning was done it projected a 300-page volume costing $1 million and taking thirteen man-years to produce.

The Postal Service spent $168,000 to develop a safety belt for its truck drivers, then abandoned that version for an already existing one, then had to junk the whole program when new federal regulations requiring shoulder harnesses were issued. And then there is the story of the paper cups: One federal agency had a water cooler for which perhaps 1,000 cups were used in a year's time. A secretary ordered ten boxes of 100 cups each from the General Services Administration. A few days later ten cartons arrived, each containing 100 boxes of 100 cups—a century's supply. The secretary phoned GSA, but no one there would admit to having made a mistake; the mountain of cups was removed some time later, at considerable cost. The Department of Health, Education, and Welfare paid $900,000 to a research firm to determine "whether college students and other young people are capable of gathering information." ("A congresswoman said she could supply the answer for a nominal fee," says Vassar. "'Some can, some can't.'") The National Institutes of Health spent large sums to study the causes of gout, only to discover—upon announcing the results of their investigation—that a British research team had done the same study five years earlier.

Vassar picks up the folder containing his multi-layered presentation at this morning's meeting and writes on the top, "Please File."

My first experience as a management analyst came in Harrisburg in 1966. I had been kind of working up toward this. One of the big requirements of a management analyst used to be the ability to write, and I had always been able to get my message across. When I was a kid, I'd always wanted to write.

I spent two years at this job. Then a guy from the governor's office came in one day and said to my boss that he wanted to borrow somebody for a special assignment at the Sales Tax Bureau. I was elected, and spent my last seven years in state government in the governor's office as a management analyst.

In the late '50s I had people push me for political contributions, despite the fact that I was a Civil Service employee. Regardless of which party, Democratic or Republican, I refused, because I never made political contributions. I lost an increment of at least one year as a result of this and I had a confrontation with the deputy secretary of revenue, my boss. He called me in and started saying that I was being disloyal to the governor and wasn't showing support for the administration. I said I was fully in support of the things that the governor was doing, but that had nothing to do with whether or not I made a political contribution. I said I knew that as a result of this he could fire me, but he knew he wouldn't have heard the last of it if he did fire me—I could talk to a lot of people. I never heard a thing after that, not a word. And I never contributed a cent. Every year the request came through and I turned them down. However, I did lose my increment as long as I was on Revenue's payroll.

At ten-forty-five Vassar gets up from his swivel chair and leaves the office through its own door, which has the words PLEASE USE OTHER ENTRANCE painted in black on its frosted glass. He prefers that the secretaries do not always know when he leaves his desk, especially when he is doing nothing more than going to the men's room. He walks down the corridor to the lavatory. Inside, the stenciled letters STANDARD CHINAL stare back at him from the porcelain urinal. He wonders how many men are at this moment gazing, blank-minded, at STANDARD CHINAL.

Back in the office, Vassar sits down in his chair and opens the bottom left-hand drawer of his desk. Inside is a tape recorder. He pulls a cassette from the top right-hand drawer, clicks it into the recorder, and depresses the PLAY button. A Rossini overture muffles its way out of the speakers on either side of the window. Vassar closes the drawer, gets up, and moves to a portable green-slate board standing against the wall opposite the window. With a piece of yellow chalk he begins to write:

Sub-Goal 2
  Management Systems
Objective 2a
Objective 2b1—PAS
Objective 2b2—Output
Objective 2c—MOA 4-1300
Objective 2d—Consultation Studies
Objective 2e—Project Method
Objective 2f—Management System Plan

He steps back, examines the last two objectives, and then crosses them out.

What is life if not drudgery, he asks himself. (*Vassar, you rail against bureaucracy, but you are the consummate bureaucrat. How many memoranda have you penciled and stenciled in the past seventeen years?*) But he feels the twinkle of an inward smile. When Nigel Vassar gets to berating himself, which nowadays happens about once a week, he usually manages to dissolve the momentary depression by thinking back to some of the articles he has written. (*Those of thee that will be hoodwinked and put on, suffer ye the damnation of eternal double-talk.*) One piece he wrote a few years ago now smacks him with perverse satisfaction: "The Successful Systems Man's Success Sales Cycle" began with lines that, if the journal he wrote them for were more widely read, would now be Classic Gobbledegook:

The Approach

This is something a little different from the conventional approach to selling systems. Here we are approaching selling systems from two angles. One, we are selling the idea of systems, the *systems concept*, the fact that we in the systems field are competent in the analysis and design of Management Systems. We are selling ourselves to management. Two, we are selling *Specific Systems*.

These two go hand-in-hand. We will not sell the systems concept, the idea of systems, as an important management tool, if we do not sell the specific systems on which we are working.

By the same token we cannot avoid selling the systems concept if we do a good job at selling specific systems.

It would be nice, thinks Vassar, if that could be read by an owlish man with a lisp.

He is half wistful, half sheepish when he thinks back to an article he has just finished reading by James H. Boren, president and chairman of the board of the National Association of Professional Bureaucrats (NATAPROBU). Boren beat him to it in describing the arts of "articulate fingertapping, orbital dialoguing, prodigious pondering, and maximum interface avoidance—all instruments of dynamic inaction." NATAPROBU has called for a Bureaucrats' Olympics that would include events in fingertapping, mumbling, memo drafting, shuffling (paper), shuffling (feet), filing (two classifications: retrievable and irretrievable), and red-tape cutting ("Contrary to public opinion," says Boren, "professional bureaucrats [probus] do not oppose cutting red tape . . . as long as the tape is cut lengthwise"). There would also be heats in office evacuating (contestants measured for ability to maximize exit speed with optimal dignity). NATAPROBU's official motto is "When in charge, ponder. When in trouble, delegate. When in doubt, mumble."

Maybe, Vassar muses, he will do an article on the whole thing—about how decisions are *firmed up* (as opposed to being made), how they *impact upon* the existing system, how new *input* leads to *options*, how ideas are *restructured*, how committees are formed when memos fail, how the government accumulates more than a million cubic feet of records each year, most of it intelligible only to a select few. But what's the use? It has been done before, and Vassar really does not care very much any more. Hasn't the public already been educated to ridicule? The era of Vietnam spawned overt cynicism in even the dullest segment of the citizenry, which found something rather humorous in language that rendered bombing villages as "protective reaction strikes," made a parachute an "aerodynamic personnel decelerator," and called an empty oil drum an "impact attenuation device."

I left state service mainly because of the salary—at that time, the difference was considerable. I'm making twice as much money now as I was when I left Pennsylvania.

In our management system here, we have goals and objectives and expected output. My expected output is measured in terms of producing a particular document at a particular time or actually finishing a particular project. It's not like in the program area of the department, where they will be taking action to place X number of people in jobs or to train X number of people. My main responsibility concerns the service's management system, which gets a high priority in the view of my boss and some of the people over him. I do not agree with this high priority status for the management system and my boss is well aware of it.

We get bogged down in a lot of internal navel contemplation. My boss says, "Here, Nigel, work this up; we've got to get something out." He gives me what is actually already a detail of the management plan for FY '77. Now, I'm not saying that we shouldn't be doing this sort of thing, but we go into too much detail about it.

The assistant commissioner for administration required a programmed plan for each fiscal year, and I think this is a good thing. But he has his way of arranging the plan and my boss's boss has a slightly different way, so we have to arrange it the way he wants it and then we have to arrange it the way the other wants it.

I am a firm believer in planning but I feel that the management system is less important than some of the other things we should be doing. When I came here it was my understanding that I would get involved more and more in analytical conceptual and developmental work. I've done very little of that.

Vassar takes the commissioner's memorandum to a table in one corner of the room, spreads out blank sheets of yellow paper, places a few charts on top of them, and stares out the window, daydreaming on little dust particles as they float through a shaft of sunlight, while he waits for the phone to ring.

In a few minutes it does. Vera asks him to recite what he is to pick up for this evening. Vassar mentions the St. Veran. Then, echoing Groucho Marx in *A Night at the Opera*, he adds, "And two hard-boiled eggs." Vera ignores him; she has never seen the movie. Vassar tells her about the meeting he has just come from, and Vera reminds him that Jane has to go to the dentist after school today. "If she needs braces," says Vassar, a wry grimace forming on his small face, "there goes everybody's vacation next summer." They ring off.

He returns to the table but he cannot get his mind to settle on the work at hand. He keeps looking across the street, his eyes resting on the Museum of History and Technology. Try as he will, he cannot extract a thought on budgetary needs. His eyes come to rest on a reprint of an article about "chains of command" by Carnage. He knows this piece. He opens it to a dog-eared page where, circled in red, is a paraphrase of Clemenceau's famous remark about war: "Bureaucracy is too important to be left to administrators." Vassar determines to work into his own report some variation of that comment, not because he agrees with it but because he hates to pass up a good joke.

The buzzer beneath Vassar's desk rings. He turns down the tape recorder and picks up the phone. Sam Fleesum, an old friend from the Army, has dropped by to say hello. Vassar smiles and tells Maggie to send him in, half expecting to see him arrive wired for sound and carrying sophisticated detecting devices. Fleesum, who takes himself so seriously, is always a favorite target for the Vassar needle. When he enters the office Vassar shouts "Hello," leaps out from behind the desk, and asks if Fleesum objects to being frisked. Just a routine security precaution, Vassar explains seriously. Fleesum at first raises his arms to cooperate, then realizes he is being kidded, and sits down in the easy chair near the window. Vassar's masquerade is not over. He walks methodically around the room, looking behind the curtains, raising the blinds and then lowering them, opening and closing doors and desk drawers. Fleesum says, "Aw, come on, I was never that bad, cut it out," and Vassar finally desists, but not before explaining that he just wanted to illustrate how paranoia-inducing the presence of electronic detection devices can be.

They talk about old times for ten minutes, and when Fleesum rises to leave, Vassar walks him to the door, putting his arm around his friend's shoulder. Then he asks him how he would react to this gesture if he thought there was a good chance that a bug was being planted on him. Sometimes Vassar's sarcasm can be overwhelming. Fleesum smiles, but he is clearly disconcerted.

He says goodbye. Vassar laughs quietly to himself as he walks back to his desk, where he picks up his notepad and scribbles something on it.

I become very dissatisfied with the ordinary government employee. I don't like yes-men, and we're loaded with them around here.

I guess the thing I'm most disturbed about right now is the layering that has occurred in our own organization. The traditional pyramidal organization now has an additional layer. Originally I said it was going to cost a couple of hundred thousand dollars a year, but my God it's going to cost a hell of a lot more than that. We've got four new what they call associate-assistant secretaries in the office of the assistant commissioner for administration. These four guys come in as an intervening layer between the assistant commissioner and the office directors. It's unnecessary. I fail to see any payoff whatsoever in this type of thing. And not only are there the four individuals but each one of them has his own staff. The one who's over our own office has a tremendous staff and has spent thousands of dollars in remodeling the space that he is using.

What's given priority is the Program Activities Structure for the fiscal year. It's supposed to be the basis for carrying everything out, reviewing and analyzing, evaluating. I don't want to minimize its importance, but I would like to minimize my role in it. What we've had to do with this over the last several months has been largely a clerical chore. I had to participate in many meetings with people to iron out the details of the configuration here, the coding system, the wording, the actual goals and objectives. Just too damn often I get bogged down in papers and numbers. I try to get out of this kind of thing, but I can't.

I think this is something I have felt in most of the jobs that I have had in government over the last 25 years or so. I fight it but I don't know how to avoid it. For example, I've been trying to see my boss's boss ever since he came here seven months ago. The other day I was leaving a message for him with one of his girls, and he was standing beside me dictating something to the other girl. That's how difficult it's been for me to get through. But he saw me coming out of his office as he was coming out, and he said "How are things going, Nigel?" I said, "So-so." "Why do you say 'so-so,' why don't you say 'great'?" I said, "Why should I say things are going great when they are going so-so?" He said,

"What would it take to make things better?" I said, "It would take decision. It would take action. It would take willingness to take a chance." "Well," he said, "I'd qualify on all of those." I said, "So would I." He said, "We'll have to get together one of these days and do some brainstorming." Well, he has said this before and we never get around to it.

It is time for lunch. Vassar flicks off his tape recorder in the middle of a Vivaldi concerto and leaves the office, stopping by Maggie's desk on the way out. He gives her the piece of paper on which he wrote Fleesum's name and address and asks her to please send his friend some of her homemade wire flowers. She looks at him quizzically, and he tries to be inscrutable. With a preoccupied air he says he will be back after lunch, and leaves. He has learned not to be too specific about a time of return— occasionally he likes to spend an extra thirty minutes or more in the cafeteria, or on a nice spring day like this he sometimes strolls across the street to the Museum of History and Technology.

In the corridor, Vassar waits outside the pale orange elevator doors. When the cab comes it is already filled with people going to lunch. At the basement level there is a long low winding hallway, its beige walls chipped and flaked. At the end, just before the exit leading to a driveway that separates Customs from Commerce, is the building's only cafeteria. It seats 480 people.

Vassar goes inside and moves to the hot-plate line, which he sees means at least a ten- or twelve-minute wait. Now he is sorry he did not accept Grafton's invitation to lunch. No one to talk with here. The sandwich line, separated from the main dining area by a gold plastic filigree partition, moves faster, but he is tired of sandwiches. A lone cashier sits in a booth off to the right, serving patrons sliding by on either side (*a double veronica*, according to Vassar's muse). He passes the time by observing the walls, his gaze diverted by a selection of large seascapes, perhaps intended as a distraction from the sweltering Washington summers. The walls are an attempt at cheerfulness and color, with alternating blocks of bright red wallpaper and yellow cement. A matted red carpet covers the floors and six wide square columns interrupt the open table space in the large room. Three of the columns are papered in red; three are painted institutional beige.

Vassar chooses the special lunch of the day: broiled liver, a salad, mashed potatoes, and dessert for $1.40. Behind the hot plate counters three black women serve from stainless steel trays. Their green uniforms are flecked with splattered food, and the hot steam has coaxed small beads of perspiration from their brows.

The problem now is to find a place to sit, because the cafeteria is already crowded. Vassar weaves through a jungle of brown vinyl chairs, steel used-tray racks, and beige plastic trash cans until he finds a table being cleared by black men in white work shirts and pants and white cardboard sailor caps. They go about their business with a measured efficiency that somehow reinforces Vassar's suppressed sentiment to make everyone on welfare work.

He sits down with his tray and pulls out the "Style" section from the *Post*.

Occasionally, I'll go to what they call the executive dining room downstairs, although this is something else I criticize. In the first place there shouldn't be such a thing as an executive dining room; in the second place, although they claim you have to have a membership card to get in, anyone with $1.85 can buy a meal there. I eat there occasionally with some friends. My preference is to go out to one of the restaurants nearby, but there are not many of them around here anymore. Frequently my lunches are an extension of a business discussion or just a meeting with someone in order to carry out some business. I'm not rationalizing it, but I can often accomplish a lot talking informally over lunch.

Sometimes I don't get back to the office until the middle of the afternoon. Our regular quitting time is four-forty-five but I seldom get out of here until five-fifteen. I usually stick around and do a couple of odds and ends. I find that I can get a lot of phone calls in at that time, because we quit earlier than a lot of other agencies.

Even at five after one there is no hurry to leave the cafeteria. The place is casual, undisturbed except by the clanging of dishes and the hum of vacuum cleaners beginning their afternoon rounds. People may straggle in for coffee until three o'clock, when the doors close.

On his way back to his office, Vassar stops to joke with a young typist, then enters his room and goes straight for the table in the corner. Fifteen minutes into his budget estimates, the phone rings. Somebody from Labor Statistics wants to know about the announced cutback in supervisory personnel for the joint labor–management commission on minority hiring in the building trades. Vassar tells him he is talking to the wrong man and refers him elsewhere. A few minutes later Maggie returns and puts three more phone messages on Vassar's desk. He is always thankful for these pink slips; he prefers to occupy his time responding to others rather than in introspection even though he knows that most of the calls are unimportant.

By one-forty Vassar is caught up with his messages, but he decides to put off the budget estimates until tomorrow. He goes to the middle of the small office, loosens his tie, squints, and closes his eyes, relaxing without opening them, and finally sits in the middle of the room for a few minutes, in a half-lotus position, doing deep-breathing exercises. The phone rings twice, but he does not answer.

Too many times I find an unwillingness to make a decision. I run into this problem of cutting through a bunch of layers in order to get at the people who should be involved. For example, after two months of working on a problem I send something to my boss. Well, my boss sends it on to his boss, and it goes through all the layers and comes back down to my level, where another guy finds problems with it. What does he do? He writes a memo, which goes up through the channels again. Hell, it took me two weeks to untangle the mess. All he had to do was call me on the phone. I went over to this guy and I told him.

I guess one thing that keeps me here is inertia, but that's not all of it. I've had some very pleasant associations with the people. And my salary is pretty damn good. Since last November I've been making over $30,000 a year. Frankly, sometimes I've wondered if I'm earning it, although there's no question in my mind about my capability for earning it.

I am a maverick. There's no question about that, you can ask anybody. Some people feel that I am rocking the boat and they don't like it. Others will give a lot of encouragement in informal discussion but none whatsoever in group meetings.

There are a lot of yes-men here, a lot of people who just go along. I don't want to downgrade my fellow workers; there are some good people in the Service. But to some of the others I say, "Look, you're half my age. You're the ones who should be thinking about new ideas, not me." But these guys, they don't express themselves. Hell, I'm 54 years old and these guys are 27 and 28 just sitting around on their asses.

Vassar emerges from his half-lotus to the ringing of still another call. Grafton is on the phone, pressing again for a promised memorandum about the quality of working life at Customs. Vassar assures him that he is working on the final draft, and they hang up.

From his In basket Vassar pulls a typewritten, blue-penciled sheaf of papers. It is the first and, he hopes, final draft of his current pet project, and he reads it slowly:

MEMORANDUM FOR I.M. GRAFTON
Subject: Quality of Working Life in Customs

As an employee of the Customs Service I too am concerned about developing the very best labor–management relations in the Service. I believe that the mission of the Service demands that it be a model employer that other employers would want to emulate, and of which its employees would be proud.

As management analyst, I am concerned about uses of some of the evolving concepts of management and the effective use of our human resources.

As an American citizen, I am concerned about the manner in which my government carries out the public business.

These concerns prompted me to develop the attached proposal for approaching improved labor–management relations thru a Quality of Worklife Program. I would be pleased to discuss these thoughts further with your panel and to develop them into greater detail if you so wish.

Congressional Interest

In 1976, the Senate Subcommittee on Employment, Poverty, and Migratory Labor conducted hearings on Quality of Working Life in America. In testimony before the subcommittee, the Assistant Secretary of Labor for Policy, Evaluation, and Research made reference to many of the characteristics that are a part of the quality of working life, including the issues of: job satisfaction, work structures and schedules, the work environment, managerial styles, employee motivation, and productivity.

During the early part of the testimony the committee chairman suggested to the Assistant Secretary that individual departments should "begin innovative work environment experimentation within existing components." That is, the Federal Government should lead the way. This was consistent with that part of the Assistant Secretary's testimony that contained a statement that, as a major employer, Government can be a model "demonstrating by its own progressive policy and practice how work can be made more meaningful and more effective."

The Concept

The concept of Quality of Working Life is rapidly becoming one of the more significant issues relating to employment.

—The Congress enacted, and the President signed, the "National Productivity and Quality of Working Life Act of 1975," establishing the National Center for Productivity and Quality of Working Life. The act defines the term Quality of Work as "the conditions of work relating to the role of the worker in the Production Process."

—The Work in America Institute has been established with support from Ford Foundation, other funds, corporations, Government Agencies, and the AFL–CIO and other unions. The goal of the Institute is to facilitate and accelerate changes affecting work, work performance, improving productivity, and enhancing quality of work and life in today's society.

—Another center, the National Quality of Work Center affiliated with the Institute of Social Research, University of Michigan, is located in Washington, D.C. That Center seeks to enhance both human productivity and quality of worklife thru experimenting with restructuring work, measuring and communicating the results, and providing technical

comes in and sits next to him, Vassar grunts a greeting; he is staring at his blank notepad. After a minute Flurry leans over and whispers in Vassar's ear, "No jokes." Vassar grimaces, frowns, looks Flurry in the eye, smiles, nods, and frowns again. He writes NO JOKES at the top of the notepad. Flurry chuckles and whispers, "What are we going to do with you?" Vassar inquires, with a serious expression, whether Flurry is asking the question as a futurist or a human being. Flurry laughs. As soon as the meeting begins Vassar's mind begins to wander, as he knew it would (*I'm quicker than Pavlov's dog*).

I spend a lot of time with my children up at the mountain campsite in Shenandoah I bought last year. It's a beautiful area up above the valley. There's nothing except the land. We use tents and camping gear. I keep the gear stored in a couple of surplus Army medical chests. The kids and I have a lot of fun up there.

At five to four, having behaved moderately well, Vassar emerges from the conference. He thinks the discussion, or at least what he heard of it, could have been worse. The group will meet again in four weeks to re-exchange thoughts.

Maggie Cragg buttonholes him just as he walks past her desk. One page of the memo she is typing is missing. Vassar leads her back into his office, rummages around among the papers on the corner table, peers in vain beneath his desk. Then he looks in the wastebasket. "How did it get in there?" he asks, with a smile. Maggie, frowning, takes it from him.

He calls the liquor store to ask about the wine he needs, then decides to call Vera and see if she has thought of anything else for the dinner party. No answer. He remembers that she must still be at the dentist with Jane. He will phone again just before leaving the office.

Vassar stares out the window for the last time today. Compared to the great steam locomotive in the transportation exhibit across Constitution Avenue, he muses, managerial hierarchies pale into insignificance.

Maggie comes in with the finished memorandum. After a glance he hands it back: fine. He knows that ten minutes later it will leave the office for what will probably be its first and final destination—the desk, and then the ever-dustier files, of Grafton. Vassar does not mind. It is well typed, in triplicate.

Four-forty. Maggie calls on the intercom to remind him of his conferences the next day, the first one to start at nine o'clock. Vassar thanks her. He has the *Post* open to the crossword puzzle, which he begins to fill in while listening to the sound of the phone ringing at his house. Vera is still not back.

A few minutes later he gets up, takes his coat from the closet, and heads for the elevator.

3

The Physician

> He's the best physician that knows the worthlessness
> of most medicines.
>
> Benjamin Franklin

ANYBODY AT Food and Drug who does a good job and looks below the surface and exposes the dirt is a maverick. He rocks the boat. He's controversial, he's a stormy petrel, he causes trouble. That's the situation we're in now. It's the incompetents at FDA who get the key spots. There's a premium on not rocking the boat, on not turning out problems. The man who comes here and does a good job is in hot water from then on.

Dispensing alternate doses of benevolence and choler, John Nestor strides to lunch down the narrow corridor on the tenth floor at Parklawn, the Food and Drug Administration's Rockville headquarters. It has been a short morning, quickened by the exhilaration of vent grievances. "A bull in the medicine chest," whispers J. Hamilton Browning to one of the small group heading for lunch. He twinkles at the man waiting outside the elevator, apart from the others. "I think that describes him admirably." Dr. Browning is pleased with his turn of phrase. So no doubt would its intended beneficiary.

There he stands, in all his unsung notoriety—John O. Nestor, medical officer, FDA—the perpetual furrow on his brow hovering over quick, piercing, suspicious eyes. He looks shorter than five-feet-ten, perhaps because his face is round, perhaps because a poorly tailored dark brown suit does not hide a middle-aged paunch. Signs of white hair almost form a laurel around the back of his head. There is also some sadness in his eyes, a trace of melancholy partly concealed by brown horn-rimmed glasses. Except for those eyes, belying a demeanor too frequently burdened by righteous indignation, Nestor could be mistaken for a cheerful man.

Nestor says something to Browning and the two of them laugh. Bull in the medicine chest, troublemaker, hero. "Most of the people around here," says the doctor of himself, "probably think I'm an s.o.b." All the labels fit with little more than fleeting accuracy but the consensus always seems to emerge that testy, petulant, curmudgeonly John Nestor has forever been, at bottom, a man of principle.

The elevator is slow in coming. *Like the rest of this building: crap*, thinks Nestor. Such irascibility often perplexes those around him, though it is expressed practically by rote, and though it is but one side of a prismatic temperament, reflecting at all angles ego and compassion, virtue and bombast. There is a touch of anguish in his belligerence. Forget the way he goes about things, say his believers, it's *what* he's going about that's important. Nestor taps his foot.

I was number three of ten children, seven boys and three girls. I was born in Franklin, New Jersey, in 1912. It was a small town at the southern tip of where the glaciers dumped a deposit of the highest grade zinc in the world. Now it's vacationland there, low mountains and lakes and countryside, but my God even when I was a kid we had tennis courts a hundred yards away and a nine-hole golf course. We lived such an open life. People were not crowded then. Even the poorest miner with the minimum wage had his individual home.

It was a wild, rip-roaring place. We had practically every race, color, creed, and nationality under the sun, and many of them were immigrants who came right off the boats from Europe and got jobs. We had Hungarians, Lithuanians, Estonians, Turks, Russians, everybody. It was a true melting pot. Nobody paid much attention to your race, color, or creed. There were so many ethnic groups that nobody was really a majority, not even the WASPs.

We had a very high murder rate when I was young because these men worked twelve hours a day, six days a week. After all that time in the mines and the mill they either got drunk or played cards. What else was there to do on Saturday nights or Sundays? I remember one tragedy where three greenhorns—I don't know whether they were Hungarians, or Poles, or Russians—hired this local fellow to take them to Paterson on a Saturday night. They went into a cheap little hotel and blew out the gaslight before going to bed. They didn't understand that you turned it off. Of course, they were dead the next morning. This is the sort of atmosphere that I grew up in.

Practically everybody in town was lower class. They were laborers. Most of them couldn't even speak English. My father would fit what would probably be lower middle class today, but back then he was upper middle class, which was about the top rung of the ladder. He could talk to the Hungarians and to the Russians. How he picked it up I don't know. He had an office at the company and he worked behind a desk and he hired and fired. He was the personnel manager. That took a great deal of diplomacy.

He was also the Democratic leader in the county for many years, and he became powerful enough in state politics to have introduced and passed in the New Jersey State Legislature laws which the New Jersey Zinc Company wanted passed. Still, my parents would be very much disturbed if our name got in the papers. I never quite understood why. They were prominent people in the community and county, but they didn't like publicity at all.

Politics was more of a hobby with my father than anything else. He earned his living from the zinc company. He never went beyond the sixth grade in school but he was endowed with a great deal of natural intelligence and ability. He was third-generation Irish from County Clare—a "two-boat Irishman" (first to Newfoundland, then here)—and very well liked.

My mother grew up in eastern Pennsylvania on a small farm. She was a teacher. She converted—my father was a devout Roman Catholic. I suppose that's why there were ten kids; they practiced what they preached. She was pretty busy taking care of ten kids, but she was a very intelligent woman with a strong sense of her duty and obligation and doing what is right.

My father was for the working man and he fought for him. He was the *padrone*. If some of the men went hunting and killed a couple of pheasants or if they went fishing and caught some big fish up in the lake, they'd drop a couple off at our house. I remember an incident in the '20s, it might have a lot to do with my fighting the establishment here. I was twelve, maybe fourteen years old. The company tried to freeze out the unions. It was back in the days when anyone who was for a union was supposed to be a Communist. (I guess many of them were, but that's beside the point.) Several union organizers were just rounded up, taken down to the railroad yards, put in a boxcar, locked up, and sent out of town. I remember it bothered me. A few years later I said to my father, "I can't understand. I know how you were for the laboring man and for you to take part in that." He said, "I saved their lives. They were going to kill these guys. I convinced them not to."

Browning breaks away and returns to his office as the rest of the group—Drs. Tagley and Jackson, Macht and Nestor—wait in a long moment of awkward silence for the elevator. When it finally comes, Nestor ushers the others in and then extends his short arm to press the third-floor button. All the men in the cab look up at the indicator panel above the doors, and for a few more seconds no one speaks. Nestor taps his fingers against the railing behind his back. *I should have taken the day off,* he thinks. The elevator descends to the seventh floor, where two women in pants suits enter followed by a maintenance man pushing a large-wheeled trash receptacle.

When I was a kid in grammar school we traveled in gangs. You never went to school alone because you'd get the hell beat out of you by a rival gang. I had my gang, and Danny Stevens, who later became mayor of the town, had his. Everybody in town knew me as "Cakey" Nestor—my nickname must have started as "Johnnycake," I don't know—and so it was "Cakey's Gang." Usually there wouldn't be any mass battles—it was individual fights, maybe the two leaders. There wasn't any knifing. They were all fist fights, and fair.

The zinc company was taking millions of dollars out of the soil but what they returned to the people was damn little. They had what was called a Neighborhood House where you could bowl, play cards, or read. They had a kindergarten, and in a pond they had a raft. There was also an annual picnic—they would always have something scheduled to give people something to do. On July Fourth the Fire Department usually paraded and they had a band concert and athletic contests, such as climbing a greased pole or catching a greased pig.

We didn't have any of the flag-waving kind of patriotism. When I grew up patriotism was just taken as a matter of course—your duty. I've always been amazed by this tendency to parade at the drop of a hat. Maybe there's a blind spot in my personality but this sort of thing doesn't appeal to me.

We all went our own way, but everybody knew everybody else in town, and the neighbors felt a responsibility. If I misbehaved somewhere and somebody saw me, they'd call my mother or father and tell them. That's one of the things I think is missing today, this neighborly responsibility, helping each other. My father would damn well know if I'd done something wrong and somebody saw me because this was the way things ran. Everybody looked out for the other guy.

I remember our open touring Model T Ford. We'd go out to my grandfather's place, just below Wilkes-Barre, Pennsylvania. It was an all-day trip, about a hundred miles, with half a dozen blowouts. I used to spend summers on my grandfather's farm. We went down the Susquehanna River and then up into this beautiful countryside. He had a small place and he used to plough with a single horse. He would take vegetables and fruit into town. We'd leave early in the morning, with one horse pulling us, and we would eat lunch in town, and he would sell his produce, whatever it was, and we'd get back in the wagon and we'd go to sleep in the back. That old horse knew every turn and we'd wake up back in the stable.

Things weren't all that idyllic, though. We once had a tremendous typhoid epidemic that wiped out a good many people we knew. There was an error made, typical of a company town, where somebody hooked the crude water system that was used for washing ore into the drinking water system. I also remember the flu of 1918. I was six years old. I remember the church bells, the plant whistle, and all of the celebrating on November 7th—it was my birthday, and it was the false armistice of 1918—and then this tremendous flu epidemic. My mother got it and the complicating pneumonia that went with it, and they thought she was going to die. I remember my father calling us into the room and telling us my mother wasn't going to live. But she did. They had the firehouses filled, they had the Neighborhood House filled, they were using the schools for hospitals. I saw it twice, with flu and with typhoid fever. They'd come up the street with these Model T trucks with hot chicken soup. They would have soup kitchens on wheels because maybe both parents were in the hospital and there was nobody to feed the kids.

Two more people enter the elevator at the fifth floor. Nestor and his small entourage move to a corner in the back of the cab. Its wood-grain paneling is finished to a high gloss, and there is a deep scratch running down a side wall. Now all nine passengers have stopped talking and are looking at the floor indicator, which goes blank for a second before lighting number three.

Outside, the narrow hall is already crowded with lunchtime passersby, and the conversation is more animated. Nestor points Macht to his left, and Tagley and Jackson follow down the corridor. Inside the two wide glass doors on the right is the main cafeteria.

I played varsity football. I was always a little fellow and I was a quarterback. In my senior year I broke a leg playing football, and that finished my athletic career.

My family wanted me to go to Seton Hall, which primarily trains

men for the priesthood, but I had made up my mind I wanted to go to
Rutgers. I had saved the money. It wasn't much, something like $1,200
for the whole year, and that had to include tuition.

At Rutgers I got into a fraternity, which was a mistake. I had a
wonderful time for a year and didn't do any studying and failed practically everything. At the end of the year I got home with just a few cents
in my pocket. My parents said, "You obviously don't want to go to
school. You go to work." So I got a job with the New Jersey Zinc
Company, and I worked with a mine and surface surveying gang for two
years. I realized this wasn't for me. So I went back to Seton Hall this
time and made the dean's honor list. Somewhere along the line I
decided I was going to be a doctor.

In my third year at Seton Hall, in 1936, my father died. There was a
question whether I'd be able to go on or not. I knew that if I was going to
medical school I couldn't spend another year in college. Because I was
on the honor list I got into Georgetown with just the three years of
college.

But when I came down to Washington I had no money at all. I didn't
know how I was going to get through. I remember the treasurer up at
Georgetown, a man by the name of Doc Hurd, said "Well, why don't
you get out and work for two years?" I said, "By God, I've already lost
two years that way. I want to get through now. I want to borrow money.
I'll pay it back later." So this man loaned me his personal funds, at 6
percent interest. I paid it off finally from North Africa, when I was in
the service.

Washington was a very pleasant town then but we didn't get too
much time to enjoy it. We were really still in the Depression. I was
having a rough time getting through. The last two years of medical
school I lived in a private home over on Webster Street. This friend of
mine had an old Chevy and the two of us would ride to and from school
and then out to Silver Spring. At that time it was only a little crossroads,
but there was a diner there and you could get a meal of meat and two
vegetables for 65 cents.

We thought of Georgetown then as contiguous with Washington, but
it was a slower-moving, more peaceful town. They had the electric
trolleys, which were quieter and faster, and you didn't have all the
fumes. And of course you didn't have the place infested with hippies. It
was a relaxed atmosphere.

I was fascinated by medicine, and I found that was true of everybody in my class. A few years later when I was in the military many men went to medical school under special programs just to stay out of the fighting. When you went to medical school in my day, you and your whole family sacrificed because you wanted to go into medicine.

I really lived a very isolated life around the medical school. It was going to classes or working like hell at home. I could have taken a part-time job, like running the elevators in the Senate or something, but I spent a minimum of four hours every night studying. I didn't go to a single social event the whole four years. I didn't go to a dance because I couldn't afford to. Summers I would go home and work. It probably was a mistake to say there's nothing else that counts but medicine, but that was what we did. And as the result of it I got a grounding in medicine and in science that is the basis for everything I do.

Nestor holds open the large glass door to the Parklawn cafeteria as his group and one or two others pass through. At first glance the room looks inviting, a tastefully furnished restaurant with subdued lighting and dark wood. It is a carefully manufactured illusion. There is no wood. The elegance is all plastic, even the black and gold painted sculpture attached symmetrically to the walls. Everything else seems to be tan, salmon, and orange. Nestor follows his companions in.

I grew up in a completely different era and I've seen all these changes in medicine take place. When I went to medical school, between 1936 and 1940, we were witnessing the first of the so-called miracle drugs— the sulfonamides. If we saw a septicemia patient we knew we might as well put him in a corner and let him die. When we saw meningitis cases we knew they were going to die. When we saw a scarlet fever there was nothing much to do with it except sulfanilamide and so we had to let the fever go through its full stages. The same with pneumonia: it had to go through the classical stages because we had nothing for it really, except the sulfonamides and rabbit antiserum, and if it wasn't a sensitive bug they didn't work. There hasn't been a medical student for years that's seen a pneumonia go through the classical four stages, untreated, as it used to when I was a kid.

It was difficult enough to get into medical school and then the first year it was hard as hell, because there was an arbitrary rule with no exceptions—if you flunked one examination you were out. The president of the freshman class was a very well liked fellow. He would have been a magnificent physician, if you take into consideration those things that should make a physician. It's not just technical knowledge but your morals, your ethics, your personality, your dedication to your job and to your principles. But he flunked one examination and he was out. He's now a dentist. He's been grateful about it ever since but he would have been a wonderful physician.

In the first year we lost one or two men with tuberculosis and one with scarlet fever and acute nephritis. At the schedule we were working, the morbidity and mortality rate in medical schools was pretty high. Illness was very common. They had no provision at all for taking care of students' health. I remember once we went to the administration and said, "Look, we think we ought to have routine physical checks," and they set up a mechanism where we would all examine each other. Now here we were, all students doing exams on the other fellows. I don't think we did any laboratory work. It was dog eat dog. You survived on your own, you got money on your own. The school just didn't seem to give a damn.

Later on when I was over at Johns Hopkins I was so impressed that I joined the alumni association there. That's where I give money, and my family have instructions that if I'm sick, if it's not an emergency, I'm going to Hopkins. If it's an emergency, as soon as they can move me out of a local hospital, I'm going to Hopkins because there's nothing in Washington to compare with it.

Nestor and the others view the dining area to the left through a plastic grillwork, which keeps incoming eaters headed in the right direction, toward the food pickup sections. Today they are lucky: the line is short leading to the ice-covered island with salads and cold plates. They pick up salmon-colored or tawny yellow plastic trays from a still-hot stack and load them with forks, knives, spoons, and paper napkins. Nestor takes a little longer than the others, holding up his utensils to the fluorescent lights and rejecting the fork. It has some egg on it. Sometimes he has to go through three or four knives before finding a clean one. (Not much different from a mess hall—probably worse, he thinks.) They kid him about this around Food and Drug, but Nestor feels that if he can take the flak from upstairs he can certainly abide a little of what goes on here, and, besides, he notices that some of his colleagues are themselves starting to examine their cutlery.

Unmoved by the choices facing them, Tagley and Jackson head to the hot-plate counters, passing by the grilled food and submarine sandwich area against one of the side walls. Nestor and Macht, making small talk in the midst of the organized commotion, decide to stay in the cold-plate area.

I chose my internship at St. Michaels in Newark, New Jersey, simply because they paid $25 a month, whereas Georgetown, where I was also offered an internship, only paid $10 a month. Today interns are getting $11,000 to $18,000.

I started immediately after medical school, July 1, 1940. Less than a year later I was in the service. Since I had four years of ROTC I was a Reserve Officer when I was called. They didn't let me finish my internship. I had to report to Fort Jackson, South Carolina, as a first lieutenant. A friend of mine who never went into the ROTC in medical school stayed out, and he got an extra year of training in surgery and then they brought him in as a captain. I did the physical examination on him. All life is unequal and war is particularly unequal.

I was brought into an infantry division in a medical battalion. I had one of the ambulance companies: twelve ambulances, a couple of trucks, a jeep, and a hundred men. But I didn't want infantry, I wanted the Air Corps, and I started trying to get it. I'd send requests up through channels and they wouldn't get anywhere. I remember I was riding downtown with a friend and we had the car radio on when we heard the news of Pearl Harbor. I was temporarily serving as the surgeon in the field battalion and they rushed that battalion down to Charleston. They got hysterical, as though the Japanese were going to invade Charleston. Right after that my transfer to the Air Corps came through.

I was a squadron surgeon in a B-25 outfit, doing physical examinations and immunizations. The commanding officer came to me and said, "Now they've only permitted me to have one doctor going over with the flight echelon and I want two—one in the first squadron, which will be in Cairo about the time the last squadron is going to leave West Palm Beach. Would you like to fly?" I said, "Heck, yeah, I'd like to fly." He said, "I'll get you your promotion to major, if you'll stay with the outfit." He said, "I can't list you as a doctor. You go down and qualify as an aerial gunner and I'll list you as a gunner and you go in the last squadron listed as a gunner." So I went down to Myrtle Beach and I checked out on the 50-calibre machine gun and became a qualified aerial gunner. He listed me as a gunner and I went overseas in the last squadron.

The B-26 at that time was a much more dangerous plane than the B-25. It was later modified and made safer but there was this old saying, "A B-26 a day in Tampa Bay," and that was just about right too. We lost a few planes going over. We were so overloaded with parts and we had seven men in each crew. When we got to Natal in Brazil, in order to make that jump across to Ascension Island and over to what was then the British Gold Coast, we had to take two men and a lot of equipment off each of the bombers. I was one of the two taken off of my crew and I had to fly from Natal in one of those old Pan American Clippers that had the short lower wing. They were like kites. It took us thirteen and a half hours to fly 1,800 miles. We landed in Fish Lake, Liberia. We had to go over at night because the Nazi submarines were out there waiting for us with their 88 mm guns and these old planes cruised at only 5,000 feet. Then we flew across central Africa through Lake Chad and Khartoum, stayed overnight, flew down to Cairo and then out to the Suez Canal to wait for our ground forces. Then we went on up through the desert.

I was in combat for nearly two years. My outfit was the one described in *Catch-22*. Now that is a very distorted and dishonest book. This guy took all of the bizarre incidents and made it look like it happened every day all day. We were a magnificent outfit. (My bomb wing still gets together once a year.) We joined Montgomery's army in the North African desert. We went right on through Tunis, through Sicily, to southern Italy, then over to Corsica and southern France.

One of the worst things was a bombing raid in May 1943 when we were in Corsica. The Germans hit us one night and they did a beautiful job. They killed 38 outright. We hospitalized 138 seriously wounded, and a lot of minor wounds that we didn't bother with.

Once at Natal one of the men walked into a propeller, which just chewed the hell out of his left arm. I took off what was left of it. We were in a little pyramidal tent. I had him on a litter and on two orange-crate type of boxes with his foot held up because he was in semi-shock and we had some plasma running into him. But that's the kind of facilities I had to take this guy's arm off. Two years later when I came back through Natal on my way home, you wouldn't have recognized the place. Here was a beautiful hospital, a beautiful home for the doctors and nurses, a tremendous cafeteria. It was just unbelievable, a result of the war effort.

We went through some pretty rough missions, particularly in the early days. Our supply line hadn't joined up in North Africa—our line came by way of Australia, the Red Sea, and to Cairo. We didn't have replacements. We were fighting a tough battle against the Nazis.

What I learned more than anything else during the war was something about psychosomatic medicine. It was a fantastic education. I saw men acutely develop hypertension. To this day if doctors are asked what causes essential hypertension, they say it's unknown, and then they give you all the theories. But I know what causes essential hypertension because I saw it produced in combat and I saw it disappear when the man was taken off. I saw men who developed severe headaches strictly as the result of stress and strain of battle, or a particular urinary frequency, and it was all subconscious. Of course if I'd told them, "It's just because you're scared to death," they might have poked me in the face. I saw low back pain which was in effect the man saying, "This situation is a pain in the ass to me." I saw men who were unable to swallow as if they were really saying, "I can't stomach this."

To a great extent it was our advice that determined whether a man flew or not. We were in North Africa, first in Libya and then Tunisia, we weren't getting replacements, we were having heavy losses, and we were at the stage where a lot of the men were coming in and saying, "Doc, I can't fly any more, I'm finished, I just can't do it." Very often a man thought he was finished before he really was in our opinion. And we'd say, "Man, you're not finished, and anyhow we don't have any replacements." The first thing we'd get thrown at us was, "You haven't been through it, what do you know about what it's like?" So every two or three months I would go on a mission, so that later on nobody could say to me, "You don't know what it's like up there, you haven't been through it." I went on three of the worst missions my outfit ever flew, when the flak was so thick you could get out and walk on it.

Three black women, their netted hair glistening beneath strong overhead lamps, glide along, aligning cold plates on a bed of crushed ice behind a long glass panel. From a few feet away each plate appears to be an abstract creation of precisely arranged colors; even Nestor is occasionally impressed with how neat things are here, but then he thinks about the food itself and his dyspepsia quickly returns. Last week he ate something here that upset him for three days. Usually the food is no worse than bland. As it is he uses the cafeteria only for convenience; if he had the time he would rather go to a McDonald's.

One of the women behind the counter asks Nestor if he would like a fruit salad. His mind is elsewhere, but he nods. She looks at Dr. Macht, who is eyeing a tuna fish plate. She points to it. "Yes, thank you." Both men slide their trays along aluminum pipes to the dessert section, where Nestor picks a pale orange from a plastic bowl and Macht pulls a piece of apple pie from the glass shelf. They move on to take milk and a coke.

After the war they had attached me to an anti-tank outfit. I said, my God, here I was trained as a flight surgeon, two years in combat. You can send a man to the School of Aviation Medicine for twenty years and not duplicate what you learn in combat. So I got out of the Reserves.

The military had no plans for us after the war. I had had only a year of internship and I knew I needed more. But all of the openings were filled by men whom the government now paid to go through medical school. I got a letter of commendation from the surgeon general, the kind they send to you after you're separated from the service, that said "what a magnificent job you've done" and so on, "you have the gratitude of your country" and so on. I sat down and wrote back to this character and said, "Well, I'm glad I did my duty and so on, but by God my training was interrupted, and now there isn't any place for me."

I decided I'd loaf for a while, just take it easy. I had no choice. There just was no place for the returning veterans. I went up to Children's Hospital and met a man I knew from medical school. (I had met him on the way to the train one night with his bags. He was going to quit, and I talked him out of it. He later became professor of pediatrics at

Georgetown.) He was running the show up at Children's Hospital in Washington, and he said, "Why don't you come in here and work with us?" So I got a job at Children's Hospital and they made me assistant chief resident. Soon I became fascinated by pediatrics. Thinking back on it I'm glad, because I realize that I never could have stomached adult medicine after having gone through the war. It's a difficult thing to explain, but with young people there's rapid healing and there's optimism and there are years ahead.

I spent two years there, and in the fall of 1947, when I got my board certification in pediatrics, I went out into private practice in Virginia. I did well, but I was working on call twenty-four hours a day, seven days a week. I found that routine practice is 99 percent snotty noses, diaper rashes, infant feeding, and growth and development. I didn't like it. After three years I tried to solve the problem by forming a partnership with another pediatrician, so we could alternate nights and weekends and vacations and so on. We got along fine except it still bored the hell out of me. So one day I walked in and I said, "Cliff, the whole practice is yours. It won't cost you a penny."

Now, while I was a resident I became very interested in pediatric cardiology, and I saw every kid in the hospital who had heart disease. So I got a fellowship in cardiology at Cornell. I went up there primarily because I wanted to do electrocardiography. Then I came down with Helen Taussig at Hopkins for seven months. After that I came back to Washington, where I got a three-year grant from the National Heart Institute for research and teaching at Children's Hospital. NIH wanted me to renew it, and I said, "I don't have the space; the facilities aren't sufficient." They said, "Well, we'll give you a grant for a wing on the building." I said, "Well, the real problem is the mentality of the people who are making the decisions. There's an impossible situation here."

Then I did a combination of pediatrics and cardiology; you lose money at pediatric cardiology alone—you have to support yourself from the pediatrics. Young people who have kids with heart disease, who are trying to buy a home and a car and feed the other kids and buy shoes, you can't charge them the type of fee that would make a decent living.

Nestor and the others continue along the line toward the cashiers. All the employees behind the other counters are female, too, except for one white man at the grill, who is shoveling french fries into waxed paper bags. The women all wear hair nets and green uniforms that look freshly starched. They seem bored. A line Nestor once read passes through his mind, he's not sure why: "A bachelor's life is a splendid breakfast, a tolerably flat dinner, and a most miserable supper."

Over at the hot-food section the steam from the trays has reached the serving people; beads of sweat appear on their foreheads, the collars on their uniforms begin to droop, and their aprons now show splattered food. All the while a procession of replacement trays rolls back and forth from the kitchens.

It wasn't long after that I came to Food and Drug. In the late fifties I was being detailed for drugs that just didn't make sense to me. I would say to these detail men, "My God, you mean Food and Drug has approved?" "Oh, yes, they've approved." "Well, where's the evidence? I haven't seen the literature." Well, they'd have the medical director of the company send me something of his choosing, usually one or two articles, testimonials that he wrote.

Sometime in February of 1960 I decided to drive to Florida for a couple weeks' vacation, and when I was just about to leave I developed a sore throat and fever. Now I had been given some samples of this new antibiotic put out by Lederle called Declomycin—I always took my medical bag along—and I took the pills for the next three days. I went down to Bradenton and I seemed to be responding. The next day I drove over to Pompano Beach. The following morning was a very clear day, a little chilly, and I went out fishing. After about an hour I just started to burn all over, every exposed part. That evening I developed blisters, my face was swollen, and I couldn't sleep all night long. I went to a dermatologist in Fort Lauderdale the next day and he put me on steroids and nonallergic soap and he said, "You better get out of Florida." I said, "Could this be something like poison oak or poison sumac?" And he said, "Oh, no, I'd be able to see that." I said, "Could it have been this drug that I took?" He said, "We don't know anything about reactions to Declomycin. It's new." Fortunately the next two days were overcast and I drove back out of Florida and came home.

Three weeks later it came out in the *Journal of the American Medical Association* that Declomycin was producing severe toxic reactions and there were second-degree burns. My own blisters took weeks to heal. So I called Food and Drug, and was shunted aside. Later I found out that both the FDA and the drug company knew tests had shown that Declomycin produced phototoxicity, but it hadn't been put in the labeling. Why didn't the company itself put it in the labeling? They had two tests on prisoners: one in Philadelphia and one out in McAllister, Oklahoma. If they took a hundred prisoners getting the standard dose and put them out in the sun, whether they were tanned or not, 30 percent would develop phototoxicity, just as I did. They mentioned all this afterwards. It wasn't in the original labeling. But only the first time a doctor uses a new drug does he look at the package insert; after that he doesn't because he already knows what this drug does and how it differs from the others. To come along a year later after you've introduced a drug and put in the warning is ridiculous.

This, plus the fact that they were always excusing themselves before the Kefauver committee and others, saying, "Well, we don't have enough men, we don't have enough money, and we particularly need specialists," bothered me. So in May of 1961, thinking this would be a good way to get out of the routine pediatrics and still keep my cardiology, I came to FDA.

The cafeteria is beginning to fill.

There were serious rumblings at Food and Drug barely a year before John Nestor arrived with his carpetbag of outrage. In early May of 1960 Dr. Barbara Moulton, a respected physician who had resigned a few months earlier from the Bureau of Medicine in protest against its policies, testified before the Kefauver committee. She stated her belief that a strong, militant Food and Drug Administration was necessary for the welfare of the American people, and that in turn a strong, militant Bureau of Medicine was necessary for the welfare of the Food and Drug Administration.

> I believe also that hundreds of people, not merely in this country, suffer daily, and many die because the Food and Drug Administration has failed utterly in its solemn task of enforcing those sections of the law dealing with

the safety and misbranding of drugs, particularly prescription drugs. . . . I have watched with deep regret as more authority has been removed from the one group within the Administration with the training, experience, and wisdom to advise you on medical problems. I have watched with deeper regret as promotions have been given almost exclusively to those individuals within the Administration who have, in my opinion, allowed considerations of private gain to becloud their intellectual honesty and pervert their sense of duty to the public. No well-trained, public-spirited physician can in good conscience remain for long in the Food and Drug Administration under present conditions.

Dr. Moulton told Senator Kefauver that it was time to remove "all those officials who either for personal gain or by reason of too many years of close association with and brainwashing by the industries they regulate have come to place the welfare of the industry above that of the consumer." Further, she pointed out that (1) then commissioner George P. Larrick was without either legal or scientific training; (2) that a medical officer in the New Drug Branch had power to release any new drug on his own initiative, without review by his colleagues, but refusal to release a new drug must have the unanimous support of the chief of the New Drug Branch, the director of the Bureau of Enforcement, and the general counsel's office; (3) that her outspoken comments about antibiotics (which continued to be used widely in inadequate dosage, for diseases in which they had been proven ineffective, in irrational combinations, and without adequate diagnosis) were decidedly unwelcome; (4) that—after a request from Pfizer and Company—she had been transferred from the New Drug Branch to the Drug and Device Branch because she "was not sufficiently polite to members of the pharmaceutical industry" and had been replaced by physicians with no clinical experience; (5) that the industry exerted tremendous pressure on FDA medical officers to certify new drugs; and (6) that the decision makers at Food and Drug frequently pick an isolated statement by one scientist that supports the industry point of view and disregard a vast amount of material by medical leaders in the field who take an opposite point of view. (*We are worse off now*, thinks John Nestor, *than in 1960.*)

Nestor pays for his lunch and moves toward the tables.

It wasn't long before I realized the connection between government and industry. Kefauver's hearings were moving into high speed in 1960 and '61. Dr. Moulton had raised all of these questions and had been shunted around. Larrick was an out-and-out industry man. We know how he was appointed: the man who led the campaign for Eisenhower in the Midwest—he's now an attorney in town—went up to the White House and said that industry wanted Larrick, who was a Food and Drug inspector. He had only two years of college. And they made Larrick commissioner. Now here was the head of a regulatory agency that depends on science, and the man didn't even have a college degree. He became commissioner of Food and Drug because the food and drug industry *wanted* him as commissioner. And what do you think of FDA hiring a medical officer who has not had an internship or a medical license? Well they did, and he eventually became assistant chief of the New Drug Division! How do you like that?

Kefauver had asked me to come on his staff as an advisor. He knew Food and Drug was scared to death of him at the time, and he could force them to give me a leave of absence. And I had agreed to come on. But I said to him, "You know the Humphrey committee wants me to appear in open session." Kefauver said, "You've got to make a choice. You'll ruin your value to me because you'll be labeled anti-industry. So if you decide to go and testify for Humphrey's committee, I can't take you on." I went back to the Humphrey committee and said, "I don't want to testify," but they said, "Look, we've got to have somebody from inside Food and Drug. We've got to crack the thing. Somebody's got to throw the bomb. We think it's your public duty and your obligation to do it, to make the sacrifice and do it. And we'll do the best we can to protect you." So I decided I would testify. Barbara Moulton threw the first bomb but then she made the mistake of getting out and therefore she was neutralized. I threw the second bomb and it hit the fan and I stayed in and fought.

Tagley and Jackson pass by the cashier's stand and pay for their lunches. They look blankly through the dining area, seeking Nestor and Macht, who are already seated in a corner near the gold plastic grillwork. The two men weave their way over to the small table and put down their trays. The table has been cleared except for the salt and pepper shakers, a jar of sugar, and an ash tray. Almost blending in with the background noise are four or five black men in white uniforms and round cardboard caps; they are scattered around the orange-red and yellow room clearing dishes and wiping off tables. Nestor stares at Tagley's rice pudding.

In March 1963, eleven months after he had arranged a noteworthy meeting between his erstwhile mentor, Dr. Helen Taussig (who had returned from West Germany convinced of a correlation between thalidomide and deformities in the newborn), and his FDA colleague Dr. Frances O. Kelsey (to whom President Kennedy later awarded the Distinguished Federal Civil Service Medal for following up on that correlation), John Nestor was welcomed by Hubert Humphrey, chairman of the Senate subcommittee investigating the FDA. "The Food and Drug Administration should be proud of you," said the senator, "and I trust that it will accept your testimony as testimony to improve the service and not in any way injure it."

Dr. Nestor wasted no time. First he said that certain new drugs should not have been permitted on the market since the data on their new drug applications did not substantiate safety. He said that there were needless delays in suspending new drug applications and withdrawing certain items from the market. He said there were new drugs on the market that had never been demonstrated as safe, and that often the data necessary to establish a drug's soundness and efficacy were submitted in the form of anecdotal or testimonial letters. And he said that questioning of past decisions by the FDA or of its commitments to the drug companies is met "with indifference, disapproval or even hostility."

To these charges Nestor added that the FDA frequently neglects the fact that the metabolism and action of drugs often differ in children; that despite requests from physicians in the Bureau of Medicine, panels of consultants had not been made readily available for advice and opinion; and that there should be a prompt and thorough reevaluation of such over-the-counter products as antibiotics, antihistamines, vitamins, sedatives, and cold preparations.

Then the doctor let go with specifics, naming names and scorning confidentiality. He cited one of his first cases at FDA, which involved Entoquel—put out by White Laboratories for symptomatic treatment of diarrhea in infants. Shortly after the drug was released two infants for whom it was prescribed experienced severe toxic reactions. Nestor investigated the general practitioner responsible for some of Entoquel's clinical evaluations and concluded that the results were "impossible" and that the man was "a fraud." (The physician later pleaded *nolo contendere* and was fined.)

But why didn't the drug companies find the results "impossible," asked Senator Humphrey, and why didn't the FDA discover the fraud before it released Entoquel? Dr. Nestor suggested that the fraudulent data were just one example of a large proportion of clinical evidence submitted in support of new drug applications, which consists of little more than "medical testimonials from practitioners." Food and Drug had rejected his, Nestor's, recommendation to keep a file of *all* possibly suspect clinical investigators, choosing instead to list only those who gave signs of untruthfulness, psychosis, or dangerous incompetence and irresponsibility. Even with such stringent screening a number of scientists soon made the file.

Humphrey was attentive. Nestor also mentioned Altafur, Menadione, Mylicon, PRN. Altafur had been passed by FDA for the treatment of severe infections, for which it later proved to be ineffective. (Subsequent hearings on the case established the principle that medicines promoted for use in serious infections and which prove to be ineffective are in fact "dangerous.") Even though the recommendation of an HEW hearing examiner to suspend the new drug application on Altafur had been reviewed and upheld by the FDA commissioner, there had been no internal appraisal to determine why the drug was cleared originally, or to discover how its producer could be allowed a three-month period of grace for further marketing after the risks became known.

Menadione, or Vitamin K_3, had never satisfied the regulation that a food additive requires prior proof of safety and efficacy, yet it was allowed to remain on the market, against the recommendations of Nestor and his colleagues. Nestor complained that during the whole course of the controversy it had been necessary to present highly technical medical matters to lay administrators for decision. (Menadione was removed from the market two days after he testified.)

Mylicon, a drug advertised "for gastric distress due to gas entrapment," had not met the standards required of a drug for children and had been ordered withdrawn from the market for pediatric use. Yet the producer, unmoved, persisted in advertising it for children under twelve years of age.

"Is that a fact?" asked Senator Humphrey. "That is a fact, Senator."

PRN (phenyltoloxamine), a tranquilizer containing an ingredient of many over-the-counter products, had been passed before the required chronic toxicity tests in animals had been performed or reported. In addition, Paremycin, Formulase, and Coldaid (along with Mylicon) had never been subjected to the necessary safety-testing procedure of a new drug application.

John Nestor listens as Tagley asks Macht, "What is life if not a conglomeration of cross-purposes?" (*The only disadvantage of an honest heart,* Nestor thinks to himself, *is believing in others.*) He reaches for the salt.

The most shocking revelation of all that Nestor offered Senator Humphrey involved MER/29, a cholesterol-inhibiting agent produced by Richardson-Merrell and marketed in the early sixties. Nestor testified that he had been given responsibility for handling the new drug application after MER/29 had been cleared by FDA for general prescription use by the medical profession, even though side effects and complications were being reported. In consultation with other experts, Nestor had determined that the drug as cleared by FDA did not have even a *reasonable* amount of data proving that it was safe or useful. Analysis of test cases had already proven that the capability of MER/29 to lower cholesterol was significantly less than the company was being allowed to claim in its labeling and promotional literature. Furthermore, work done at the National Institutes of Health had shown that in blocking production of cholesterol, the drug permitted another fatty substance to accumulate in the blood. Moreover, rats heavily dosed with the drug bore stillborn litters.

Nestor told of other serious side effects that came to light after MER/29 went into general use, among them severe skin rashes, loss of hair, cataracts, and impotence. He had, he recounted, urged lay decision makers to halt marketing of MER/29, pleading that physicians be alerted immediately to the severe reactions it caused and that conclusive evidence of its efficacy be required. Richardson-Merrell, meanwhile, was asking in one of its marketing circulars: "What is influencing *your* MER/29 sales? *This?* [collage of testimonial articles] or *this* [cartoon of physician, saying 'I don't know, Merrell, Dr. McCynic said it may be toxic.']" The ads went on to say, "MER/29 already has more excellent clinical backing than most other drugs can ever claim. Don't let a few questioning doctors throw you! Know the answers ... Sell positively."

Although John Harvey, who was then deputy commissioner of the FDA, later publicly admitted that there were enough hard data in the new drug application for MER/29 to insure that it would never be marketed, the administrators overruled Dr. Nestor and allowed prescription of the drug to continue. The FDA ultimately required Richardson-Merrell to issue a warning letter to physicians. This slowed but did not stop the use of MER/29. Two weeks after the warning letter, Merrell, with a $2-million inventory of the drug on hand, wrote pharmacists that "physicians throughout the country are prescribing MER/29 and we urge you to make sure your stocks of this high-volume specialty are adequate."

What Nestor did not tell the Humphrey committee—because at the time he was working with a grand jury investigating the whole MER/29 scandal—was that an FDA supervisory inspector in Cincinnati had reported the defection of a Richardson-Merrell lab technician. Early in 1962 she had left the company because she could not in good conscience participate in some of its testing practices. The FDA delayed six weeks longer before acting on its suspicions, and finally dispatched Nestor and a pharmacologist colleague to Cincinnati.

Food and Drug really never wanted MER/29 to go to court or anything else, in my opinion, but events and my action in putting things on the record gave them no choice. I received the assignment on or about October 1, 1961. Before the end of that month I had reviewed the whole thing, and I'd said that the drug had all this toxicity and ought to come off the market, and I'd gotten the Bureau of Medicine to support me. We went upstairs to the commissioner's office, where Harvey overruled us, and instead of taking the drug off the market, he prescribed a warning letter to doctors and a crash eye study.

Shortly afterwards we received a tip that there had been falsification of the laboratory work. I felt that somebody should go right out there and walk into the firm, pull an inspection and look at their records. Well, it took the FDA a couple of months and multiple meetings before it finally decided, yes, we'll send somebody out there. They picked Dr. Nestor to go because he was handling MER/29. But they wanted to send me alone. 1 said, "That's ridiculous, what we are looking for is animal data and I want the pharmacologist who worked on MER/29, Ed Goldenthal, to go with me." They said, "Oh, no, we can't afford to send two people to Cincinnati." Now they send people all over the world, every year, but what they wanted to do was to get me out there alone, in a field in which I am not an expert. I told them flatly that I refused to go "if you don't let me take the pharmacologist." So reluctantly they let Goldenthal go with me.

We flew out on Sunday, April 9, 1962. We met with the inspector who had been tipped off by a member of his motor pool, whose wife had quit Merrell in disgust because of the falsified data. We appeared at the company Monday morning and we pulled a two-day inspection. To make a long story short, we caught them with their pants right down around their ankles because they didn't really know what we were after. I planned the whole strategy. They asked why we were coming out for the inspection and I said, "Well, you know this is a hot potato and I want to know right up to date all the adverse effects." We spent two hours in the morning doing nothing but talk about clinical work. And then around noon we went out to eat. (They offered us lunch but we wouldn't even take a cup of coffee from them.) When we came back I said, "Well, I guess that's about all I need." They said, "We'll be glad to show you anything." I turned to Goldenthal and said, "Do you think there's anything you want to see in the animal data?" Goldenthal said, "Well, there are a couple of things I would like to look at." We went down in the laboratory and we had them pulling out the raw data, and we saw what we wanted. We got the evidence.

That night we went into the Food and Drug office and spent two or three hours dictating a summary of our experiences. When we left we hadn't told them whether we'd be back or not. Now we decided we'd go back the next morning, to see if we could find any more data, to confirm what we had seen, and to give them a chance to come up with any answers. It was obvious to them by this time that we knew they were withholding data from us.

But when we came the next day they refused to give us anything more. They realized that we had them. At the end of the afternoon we said we were going back to Washington and they wanted to know what action we were going to recommend. I said, "Well, we'll simply recommend that when we get to Washington." So we dictated our memo that night and then got on a plane and came back.

Two days later their attorney in town called John Harvey at his home and said they were withdrawing the drug. They realized we had the goods on them. But that'll always be listed in our files as "voluntary withdrawal" of the drug. This is the case so many times. The drug company realizes we've got the goods on them, then they voluntarily act. It's the most involuntary voluntary action you'll ever run into.

Nestor looks at Tagley's rice pudding and notes aloud, with a barely hidden smile, how similar it appears to curdled yak's milk. The others wince and chuckle.

The subsequent indictments and trials emanating from the MER/29 affair resulted in numerous convictions and out-of-court settlements. In March 1964 Merrell entered pleas of *nolo contendere*, which served to avert the publicity that would have attended a trial. Maximum fines of $80,000 were levied against the company (which in that fiscal year had a net income of more than $17 million). Three of its employees also pleaded *nolo* and were put on unsupervised probation for six months.

Later on came a barrage of successful damage suits for injuries suffered because of the side effects from MER/29—the cataracts, loss of hair, severe skin rashes about which Nestor had warned. One was for $1.2 million, the largest in U.S. history for a personal injury not involving death. Total damages paid came to approximately $50 million. The whole nasty business was reported extensively in the newspapers and later on in several books, yet either the public's threshold for shock was too high or its capability for grasping a scientific scandal too limited for it to raise a hue and cry. The principals at Richardson-Merrell held on to their jobs. Some were promoted.

When Nestor finished testifying before the Humphrey committee, Senator Gruening congratulated him for a great public service and said that if even a fraction of his testimony was correct and substantiated, it constituted a shocking indictment of the Food and Drug Administration.

Though Nestor's efforts in the MER/29 case were likewise commended by the Department of Justice, almost immediately after his testimony—later the same day as a matter of fact—the Food and Drug Administration issued a brief statement that denied the import and accuracy of virtually all the doctor's charges. Commissioner Larrick said Nestor was referring to incidents that had occurred before new and tougher drug control laws had gone into effect. He said,

> We operate under the terms of a law. Administrators and attorneys are properly entitled to evaluate the medical facts before embarking on a regulatory program that must be sustained ultimately in the courts.... Arousing fears and challenging actions on the basis of a partial statement of all facts and considerations involved will not improve the lot of the American consumer. We have done well, even in the troublesome instances highlighted by Dr. Nestor's statement, to discharge our responsibilities to the public.

One day later Senator Humphrey responded, saying he wished the FDA were as quick to change its procedure as it was to issue rebuttals of criticism. He particularly supported Dr. Nestor's testimony concerning Menadione, Mylicon, and MER/29. The senator added that "Dr. Nestor's case remains fundamentally unchallenged," and that FDA had not refuted a single major point he made but had "avoided and side-stepped most of the major issues."

For his part Nestor said he did not consider himself a crank but rather a man of "very positive opinions." Humphrey went further. On the Senate floor he pointed out the doctor's repeated attempts to remedy the frauds being perpetrated, adding that the day after Dr. Nestor's testimony Coldaid and PRN were withdrawn by their manufacturers (and Menadione two days later). It was a strongly worded statement, which would take up eleven full pages of the *Congressional Record*, and in which Senator Humphrey supported virtually every charge made by John Nestor. To this day none has been proven inaccurate.

At the time, the drug industry appeared barely fazed. *Drug News Weekly* carried a banner headline, "Humphrey Report Has Praise for FDA, Industry But Also Cites Weaknesses," and reported that the senator lauded "in the highest terms" both the agency and the manufacturers. Meanwhile, HEW Secretary Anthony Celebrezze ordered that any employee called to testify before a congressional committee inform his superiors and disclose what he will discuss, so the Department would be able "to ascertain whether the employee has been asked to testify in his official capacity or as an individual stating his personal views."

When Ralph Fine ran for Congress, he had quite a bit of television and radio exposure on the basis of his book about MER/29 and thalidomide (*The Great Drug Deception*). The publishers arranged these interviews, but when the people at a station in Cincinnati—the home of William S. Merrell, which produced both of these drugs—heard what was being proposed they just hung up. They weren't going to have it in Cincinnati. Some of the drug executives and scientists get away with murder. The MER/29 case is the best example in the world that there is a double standard of justice: evidence of toxicity withheld, and all they get is a slap on the wrist—six months' probation and not even a fine. Somebody else goes into a corner grocery store and robs them of twenty bucks and he gets twenty years in jail!

Congress has done a wonderful job, but one of the most amazing things is that all of this has been exposed and it's in the public record and nobody ever reads it or pays attention. The first thing I said when the General Accounting Office came in here was, "Hell, all this work's been done for you fellows. You don't have to dig it out." This crew at Food and Drug would come down to Capitol Hill and be cut to ribbons. But you could get on an elevator with them when they came back and their whole attitude was, "Well, we got through another one." They had no intention of changing or correcting any of these things unless it hit the fan. We've had committees that have done magnificent jobs, like the Kefauver committee, the Humphrey committee, the Fountain committee, the Nelson committee, and now the Kennedy committee. They've exposed a great deal of skullduggery and put it on public record and nothing ever happens.

But the senators aren't in the executive branch, so all they can do is expose. Because the budget is so complicated and things are now being appropriated for years in advance, Congress has even lost the power of the purse string—that's why it's important now. The executive branch of the government is running the country. We in effect have a dictatorship.

Nestor eats more quickly than the others but his conversation is not as animated as usual. *What am I doing here?* he asks himself again, and for a second, as he sees Jackson's cherry pie his mind goes back to his grandfather's farm in Pennsylvania. The casual talk of the other three, first about the pending transfer of another medical officer, then on what happened with a new drug application from Pfizer, then about the saccharine controversy, mingles with a summer smell on the porch at the farmhouse. But the new drug application has tripped a switch in his memory, and, back in the present, he makes a mental note to look up an item in some old files when he returns to his desk.

While I was working with the grand jury in 1963, I came back to my office one day to read my mail and I found an empty room. They had moved me out of New Drugs into this Surveillance Division, which dealt primarily with drugs *after* they got on the market, not my particular interest. There was no prior notification. How's that to treat *any*body, much less professional people? There didn't seem to be a chance to get back at that time. I was new in government and I didn't know anything about appeals so I just accepted it and went to work there. They also tried to get by without giving me a step up in grade and a pay raise to which I was entitled, by withholding the necessary certificate of competence. On that I threatened them and I finally won.

They had moved me because I was being too effective. My God, I had already upset half a dozen applecarts with Entoquel, the MER/29 drug, and so on. I was just being too darned effective. They wanted me out of the area of passing on drugs before they went on the market. Now with all of this I couldn't afford to be wrong or they'd have landed on me like a ton of bricks. But then I started being too effective in my new area, surveillance. It's a very complicated thing. I had worked on two Vitamin K_1 products put out by Merck, and a woman doctor who used to work for Merck came down to Food and Drug and into my division and she inherited both products—after she had worked four years for Merck! Shortly afterwards I was moved out. Now how can I prove that anybody deliberately did anything? But it was damn peculiar that I was moved out of there and she inherited it, after I had been demanding that we stop giving the stuff intravenously because it was causing anaphylactic shock and death. To this day nothing's been changed, but you can't make these accusations in public without documentation.

Nestor removes his glasses, exhales on them, and wipes them with his napkin.

By 1964 Nestor had begun to make new waves at Food and Drug, having reviewed the new drug application for Contac, put out by Smith, Kline and French. Commissioner Larrick had testified before Congress that FDA never permitted a new drug directly over the counter, but Contac, an exceptionally popular cold medicine, presented a glaring violation of that policy. The FDA had likewise ruled that fixed drug combinations were "irrational and indefensible," but Nestor had found a fixed combination of five ingredients. Moreover, there were numerous side effects being reported, including evidence of thrombocytopenic purpura (extremely permeable and fragile capillaries, bleeding into the tissue) and convulsions, as in the case of a commercial airline pilot who had taken less than the standard dosage. A thirteen-year-old boy who had swallowed one Contac had been hospitalized, semi-conscious. A young woman had died. Cases of glaucoma and urinary retention were also precipitated, both attributed to the atropine in Contac.

Nestor wrote an honest report and recommended action, but adhered strictly to departmental regulations concerning confidentiality of new drug applications. Documents later made public disclosed his role, but no action was ever taken on his recommendation.

I was in Surveillance turning up various things and asking questions about cyclamates, and all of a sudden they moved me out, against my will, into the Division of Medical Review, which was away from new drugs completely. I think I was just being too effective in Surveillance. At the time I wanted to protest, but I was moved without anything in writing. When I finally got the official papers, it was more than a month after they had become effective. I felt trapped. It looked hopeless to try to do anything through the Civil Service. (And looking back on it I think it would have been.) I finally became desperate. Humphrey was Vice President, and Julius Cahn, who had been his staff director when I testified, was over in the White House when I reached him. I called from a pay phone and said, "Listen, Julius, I'm about at the end of my rope." I said, "I know you people didn't promise me anything, but you told me that you would do your best to see that witnesses who testified wouldn't be harassed." I said, "I've been taken completely out of new drugs and completely neutralized, put under these jackasses, and I'm desperate. My God, all you have to do is call from the White House and simply ask them where I'm working, and is it where I want to be. All you have to do is make an inquiry. You don't have to do anything else." Well, God almighty, it wasn't half an hour later that the deputy medical director came bounding down the steps. "Dr. Nestor, now where is it that you want to work?" I said, "I want to go back to cardiopulmonary and new drugs and no place else." Well, there had been a call from the White House inquiring about where I was, and hell, they moved me back that afternoon and the paper work followed.

But things were so rotten in Food and Drug that no matter what they gave me, if I looked below the surface and did a thorough job, I turned up dirt. I even did that in the Division of Medical Review. That's characteristic of Food and Drug. The man who doesn't get into trouble—who gets promoted, who gets key positions—is the guy that doesn't do his job.

Nestor reaches into his coat pocket, pulls out a full-page advertisement by the Pharmaceutical Manufacturers Association clipped from *Time* magazine, and hands it to Jackson. The text appears below a color photograph of pills, capsules, and medicine bottles:

> But our
> commitment has been made:
> To research, to
> drug education,
> and to continue our
> support of legislation
> to combat illegal
> drug usage.
> So that "drugs"
> can simply
> mean—
> good medicine.

Nestor thrusts a forefinger in the air and asks, "How cynical can you get?"

In early 1966 Dr. Nestor was instrumental in forcing withdrawal from the market of an anticonvulsant prescription drug called Elipten (put out by Ciba). FDA Commissioner James L. Goddard, newly appointed at the time, avoided commenting on why the old regime had let ten months pass after Nestor's review of the facts before dispatching inspectors to investigate. When they did they uncovered adverse clinical data reported to Ciba by physicians but not in turn reported by Ciba to the FDA, as required by law. Nestor later charged that Goddard himself sold out to the industry in permitting Serc, used to treat Menière's syndrome (a disorder of the middle ear), to remain on the market despite lack of evidence proving its efficacy.

In mid-1967 *Drug Trade News* suggested reasons why the newly enacted Public Information Act should not include data found in new drug applications: "The medical obstacles boil down to objections about disturbing the doctor–patient relationship, upsetting investigators, and the reluctance of FDA medico–scientific teams to work in a goldfish bowl. . . . FDA doctors don't want to go on record as criticizing another's clinical work or by classifying his work as useless or not well done."

Nestor felt the piece was a deception, and was perturbed enough to spew out a letter to the editor:

> I would like to know who polled the physicians and when. I have never heard of such a poll and wonder who presumed to speak for the whole group without consulting the members.
>
> Frankly, I personally have always believed that we should operate in a "goldfish bowl". . . . Perhaps if this had been the situation in the past a lot of trouble would have been avoided. Actually, the implication of your article is that investigators would submit data to FDA that they would be embarrassed to have published and that doctors at FDA would be equally embarrassed by publication of their decisions. This is hardly a scientific approach.
>
> . . . The doctor–patient relationship exists solely for the benefit of the patient and not the doctor. The patient is not protected by any policy that permits inadequate, inaccurate or fraudulent data to be used as a basis for getting a new drug application approved. Court decisions have established that this happened under the present policy of secrecy.

(That article, thinks Nestor, was as phony as a three-dollar bill. It was planted by FDA to make them look good.)

Nestor, Macht, Tagley, and Jackson rise from the lunch table after about 45 minutes, carry their trays to a nearby steel rack, and slide them in. Conversation at the surrounding tables seems to be mostly about the role of politics in the saccharine controversy. Nestor remembers another line: "All bow to virtue, and then walk away. Virtue has many preachers but few martyrs."

In 1970 John Nestor spoke out again, this time to protest "retaliation" by the FDA for his complaining about "incredibly permissive pharmacology guidelines" followed by the Bureau of Drugs. There was more to it than that. On June 11 Nestor had privately approached Commissioner Charles C. Edwards ("proof positive that I first tried to correct things within the system and failed—only then did I go outside to Congress and the press"). He called Edwards's attention to carcinogenic effects suffered by rats that had been administered Triflocin, a potent diuretic put out by Lederle Laboratories, and charged that Lederle had refused to furnish the names of human subjects who had taken the drug.

Edwards requested written recommendations, which Nestor supplied the next day. He wrote that experimental drugs should not be administered to humans until animal studies have been completed and reviewed by the FDA, and even then they should first be tested for toxic and metabolic effects on normal healthy volunteers before being given to sick patients. "If this policy had been followed in the past, we would have avoided exposing humans to carcinogenic drugs such as Triflocin (Lederle), MK665 (Merck) and a potent immuno-suppressant like Cinanserin (Squibb)."

Six weeks passed with no answer. If Edwards had thought the greatest remedy for anger was delay, he did not know John Nestor. Bristling, the medical officer fired off another memorandum urging the commissioner to take

> prompt and vigorous action to correct this scandalous situation. The present practice of prematurely exposing humans to new experimental drugs violates every code from before the time of Hippocrates down to and including those originating in Nuremberg, Helsinki, the World Health Organization and the United States Public Health Service not to mention the Food, Drug, and Cosmetic Act.

Edwards replied that the FDA was doing all it could to prevent harm to the patients involved, but he did not mention Lederle or Triflocin. That was the last Nestor ever heard on the subject.

Five years later, according to a yellowing clipping from the *Wall Street Journal* that Nestor treasures, Dr. Edwards was named a senior vice president of Beckton, Dickinson & Co., a major maker of medical devices. The article said that while with the government Edwards "vigorously defended legislation to put medical devices under the FDA's control as 'essential to quality health care'" and quoted him as now saying that certain proposed regulatory legislation "may attempt to do too much too quickly."

In August of 1970 Nestor was asked whether he would "be interested" in moving to the Division of Drug Advertising. Nestor assumed he was being offered the directorship but declined anyway. In September, though, he was told officially that he was going to Drug Advertising, not as director but as medical advisor. The assignment was called "temporary."

John Nestor sizzled his cantankerous best. He called the transfer "humiliating" and appealed it within the agency, claiming that he would be virtually useless in the Division of Drug Advertising.

This time, as before, publicity and continuing congressional inquiry and support apparently worked to Nestor's advantage. He was quietly shifted back to the Cardiopulmonary–Renal Division of the Bureau of New Drugs. But it was to be a short-lived tenure.

Perhaps because of his review at the time of a cholesterol-lowering drug (also proposed as a treatment for digitalis intoxication)—which caused him to raise "serious questions concerning the adequacy of previous tests"—perhaps because of numerous other professional or personal conflicts distressing to the hierarchy at Food and Drug, or to the industry, early in the spring of 1972 came still another transfer. On March 14 Nestor was informed that he was being moved to the Office of Compliance. The official papers had actually been signed five days earlier.

It was a bureaucratic *déjà vu*. According to Nestor, this step again effectively removed him from a position where he could evaluate the efficacy of highly complex medicines and into a job where he would oversee the marketing of things like medicated bandages. *They want me to handle stuff that any freshman medical student can do,* he thought, and he protested vigorously. The official job description advertised for his former position, Nestor pointed out to anyone who would listen, had fit him to a T: board certified in his field, author of important research papers, member of a meaningful group of medical societies, demonstrable integrity, effective in expressing ideas, productive, with knowledge of and adherence to FDA and Bureau of Drug policies. The new job required "an M.D. degree supplemented by high level experience in the medical and drug fields."

Nestor took his case to the Civil Service Commission, which concluded two months later that because his salary grade had remained the same, his transfer was not a reduction in rank but a valid reassignment. In fact, the commission further ruled, there was now only one superior officer between Nestor and the bureau director (as opposed to the two in his former position) so he had actually been *elevated* in the FDA hierarchy. Subsequent appeals to the Secretary of HEW proved futile.

But Nestor's case did attract attention. The National Health Federation organized a campaign that resulted in more than a thousand letters of protest to the White House. Ralph Nader's Health Research Group questioned almost a hundred FDA medical officers and reported that over two-thirds of them felt numerous pressures to approve new drug applications: "Unless one has the resources and fortitude of a Dr. Nestor, more likely than not, the officer will bow to the wishes of his superiors and revise his recommendations." When a thorough and conscientious review of a new drug application is performed, said one medical officer, "the only reward is what Dr. Nestor received." Another wrote that the FDA prefers physicians

who have the ability to lie with confidence and security as long as the lie is in behalf of self, administrative superior or organization; to regard patriotism, the good of the whole or others, as symptomatic of immaturity; and perhaps above all else, to disregard the higher sense of Hippocratic tradition. When Medical Officers are recognized as failing to comply with the above criteria they are selectively assigned mere meaningless tasks.

Nestor continued to burn.

They started to clean out the whole Cardiopulmonary–Renal Division for two reasons: first because they wanted people who for two or three years won't know what the score is and who'll just rubber-stamp whatever comes through. So at the same time they're advertising and recruiting for specialists they get young men right out of a residency who don't know which end is up, or doctors in their middle fifties who want to coast for a while in semi-retirement, or men who have been brainwashed for all their lives by the drug companies. The second reason they wanted to get us out of there is that we know where all the skeletons are, the dirty work done in the past. It was clear-cut to me.

In other words now I'm on staff, an advisor, where previously I was in a line position, that is, I was a medical officer reviewing scientific data and making recommendations for action. In an advisory capacity they can ignore me. I've rocked the boat too much. They're trying to put me on the shelf all the time.

The interesting thing is, FDA does finally respond when the pressure gets too hot. Then their action appears in the paper and everybody says, "Isn't this wonderful, what this FDA is doing!" Usually they've been dragged to the woodshed, but when they finally do the right thing the public thinks that it is being protected.

Outside the glass doors leading to the cafeteria, Nestor points Tagley and Jackson in the direction of the south parking lot. Dr. Macht has to go to the visitors' lot in front. Nestor, headed anyway toward the main entrance, offers to show him the way.

In August and September of 1974 Nestor and a group of other scientists, subpoenaed to testify before Senator Humphrey, openly castigated the FDA for corrupt drug-approval practices and ruthless treatment of employees inclined to blow the whistle. Again, as he had done more than a decade earlier before the

Humphrey committee, the doctor spilled all his beans. But now he was no longer a lone wolf howling at the agency from within—the others uttered a similar litany of grievances—and he could focus as much on his own experiences of bureaucratic harassment as on drug-safety issues.

Such public allegations, from such prominent and respected sources, were serious enough for both the commissioner of Food and Drug (by now Alexander Schmidt) and HEW Secretary Caspar Weinberger to launch their own investigations. Schmidt's self-evaluation proved exceedingly controversial, if not predictable. It took fourteen months to complete, cost close to $200,000, and concluded (in late 1975) that the employees' accusations were groundless.

HEW's Review Panel on New Drug Regulation, on the other hand, a select gathering of law professors and scientists, equally intent on a thorough appraisal of the charges and on full protection of their independence, labeled the Schmidt study "inadequate" and "procedurally defective" and found that the "fundamental questions raised by the allegations remain not simply unanswered, but virtually unasked." The panel hired its own staff counsel to investigate further.

Nestor felt somewhat vindicated, but he was still fully sensitive to his enforced inactivity. By totally ignoring him, he thought, superiors at FDA had chosen the path of least resistance. The year 1976, though, brought a more overt form of harassment: Food and Drug pressured Nestor into relinquishing some stock he held in a corporation that partially owned a subsidiary firm that made medical devices. This especially rankled him, not so much because the conflict-of-interest regulations were being so strictly construed, but because the same rules were not being enforced at the higher echelons of HEW, even when more direct ownership of *drug* companies was involved. Fuming, Dr. Nestor pointed particularly to none other than the chairman of the Review Panel,

Dr. Thomas C. Chalmers, whose holdings at the time he was appointed had become part of the public record. "Chalmers not only started out with a conflict by owning drug stocks," Nestor charged, "but he picked up more after he became chairman. How is he going to be totally objective? At the hearings he repeatedly shows an exaggerated solicitude for the financial well-being of the drug companies."

It is hard to say whether it was the disclosure of Chalmers's holdings or continuing friction between him and other members of the Review Panel (in a number of votes Chalmers cast the lone dissent) that finally caused him to submit his resignation, which was accepted by HEW Secretary David Mathews. Again, Nestor felt as if a battle had been won—the long dark tide at last, perhaps, turning in favor of the public interest. But he remembered the exposés of a decade earlier, and he knew full well that his personal war was far from over. During the five years following his transfer to the Office of Compliance, he estimated that he had been assigned less than five months' work. ("And I'm now making $47,500 a year!") Yet he could pull numerous clippings from his file which showed that the FDA was continuing to place ads in professional journals and newspapers for qualified cardiologists. And when the directorship of Cardiopulmonary–Renal was vacated, it was filled with a temporary appointment at a lower grade. "They advertise for people with 'interpersonal skills,'" Nestor complained. "Translated, they mean specialists who will not speak up and rock the boat. People who raise questions are troublemakers. Why is it advertising for a cardiologist when it isn't using those it already has?"

It was about this time that the director of the Bureau of Drugs, Dr. J. Richard Crout, called Dr. Nestor into his office. Though they had seldom met personally, Crout and Nestor had been adversaries over various bureaucratic shuffles and new-drug-approval procedures for at least four years. Now Crout wanted to unruffle feathers, burn bridges, soothe feelings. According to his memorandum of the meeting, he expressed concern that Dr. Nestor felt he had no meaningful work to do, and he hoped that bygones could be bygones. He acknowledged Nestor's feelings that he had "been placed on the shelf." He mentioned that a number of important hearings would be coming up in the Office of Compliance and asked that Nestor handle the medical aspects. "Dr. Nestor indicated he would willingly accept this assignment and do his best, although he did want us all to understand that he felt his best utilization would be in the Division of Cardio-Renal Drug Products."

Nestor's recollection of the same meeting differs not so much in substance as in tone, and evokes a full measure of fifteen years' pent fury. According to Nestor's handwritten memorandum, Dr. Crout had admitted sitting tight on his case, with the commissioner's knowledge and approval, but had averred that the two of them, Nestor and Crout, had communicated well over the years and there was no reason why they couldn't continue to do so. Nestor interrupted to point out that there had really been little communication between them except of a perfunctory nature. Dr. Crout agreed that this was probably so and that they should in the future communicate more often, and that he realized things had not been ideal in the past but that they should let bygones be bygones.

Nestor replied that he could not let bygones be bygones even if he tried because he was very bitter at the way he had been treated for the past four years and could not easily forget it. He mentioned that he had been arbitrarily and capriciously removed from the Cardiopulmonary–Renal Division and placed in an office with little or nothing to do, against his will. He stated his opinion that this was deliberately done to force him out of the agency, but that it had not worked. He asked if Crout realized what a waste of training and expertise this was and how destructive it was to his morale. He reminded him that the passing of time and the sequence of events had served to prove how right he had been in raising issues in the Cardio–Renal Division about such drugs as Triflocin. It was for raising these issues, he said, that he, along with the others, had been moved out. He also made the point that, despite his bitterness, he had never played dog in the manger but had always worked promptly on any assignment given to him.

Dr. Crout implied that, although Nestor had always willingly taken an assignment, there were some questions about the quality of his work. Nestor asked why that had never been called to his attention or made a matter of record, as required by Civil Service regulations, so that he could respond appropriately? He pointed out that when a consumer safety officer came to him with a bottle of 1/2-grain codeine tablets that was labeled 1/4-grain, it did not take more than three seconds to conclude this could be dangerous and that the product should be properly labeled. He said this was the nature of much of the activity in Compliance, and he asked how he could do more work when none was assigned.

The two parted after an hour, with Nestor reminding Crout that this meeting had not solved the work problem to his satisfaction.

Not long afterward they met in the elevator. As Nestor tells it, "It was only the two of us. Normally he avoids me like the plague, but now he couldn't. He asked how I was. I said fine, how are you. He said fine, but that he had been working hard. I said, well, why don't you come on down to where I am. I don't work hard at all, there's nothing to do! Just then the elevator door opened, and he left with a grimace."

Nestor and Macht walk down a long corridor outside the cafeteria. There are a lot of narrow halls in the Parklawn Building, a massive gray steel-and-glass block that rises and glares unexpectedly in the still-developing greater Rockville area. Inside, beside the office space and the cafeteria, are a gift shop, a drugstore, a florist, a bank, a cleaners, a beautician, a barbershop, a post office, and a credit union. Employees rarely need to leave the building during their lunch hour.

For all its amenities, though, Parklawn exudes signs of hurried planning and construction. Its passageways are cramped and confining, and its stairwells, thinks Nestor, must have been built according to the country's most liberal fire code. They carry barely two people at a time. Everywhere there are flimsy partitions separating offices from hallways and from one another. Normally it takes Nestor a half hour to drive to Parklawn from his home in Virginia, time he uses to figure out what he has to do that day (when to get to the Xerox machine, whom to mail clippings, which novel to read next).

Nestor and Macht take the elevator to the fifth floor, which leads to the front entrance; there Nestor a little hurriedly bids good-bye to Macht, who promises to be in touch before the end of the week.

Things began to jump again at FDA (and HEW) in mid-1976. Senator Kennedy's hearings were under way once more; some two dozen new scientists had joined the original witnesses against Food and Drug. The Government Accounting Office got into the act, charging both the agency and the industry with exposing humans to unnecessary risks in testing new drugs. Without Chalmers the HEW Review Panel was asserting its independence.

Senator Kennedy called the employees' testimony "a vital public service," adding that the witnesses were "not cranks... as some of them have been labelled," and he took the occasion to praise in particular Nestor's "distinguished record." And Ralph Nader said publicly, "Fortunately for all of us, John Nestor has persevered."

Nestor himself, perhaps recalling the congressional commendations he had received in years past and the subsequent FDA harassment to which he had been subjected, tried once again. Besides suggesting a more careful selection of people at the top (to avoid conflicts of interest—the so-called revolving door or deferred bribe syndrome), he made detailed recommendations to Senator Kennedy. Among them were that all FDA contacts with industry and actions on new drugs be in writing and on the public record, that animal and human pharmacology data of safety and efficacy never be regarded as trade secrets, that drugs be evaluated according to their *therapeutic* benefit, and that any harassment and intimidation by bureaucratic superiors of employees who expose wrongdoing should be punished. "There will always be a number of civil servants," said Nestor, "who will insist on compliance with the law."

In mid-April 1977 the Review Panel's special counsel issued his report, and even the most casual observer of the bureaucracy had to construe it as nothing less than a blockbuster. Almost 800 pages long, the study was meticulously documented and conducted under apparently rigorous standards of proof and impartiality. It concluded that (beginning in 1970) FDA management, while not dominated by industry, undertook a conscious effort to make the agency less adversarial toward and more cooperative with drug manufacturers, that (by a systematic pattern of involuntary transfers) it attempted to neutralize reviewing medical officers who followed a different philosophy, and that a number of its administrative dealings were probably unlawful.

Each of the allegations had been painstakingly investigated, with John Nestor's case receiving particular attention. Noting that Nestor is perceived by different people as "inexcusably rude," "colorful," "abrasive," "intelligent," "loud," "combative," "boisterous," "candid," or "honest," the special counsel nevertheless found that he had been unlawfully transferred from a drug-reviewing position to a non-reviewing office that "wastes his expertise." It was a matter of false pretenses: in truth Nestor had been moved because his superiors, including Drs. Crout and Henry Simmons, viewed him "as a management problem," but when he filed a formal grievance various FDA officials "testified untruthfully" under oath about his importance in his new assignment. The HEW investigators charged Crout with consciously misleading statements and others at Food and Drug with issuing a patently false press release concerning Nestor's usefulness in Compliance.

In fact, said the panel, Nestor was "severely under-utilized," and, furthermore, it suggested, the potential for his harassment was insidious and continuing—as witness a quote from the November 12, 1976 issue of the *Food and Drug Letter*:

> "A common view in food and drug circles is that a Democratic president will mean an extensive honeymoon for FDA from tough congressional scrutiny. Given a two-year mandate, if the pressure were removed, we could shove [Dr. John] Nestor and other dissidents aside and take care of other personnel problems in short order," a high FDA official told us.

The special counsel went on to recommend that Nestor's tainted grievance hearing be voided, that he be given an official apology and offered a position where his talents could be used, and that some arrangement be made to pay his legal fees.

Besides Nestor, various other FDA critics were found to have been treated with "unlawfulness, dishonesty, discourtesy, lack of consideration and even apparent vindictiveness." The chairman of the Review Panel called the report "a rare occasion on which allegations made by federal employees against the management of their agency have been thoroughly investigated by an impartial body and the results of that investigation made public."

Thus did the panel's findings differ significantly from those of former Commissioner Schmidt. Its special counsel, moreover, uncovered evidence that at least some of the personnel changes at FDA were made in response to complaints from industry, in particular by Elmer Bobst, chairman of the board of Warner-Lambert Pharmaceuticals, who was influential in the Nixon administration. And it found that many of the techniques used to neutralize complaining FDA medical officers—though they were an unlawful circumvention of government regulations—were prescribed by a specially prelared administration manual telling how the Civil Service could be rendered more "politically responsive."

The panel's report got some small play in the Washington papers and on ABC News. Two weeks after it was published, Crout, whose reprimand had been recommended by the special counsel, was given a distinguished service award by new HEW Secretary Joseph Califano.

In light of all his past testimony and the subsequent public apathy and intramural harassment, Nestor himself wondered if anything would come of this latest "piece of dynamite." He was not optimistic.

I have never found an honest drug company—although I haven't dealt with all of them. Even those that would like to be honest find out they are at a competitive disadvantage and can't afford to be. I've had offers with drug companies that I couldn't in good conscience take. I turned it down. The fellow said, "My God, why are you turning a good thing down?" I said, "I'll tell you why. One of the first things I'd say was that 95 percent of that crap that they've got out on the over-the-counter market ought to come off." Now how long do you think I'd last with an association like that? They don't want good science. You've got to make a choice as to whether you're going to operate under the scientific ethic and make decisions in favor of the patient—the consumer. You can't be on both sides. I would have to give up the whole reason I came into medicine, the whole idea of public health.

I think that the drug companies could be made responsible. We're living now in an era where the drug industry, for at least fifteen years to my knowledge, has continuously made the highest net profit of all industries in the country. There have been years when the profits of some companies are so high they could pay off their entire capital investment in two and a half years' time. It seems to me that when drug companies cut corners and use all sorts of pressures to get around doing adequate studies, they can't claim they don't have the money—they've got all of these profits. Why in the hell can't they afford to do these tests? Why do they have to go ahead prematurely administering drugs to humans before they've done adequate animal studies? I don't think you have to destroy the capitalistic system to make the drug companies responsible. The first thing we ought to do is start following the Food and Drug law, which has never been properly enforced. We've got a lot of power under it.

When I took up this problem of testing in humans, I got a routine progress report from the company on the so-called follow-up that was ridiculous—grossly inadequate. There was nothing about quality; all they did was send a letter to people. Now if they want to *sell* me a drug, they'll send a detail man—why can't they send a man out to check to see if human guinea pigs are being properly followed by a doctor? Well, Food and Drug did send two inspectors up to the company to check on the follow-up, to look at the records. When they got there, they were shunted around, told that the men they wanted to talk to weren't there, would be here tomorrow, and so on. But then the medical director, a vice president of the company, walked in and said that the FDA had the National Academy of Sciences set up a committee to look into this follow-up problem, and he said, "I'm chairman of that committee and we've been working on it and we'll hand in our report in a few months." So here is the crook himself and the company that is one of the worst offenders, and all of a sudden who is made chairman of the investigating committee? The crook himself! Now, when that hits the fan . . .

For more than sixty years the food and drug industry has had this agency in its pocket, and we're in its pocket today worse than we ever were. They control us because they've always been able to dictate who would be commissioner and who would be medical director.

If the drug companies don't get what they want, they accuse the medical officers of being unfair. Undoubtedly they were behind my transfer but they never had any face-to-face confrontations with us. Everything is done with the higher officers.

There are no morals or ethics in the drug industry. How do you explain the Merrell people when they faked the monkey data, when they withheld proof of the fact that MER/29 had caused cataracts in rats? How do you explain these humans?

I grade the Review Panel's report a C+ and no better—although they did the best with what they had. If they'd been given full investigative powers with the right to subpoena, as we asked for, they would have uncovered a lot more. This time I've got all the fingers on both my hands crossed, but we'll have to wait and see how the new commissioner [Donald Kennedy] responds. I've been disappointed too many times in the past. It's not enough that I've been vindicated. I want to see Food and Drug cleaned up.

At the florist shop a few yards down from the reception lobby elevators, Nestor stops to look for some flowers to take with him this evening. He has been invited to dinner by Browning, one of his few close friends besides Macht.

Being a bachelor, he often eats out, but usually in restaurants. *What can you prescribe for loneliness?* he has asked himself. It is a corny question, but poignant. Nestor thinks he would like to have a wife and family, but in his case things simply did not work out—not a single social event in medical school, and then those four and a half years in the Army.

Now he spends his free time reading about the Civil War and listening to classical music. He gets 26 days' annual leave, which he uses either traveling with a charter club or resting at the cottage he and his brother have on the Chesapeake Bay.

Nestor taps impatiently on the glass counter in the florist shop. Two minutes pass; still no service. He walks out and heads toward the drugstore next door, glancing automatically at the headlines on the newspaper stand. A Drug Fair like all Drug Fairs. The length of one wall is devoted entirely to colorful bottles, boxes, cards, and tubes—over 2,000 items displayed under large red labels that stand out against the white fluorescent light: LAXA-TIVES, DEODORANTS, VITAMINS, SHAMPOOS, PAIN RELIEVERS,

TOOTHPASTES. Nostrums appear to be as popular in America as anywhere.

Nestor buys a toothbrush for 69 cents and leaves the store, walking briskly to the glass-enclosed gift shop in the far front corner of the building. He browses for several minutes before asking a clerk about some wine. She shows him a small display, from which he picks a bottle of Gallo Red Burgundy. He hands her a five dollar bill and gets 49 cents change.

Drugs should not be used lightly for every minor symptom—a little bit of headache or a little runny nose. I practically never take a drug. When I'm real sick with a lousy cold I might take a couple of aspirin. Antihistamines cause a thickening of secretions, so they are not only useless but can be dangerous. The interaction of drugs is often tremendous. There are about eight drugs that aspirin interacts with. For example, aspirin modifies the anticoagulants used to prevent clotting. This is the danger of over-the-counter drugs. In the early 1950s the law created two classes of drugs—prescription and over-the-counter—and set rather rigid criteria for what could be over-the-counter. If we applied those criteria properly, 95 percent of the drugs that are on the drugstore counters now wouldn't be there. But they just ignore the law.

Of course it's true that there are many people walking around with a special predisposition to be damaged by drugs thatwon't affect the average individual. I had a little fifteen-year-old girl who survived three major heart operations, and then we lost her to a drug reaction.

A lot of folk remedies are good psychotherapy. Stuff like cough medicine works the same way. As far as I'm concerned, the only value of cough medicine is for the parents. They think they're giving something to their kid and it makes them feel better. So cough medicine for a child is good psychotherapy for the parent. Most of them are placebos. After all, 90 percent of us get well on our own from any illness. No drug ever *cured* anybody. An antibiotic doesn't cure you—you heal yourself. If you've got a streptococcus septicemia and we give you penicillin, it may kill off all the causative streptococci but you get well yourself. No drug ever cured anybody.

I was once a consultant on a children's book put out by HEW to tell kids about drugs, and boy, what a reaction from the drug industry! They didn't like the ideas I got in there that drugs can be a two-edged sword. They can be dangerous when not used properly. I got in there the principle that drugs themselves do not cure, which is a basic, fundamental, physiological truth. The drug industry didn't want that—they wanted a book put out by HEW that talked about the wonderful public service of the drug industry over the years.

Sometimes we try to do the right thing and go about it the wrong way, like with saccharine. That's been classified as a drug since the early 1900s, so it's nothing new to be able to buy it that way. The *New York Times* quoted somebody as saying that the proposed ban on saccharine in foods undermined the freedom of Americans to eat what they please. Well, its present widespread use undermines *my* freedom *not* to eat saccharine—it's impossible to avoid it. Saccharine should be available only as a prescription drug so the consumer and his physician can judge the benefit-to-risk ratio in an individual case, such as diabetes or obesity, and act accordingly, with full freedom.

Actually the Delaney Amendment, which was added to the Food, Drug and Cosmetic Act and bans all food additives found to produce cancer, is both good science and good law. It's been under attack, but it should be retained and enforced for a number of reasons: first, most experts believe that a large percentage of cancers are caused by environmental factors such as food additives, drugs, radiation, and so on; second, there's been an increase in cancer each year for many years; third, we don't now know if there is a minimal dose below which a carcinogen can be considered safe; fourth, our present animal tests are relatively insensitive, so when they are positive, they indicate how strong the carcinogen is. For example, we must pay great attention to the warning signal represented by the Canadian tests on the saccharine—we have to assume that any substance which is carcinogenic in animals could also be so in man. And fifth, a substance is either cancer-producing or it isn't. Ingesting large amounts of a noncarcinogen will not cause cancer, but small amounts of carcinogen may cause cancer. Usually a substitute can be found for those few chemicals that are carcinogenic.

Food and Drug tried to set a reasonable limit on the dosage of vitamins that could be sold over the counter, these one-a-day type things, so that the public wouldn't be exposed to toxicity which you can get from Vitamin A and Vitamin D, the fat-soluble vitamins. Well, the vitamin people—who like to put out say 50,000 units of Vitamin A because the lay person may walk into the drug store and say, "Boy, this must be potent!"—didn't want that. I disagreed, because I ought to be under medical care if I'm suffering from an out-and-out vitamin deficiency. If a doctor wants to prescribe large doses of the vitamin complex that will correct my beriberi or pellagra he ought to write a prescription for it. Those hearings went on for about two years, several attorneys made a fortune out of them, and finally Food and Drug lost and the outside experts won. But in that case we disagreed as friends, that's all. I think they respect me and I respect them. They're doing what they think is right and I'm doing what I think is right.

The clock says three minutes after one as Nestor heads back down the front corridor, past the Drug Fair and the gift store and the florist shop, to the elevators. He passes them and turns into the Parklawn post office, where he pulls two envelopes from his breast pocket and drops one through the slot marked local mail, one through the out-of-town chute. Just outside the post office there is a free scale inviting passersby to weigh themselves. Farther down the B Wing is a Visitor's Center, with plush royal blue chairs arrayed on a thickly cushioned carpet and three walls full of pamphlets put out by HEW's myriad bureaus and divisions.

Nestor moves to a front elevator that has just opened, steps inside, and pushes the button for the ninth floor.

Another attitude here is, well, I'll put it on the record and make my recommendation and what happens to it is none of my business—what I really want to do is come in from eight to four-thirty and every two weeks pick up that green check. One doctor said exactly that to me. He was one who was promoted. An officer in my division once told a congressional committee, "My job is just to write memos. I don't know who reads them or who does anything with them." This was his attitude and this is the attitude here.

We've got quite a few people here who have medical disabilities, who can't practice. So now they've got a damn good income doing damn little work. They're retired at a darn good salary. They don't want to upset it. We once had a doctor drawing full salary who didn't come in until ten-thirty in the morning and she left at two in the afternoon. Everybody knew it and nobody did a damn thing about it. Technically, you're supposed to take half an hour for lunch. A lot of people are going out and taking two hours. This is one of the ways the government shows favoritism. If some of us did it they'd land on us like a ton of bricks.

FDA is too big and cumbersome. We reached the law of diminishing returns a long time ago. Now we've got a lot of people running around stumbling all over each other and literally accomplishing nothing. When I first came aboard we had only eleven or twelve doctors and we put out more in the way of an end-product than we do now with a dozen times that number. We ought to be organized in such a way that drugs are assigned for review on the basis of the expertise of the assignee. When we get a real problem in, say, pediatrics, we should have a meeting of all the pediatricians aboard and get a consensus of in-house opinion before we start running to the outside. We're simply not utilizing our expertise. It is impossible under the present establishment to correct things from within. Impossible. You get neutralized as it goes up through channels from one level to another, distorted and neutralized.

In the Bureau of Drugs we've got too many chiefs and too few doctors who are really reviewing the applications and doing the spade work. The chiefs come out of industry or medical school and immediately they're experts and are out making speeches the next day. People are picked because of the way they will serve the commissioner, who in turn is serving the drug industry. They ignore seniority. They ignore every rule in the book. They have made it very plain they don't give a damn about the Food and Drug law or Civil Service regulations. They're writing their own laws from day to day, by nothing more than whim.

The basic problem at Food and Drug is the motivation and integrity of its leadership. If and when a commissioner, medical director, and general counsel are brought in who have not been hand-picked by industry, and who take the attitude they are going to enforce the law the way Congress passed it and not the way they think it should have been passed, then the FDA will be cleaned up in short order. But to my mind there has been no doubt about drug-industry control of the commissioner, from Larrick through Goddard through Ley through Edwards through Schmidt—except that I think Goddard was mostly influenced by the food industry. It's too soon to tell about Donald Kennedy, but I have my doubts.

The elevator makes three stops between the fifth and ninth floors. Nestor fidgets: he has a lot of clippings to mail out this afternoon. But it is the item he logged in his mind at lunch that bothers him. He can't remember what it was.

At the ninth floor Nestor heads down the narrow corridor and enters a large space that has been partitioned into a secretarial station and four very small offices. He goes to his room, filled with books and papers, and sits down behind a cluttered desk.

If the only disadvantage of an honest heart is credulity, Nestor thinks to himself, *then maybe I should become even more incredulous.* He leans over, searching for something on a side table covered with stacks of filled manila envelopes. Finally he pulls out a photocopy of a page from the HEW personnel manual, CODE OF ETHICS FOR GOVERNMENT SERVICE, from the chapter on "Employee Conduct." With a red pencil he circles the first clause: "Any Person in Government Should: *Put loyalty to the highest moral principles and to country above loyalty to person, party, or Government Department,*" and writes in red next to it: "This is the rule and the philosophy under which I operate." The trace of melancholy in John Nestor's eyes should not be mistaken for resignation. He slips the page into an envelope for mailing.

The hodgepodge of reactions that John Nestor seems to provoke in everyone who meets him usually combine to yield a grudging respect, if not admiration—even from his superiors at Food and Drug. Both Dr. Simmons and former Commissioner Edwards publicly admitted to mixed feelings about their feisty underling. Edwards called "absolutely 100 percent nonsense" Nestor's charge that the FDA was retaliating by moving him around, adding that the doctor had created "some major administrative problems." (He refused to specify.) "But nobody questions the fact that Nestor is a very conscientious, hard-working guy."

Simmons acknowledged to the newspapers: "He's very zealous. He really wants the law enforced."

In late 1977 came further vindication. Commissioner Kennedy formally vacated Nestor's 1972 grievance hearing as "fraudulent and tainted," and restored Nestor to his old position in Cardiopulmonary–Renal. "I thought he put his case well. Ultimately, Nestor showed me his terribly strong determination that that [the Cardio–Renal position] was the job he wanted. I considered the simple justice question, and I came to feel we couldn't do anything else." But Nestor still wasn't satisfied, claiming that he never received a letter of apology and that Dr. Crout had never been appropriately reprimanded.

Morton Mintz of the *Washington Post*, a longtime FDA watchdog and one of Nestor's friends, concedes that the doctor has an abrasive personality. "There's an interesting schizophrenia about him," says Mintz. "As shockingly accurate as he usually is on the facts, he goes completely overboard in finding conspiracies under every rock." But, Mintz is quick to add, "He almost has to be that way to do what he's doing. All of his faults are like fly-specks on the whole character of the man. He is a hero."

The old "Cakey" Nestor seems hardly changed.

We've often asked ourselves the question, would it have been better to let thalidomide go on the market and then have the place really cleaned up? Well you can't do that, but it's what's going to happen. We didn't get the '38 drug law until the elixir sulfanilimides scandal killed 111 people. The '62 law was dead as a dodo until thalidomide hit the fan. We never get anything done until we have a catastrophe and a lot of people lose their lives, see.

I realize, intellectually, that I have accomplished far more in my years at Food and Drug than I could have in private practice. When I helped take MER/29 off the market I did more good than a lifetime of seeing individual patients. When I took Entoquel off the market I saved a lot of lives in infants and children. I still have the satisfaction and pleasure from private practice on the side. That's the cream in my coffee. But the decisions made at FDA affect thousands more people.

Many establishment people probably think I'm an S.O.B. But somebody who knows the score has to stay in here and take the insults and do the fighting. I've never given a damn about promotion. I don't think I'm a good business manager; I wouldn't make a good supervisor. I came in here to evaluate new drugs and to make recommendations. I am peculiarly well qualified, and my whole past record demonstrates it.

I'm one of these individuals you either feel strongly for or strongly against. I think the only evidence that I'm a little childish ie the fact that I'm a whistle-blower at this age. In that respect I never have grown up. But I'm still looking ahead to the future and not to the past. I say what I believe. I think that the basic philosophy of right and wrong that I got as a child still plays a major part in determining my conduct. If anybody sees what they think is wrong, they ought to take some positive action to correct it if they have the ability and the power to do so. I think we should all be activists. I don't think we should sit back and wring our hands and say, "Oh, isn't Food and Drug terrible? Why doesn't someone do something about it?" Well by God I'm the someone.

John Nestor takes a small drug capsule from an envelope on his desk. It is half turquoise, half dark blue. Squeezing it firmly, he rolls it for a second between his thumb and forefinger until the gelatin coating becomes tacky.

Then he turns around in his swivel chair, stares out the windows overlooking a sterile courtyard and the south parking lot at Parklawn, and, for the third time today, picks up the phone to dial a lawyer he knows in Washington.

4

The Programmer

When I see the elaborate study and ingenuity displayed by women in the pursuit of trifles, I feel no doubt of their capacity for the most herculean undertakings.

Julia Ward Howe

ANDREA BAXTER stares into the big plate-glass window at the Biograph Theatre in Georgetown and adjusts the lavender scarf around her neck. A friend's words from a day-old conversation ecto in her mind: "I think we should keep in mind what's been said about our generation going into the Civil Service. It was John Kennedy's influence. He gave a new idea of what it means to serve your country."

It is a pale blue Saturday morning, although there are several large white and gray clouds against the April sky and showers have been forecast. Andrea carries a red umbrella. She has just been dropped off on M Street, and for an instant she is caught by the euphoria of spring. She looked forward to this all week: two hours to shop and browse, a leisurely junket to the top of the storefront district on Wisconsin Avenue and back down the other

134

side by noon, and lunch with Richard at either the Big Cheese or Clyde's.

Andrea Baxter has a pretty face—some would call it beautiful or classic, even for the artistic flaws: mouth a bit thin, cheekbones slightly high, once-pastel features now hardened by a businesslike demeanor. She is 34, and there are the faint beginnings of crowsfeet around her eyes. But she remains elusively attractive—a quality a suitor once ascribed in an admiring letter to "the style and simplicity with which you choose your clothes, the class and cool grace with which you carry yourself." *Damn. That* note she saved.

What is presented to the world is all very practiced yet wholly natural. Her hair is prematurely gray and she wears it short, making her look smaller than five-foot-five. She uses little makeup, pale lipstick the only visible concession to cosmetics. Her teeth are straight on the top and rather crooked below, an imperfection usually camouflaged, though, by surprisingly winsome smiles. There is absolutely no mistaking her for one of the GS-5 secretaries in the Department of Transportation.

There are some advantages and some disadvantages to being a woman in government. The advantages are more conspicuous. There are not so many females around and men like women. I find it's easy for me to walk into an office and get help or whatever I want. People are very willing to assist me.

There are a great many more female professionals now then there used to be, although they are not rising up to become heads of offices with any great rapidity. The situation is different in different agencies. This Department is one of the worst in the way they have treated females. For example, there was a woman in the Federal Highway Administration who was a Grade 14 or 15 in a temporary job; they replaced her with a man and she went back to a lower grade, making less money. But some quotas were established a few years ago: all offices had to have some women at a certain level.

I think there's been a big change in the way secretaries regard their roles. The role of black secretaries in Washington is interesting. Some of them have taken a strong stand on personal favors for men, like bringing coffee, fetching lunch, sharpening pencils, wiping desks, and all this sort of stuff. The black secretaries assessed it correctly, which was that it was not associated with the job, but it was a power play. And a certain number of them refused to do it on the grounds that they were not hired to be maids.

I always felt that, as a professional woman, I could not ask a secretary to do such things because they were based on hierarchical differences, and that those men who did it were pulling rank. In my organization there is only one guy who still does it, and sometimes the secretaries will go along with him because he has temper tantrums if they don't. But they really see it quite clearly as a power struggle. Even the white secretaries.

When I first started working here the secretaries wouldn't speak to me, because they had a lot of prejudice against professional women. That went on for three months. It upset their thinking: a secretary wasn't able to see herself as a subordinate, her boss was just a woman like any other. She couldn't flirt if she wanted to. I think that that's much less likely to happen now because secretaries are more self-conscious about playing that kind of role.

In our office we have a male secretary and I think he's marvelous. I've never left a message asking a question but that his response hasn't been almost instantaneous. There was a very interesting article in the *Harvard Business Review* called "Postscript to the Peter Principle." That's the one that says everybody rises to his level of incompetence, and if anything can go wrong, it will. The article points out that a lot of things seem to be going right, and suggests that the reason is something called the para-hierarchies of women. The secretaries are really the glue that holds everything together. And it's because they can't really rise. It says the same thing about blacks, and labor forces of various other kinds. It's a very interesting article. As it happens in our office the professional–clerical relationships are quite awful. The secretaries don't answer the phones politely; it's just kind of an all-around horror show.

The government is undoubtedly making strides for women's rights relative to private industry, but not much relative to itself. There is a girl in this office who is raucous, a very abrasive personality, and she's the big women's-lib type around here. Every other week they have a women's meeting and bring in speakers. I missed one yesterday and I got bawled out for it.

I myself have had to explain to people that when I bluster they shouldn't take me all that seriously, because I am really conditioned to the idea that blustering is part of life. I'm still regarded as a tough cookie, but my fights tend to be on sensible grounds rather than on feminism.

Andrea begins to climb up Wisconsin Avenue, heading toward the old public library at the top of Georgetown. The reference room flashes through her mind; it has been two years since she last set foot there. Impressively musty historical manuscripts about the old town are stored there. The one she used to like best was an encomium written by General Edward Braddock in 1755, and she remembers that he "never attended a more complete banquet, or met better dressed or better mannered people than I met on my arrival in Georgetown, which is named after his gracious majesty." And as she looks up now she spots a carefully contrived remembrance of things past: an *Olde Georgetowne* street sign hanging from a corner lamppost, the early glory rendered in colonial script and aged and weather-beaten enough to lend a modicum of authenticity.

Across the street a great many boutiques press in on one another, most of them catering to a still-exclusive clientele. Even though modern Georgetown has on its avenues as many dropouts as modishly genteel matrons, the fare in commodities remains fashionable and expensive (as do the town houses on the side streets). In this block alone there are several dress shops, two interior accessory stores, a jewelry appraiser, and a fancy bakery. But there are also a Roy Rogers Family Restaurant, an ice cream store, and a porno shop on M Street. In a parking lot behind the bank a group of disheveled teenagers, all in levi's but with their hair considerably shorter than a few years back, mill around noisily. For the new young professionals living around Capitol

Hill, it is almost unfashionable now to refer to Georgetown as fashionable. The thought occurs to Andrea that things have certainly changed since she first saw the place, just after graduating from college. The street people with their blankets and guitars are almost gone. The new stores seem to relate more to the life-styles of this younger generation than to those who can afford what the boutiques still have to offer.

I'm the oldest of five children—two sisters, two brothers. I was born in the Bronx in 1944. My father at that time was a physician in the Army, stationed in New York City. But I grew up in Madison, Connecticut, which was a small kind of hick town twenty miles east of New Haven. It had always been a fashionable summer resort but recently it's gotten to be a very fashionable suburban place.

I was a happy kid, had a great time, but I wanted to get on with it. I would throw myself into one activity after another. It was something that was very characteristic of me that I wanted to do everything, but my mother called me a docile child. I got along well with adults, even better than with people my own age. I got along very well with my parents. I put off conflicts until later.

When I was eight my younger sister was born and I took care of her a lot for about three years and really regarded myself as another mother of hers. I think that may account for me not sentimentalizing motherhood or children. By eleven I'd done it and it was time to move on to something else.

I lived right near the center of town and I could ride my bike or walk to town, or to the beach. I have never ridden a school bus in my life. I was able to get into New Haven if I wanted to, and even when I was pretty young, maybe like twelve, I could get a train and go to New York City by myself.

I loved school. I had a lot of free time: nobody ever gave me any homework. I spent a lot of time running around in the woods, looking at plants and flowers and sea shells. I had a dog I was always with. I took piano and ballet lessons.

And I read a great deal. Nobody ever bothered me when I was reading—that was a house rule. I can remember at the age of seven reading a lot of Nancy Drew and when I was in high school, maybe at the age of fourteen, starting to read some Sartre, and Fromm's book on analysis of dreams and Kafka's *Trial*. I really didn't understand what these books were about but I was reading them anyway. I'd already been reading a great deal before we got television. We have two pre-television and three post-television kids in my family, and that makes a difference. My brother and I were very comfortable with the written word. The other three were probably more "with it"—more interested in fads and what's happening in the world. I was very out of it. I read adventure stories, all the Nancy Drew, all the Bobbsey Twins, all the Hardy Boys. Then *Kidnapped, Treasure Island,* and into the more adult but still children's books, like *Gone with the Wind* and *Jane Eyre.*

One summer I went to a sort of homespun camp in New Hampshire, and another summer I went out West. It was fun but I always had real problems, until I was about sixteen, getting along with people my own age. So at first I would be very isolated, and then by the end of the summer people would begin to recognize that I was okay as a person. I think part of the reason was that when we lived in the country outside of New Haven I didn't go to kindergarten. I generally had friends who were a little bit older than I was and I kind of copied them. I didn't really run with a gang of people—I probably spent more time alone than most kids. But I was a Girl Scout, a Brownie, all that kind of stuff.

My father was the doctor in town, which in a sense put me at the peak of the social sector, but on the other hand he is Jewish and my mother is not. I was kind of sensitive to that. My father was the only Jew in the Beach Club. He still is, as a matter of fact, twenty-five years later. Religion was never a big deal. None of us were ever brought up with any kind of religion whatsoever.

I never went to a Jewish service at all until I was in this girls' boarding school. (Then I would sort of capitalize on my heritage during the holidays, to get out of school.) I went to public schools in Madison until I was fourteen, then to a girls' boarding school, St. Margaret's. It was a horrible experience there. Every moment was programmed and assigned. Besides that, I was somewhat sensitive about my background. At that time it was the only girls' Episcopal boarding school in the state of Connecticut. My parents sent me there because I was a very smart little girl, and it was a much better education than I could have received in Madison, where I had no competition intellectually. I think that my parents also were afraid that I would go off and get married when I was sixteen or eighteen, and they had higher hopes for me.

At some of these institutions I was exposed to I was sort of overly conscious of the fact that my father is Jewish. Not that it really mattered, but I believed that it did. For example at this boarding school most of the people had debutante parties. I was never invited to any of them, and that kind of stuff still makes me quite bitter.

We couldn't date at all. Occasionally we'd have dances with nearby boys' schools, and (an example of how strict things were) they'd pair us off according to height, we'd have dinner, and they'd send the guys to the other building where the dance was to be held—I'm not sure why they sent the guys over there before us—and then the girls would go over. At the end of the evening the guys would leave the building and they wouldn't let us walk with them to the bus and they wouldn't let us go back to our building. We had to stay in the building until their bus was away.

That whole routine of having every moment programmed was very, very bad. And there was some kind of stigma attached to being a brain there also.

I like many different kinds of people, but at that time I looked up to people who were really incredibly smart. After I left that boarding school I read less. I think it destroyed my curiosity and interest in reading and a lot of other things.

We had to wear these terrible uniforms—bright blouses with kind of green flour sacks over them—and oxfords. Every day. We also had to dress for dinner in uniforms: high-heeled shoes and stockings and dinner dresses. The only variety we were permitted was sweaters. We were allowed to wear aqua, yellow, pink, or white sweaters with our dinner uniforms. They used to check us for stockings. We had chapel every morning and prayers every night, and sometimes after prayers in the evening we had to walk through the library drawing room holding up our skirts to prove that we were wearing stockings.

The school felt that music, drama, and art were very important, so we had drama right through seventh, eighth, and ninth grades. I played chamber music, in piano quartets with strings, and I sang in the glee club. I really loved acting. I played Banquo in Macbeth.

I didn't like it there but I tend to stay wherever I am.

We all complained all the time. We bitched about everything. The whole demoralizing atmosphere of the place was really bad. College, even though it was another girls' school, was like freedom to me.

I was at St. Margaret's for four years. From that sort of school there was only one road—you either went to one of the good women's colleges or you went to one of the two-year schools for women. I went to Radcliffe. I was nineteen.

A window display of fine silver, perhaps from the early nineteenth century, lures Andrea Baxter up the steps and to the door of a quaint-looking shop with a narrow front. It is locked, but a multi-colored PLEASE RING sign encourages her. After several minutes the door is opened by a tall woman. Andrea says hello, and the proprietor asks her in. She knows Andrea has no real intentions to buy (an understanding that is in fact quickly communicated) but she will still be happy to show her around. "Actually that's exactly why we're going out of business. The young people buy stainless steel." *The lady is loquacious*, thinks Andrea. She is not paying close attention to the woman (better to avoid a long conversation, or to feel sorry for her), but smiles and continues to look around at the sterling.

"Actually, I collect stainless myself," the tall lady continues, her eyes wandering out the window overlooking Wisconsin Avenue. "Silver is for museums." That's true, thinks Andrea. Several of the displays here are tagged as museum pieces might be: "Set of twelve George IV Silver Gilt Teaspoons, London, 1822" and "Old Sheffield 6 cups egg cruet, London, 1795."

"Actually, we could stay open even now," the proprietor says, "if we were diversified. But that's a whole new problem."

Andrea is slightly put off by the woman's manner but does not know why. She wants to ask her why she keeps saying "actually." Instead Andrea says, "Maybe business is going down because of what's happening in Georgetown. It's changed so much."

"I know," says the woman, looking out the window again. "But mostly people are just not buying as much important silver." And she mentions how Georgetown had been a sleepy one-to-one community when she first moved there twenty years ago (Andrea, mesmerized by a slightly tarnished brass dish hanging on one of the walls, is thinking of Richard), how with the coming of liquor licenses, good restaurants, live jazz, and the like, the atmosphere changed—especially when the eighteen-year-olds who could not legally drink in Maryland and Virginia began to invade the night spots. "Now things have gotten so bad I put a lock on the door. I cannot get insurance. In the old days you could see little children and old people in this community. No more."

Looking into the brass dish, Andrea asks herself, *What is life except for an accumulation of experiences? Let us savor the moment.* She is preoccupied with her own thoughts, but she wonders why the tall woman said "cannot get insurance" instead of "can't." They talk a little longer, and Andrea concludes that if the business closes it would be more of a relief than a tragedy.

I was accepted at Radcliffe early in my senior year. In high school I had thought I was very suited to an intellectual environment, but in college I was intimidated—especially by the atmosphere of respect for genius at Harvard, but also by the atmosphere of respect for neurosis. To me Harvard and Radcliffe have a very weird atmosphere.

I really didn't catch on to my major, which was English. My teachers would tell me I wasn't being analytic, but I didn't know what an analysis was because that was one thing my school had never taught me. So I was at sea as to what to do, and that bothered me until my senior year, when I finally caught on.

At that time Radcliffe was isolated from Harvard, and the system was quite impersonal. I lived in a dormitory there, and we went down to Harvard for classes. The first two years I went out with guys who were not intellectual at all. At Harvard there are some real sporting types who get in because their fathers have a lot of money. I don't know how much that's true now but it used to be. I didn't start going out with people I could really talk to until my last two years, when I dated guys from the *Harvard Crimson*, a more intellectual group. Then I realized how much I'd missed by being cut off from the Harvard houses' life, and it made me mad. All of those boys knew at least some professors personally and had lunch with them every day. We had no contact with them at Radcliffe. I was jealous. I was a junior when I began to realize it, and then senior year it kind of hit me full blast. As a result I became very much of a feminist my last year—of a ripsnorting variety.

At that time it wasn't a subject that was discussed openly, and when it was it caused terrific antagonisms and hostilities. "Male chauvinism" didn't even exist then, so you couldn't even call it by a name. It was the normal way men behaved. I guess what I resented was that I had gone to Radcliffe and Harvard thinking I was stupid, and then realized a lot of that was because of an atmosphere that tended to classify women as stupid. I hadn't linked the fact that being a woman cuts you off from a whole set of opportunities that made boys seem more intelligent.

The Feminine Mystique was being passed around surreptitiously from girl to girl at that time, ad people would read it almost secretly. It had a huge impact on me because at that point I had been going out for about a year with this group of intellectual guys and I had really registered how jealous I was of them. So when I read that book it gave me a reason.

I must have driven people crazy. I started talking about it, and I can remember driving my mother crazy, driving all the girls in my dorm crazy, driving all my boyfriends crazy. I guess I stirred things up. What bothered me most was the relationship with men—the fact that in the group of boys I went out with it was the custom for the boys to talk to each other and the girls to sit in between them and be pretty. I think Radcliffe girls worshipped Harvard men in a very funny way. These guys all considered themselves geniuses and the girls had to be bright enough to be seen with them. But it didn't give you a license to be called on or to speak.

There are many different sets of values at Harvard, but there's one that puts intelligence above everything else, including accomplishment. It doesn't rate skills—like dealing with people and organizing things— very high at all. I considered myself bright enough to go out with them, but not anything more.

I always wished I were smarter than I was, and I began to resent that I didn't write. But soon I began to feel that being a genius wasn't the only criterion for being able to talk. And the conversations they were having were tremendous fun, the kind where you just stay up all night, discussing philosophical issues with lots of laughter in between. So I finally decided I was going to inject myself into the conversation. It was a particular kind of university bullshit and the kind I haven't engaged in really at all since.

In the spring just before I graduated I got a group of sophomores in my dormitory to set up a meeting with Mary Bunting, the president of Radcliffe, David Riesman, who wrote *The Lonely Crowd* and *Individual Reconsidered* (he's now called on for opinions on alienated youth and that sort of stuff), and Erik Erikson, who wrote *Childhood and Society* and *Young Man Luther*. We invited them and their wives to come to a little seminar at Mrs. Bunting's house. It was one of the first things of that kind that had ever been done.

We each prepared a little statement about why we thought this was a problem, because at that point nobody thought it was a problem except Riesman, who had brought it up in his classes on American Sociology. One of the things we talked about was masculine and feminine styles of thinking. Harvard really glorifies the masculine kind of thinking, which is very aggressive and arrogant, and puts a premium on making pat statements that you try to defend. The girls I knew were more humble and were deferential in their relationship to the people they were reading. It started a really interesting discussion, with a sense that what we were saying had an echo in older people's minds, and it gave me a lot of confidence to go on thinking about it.

But I was the only senior who was interested. All the others were in senior panic, running around saying, "I want a man." They were all getting engaged right and left or going into declines and sleeping fifteen hours a day and weeping. It was hopeless, so I gave up on them.

Looking back on it I guess Radcliffe was a high-class mating service. You mated with Harvard guys. I mean, here are these girls who have scrambled their way through high school, and then to come to that!

Other schools were different but no better. Smith would be considered homespun—able but homespun. Bryn Mawr girls were pretty intellectual and interesting, except that they seemed sort of fierce. Wellesley girls were always very well turned out. Smart, but never messy. And Radcliffe girls went in for being very messy—physically messy. Pot smoking hadn't really started then, although there was one group in Cambridge that was smoking pot.

I don't like the idea that so many women's colleges are going coed. My feeling is that women have very few things going for them that are exclusively theirs. I can't see any reason for diluting it.

My views of Harvard and Cambridge are very much colored by what happened since. It seems as I look back on my life that Radcliffe was a kind of gray interlude between interesting things, that my high school seems to be more connected to what I do now than my years at college. Somehow at Radcliffe I felt as if I was under water a good deal of time. Considering the amount of time I spent studying I was intellectually understimulated. I worked really hard and didn't enjoy it a whole lot. It seems funny to have been in one of the most privileged places and have had this reaction.

I did particularly like courses with a poet who was there. I began to enjoy creative writing. I still write poems. I was a member of a group called The Club—it was something that this poet organized and ran and it was just for girls, and we would invite other poets to read. They'd come as friends of our instructor and not charge us whatever outrageous sums they used to charge others. John Berryman once came. For some reason he took a great liking to me and subsequently called me up and wrote me a couple of poems. I still have a couple of them in manuscript form. In fact, there's one of his poems to me in the Pulitzer Prize-winning book and one of them in the National Book Award book. One of them begins, "Profoundly troubled over Miss Baxter. . . ."

In Washington people are much more practical about where you've gone to school. I get a funny reaction when I say I've gone to Radcliffe. It's hard to read what it means, like "She's not in my league" or "she's something else." It's generally not a good feeling.

Andrea leaves the silver shop and continues up Wisconsin Avenue, passing through the contemporary version of colonial Georgetown: stores called the Bootery, Pants Corral, Powder & Smoke, barbara's. She stops in the People's Drug Store to buy a magazine, leafs through *Playboy* and *Harper's*, and finally buys a copy of the *The New Yorker*.

In a crowded window display between O and P streets she spots a lilac-colored pants suit—not exactly her style, but she needs something for a wedding she has been invited to in New Haven next month. She enters the boutique, stepping onto a plush carpet. This is the store, she remembers, that she sinks into.

Richard once came in here with her and, refusing to acclimate to the place, stood instead in a corner looking embarrassed. Now Andrea loves him for that sort of thing, but she did not at the time.

Toward the back of the store, near the dressing rooms, a suburban-looking mother is telling her two teen-aged daughters that she has worn maternity blouses three times in her life and they aren't going to get her into one again no matter how stylish. Andrea finds the lilac pants suit on the rack. She does not like it, she tells herself while staring out across the street at a slim matron walking her Afghan. She browses a few minutes longer, then leaves.

Outside, it has begun to drizzle. Andrea flips open her umbrella and continues up the street, stopping for a moment to examine some cheese and wine on display behind a tinted window, and to adjust the scarf around her neck. At home she will slip into a pair of old levi's herself, and a Princeton sweat shirt. It is the outfit in which she feels most comfortable, but she would be embarrassed now, having been in government this long, to show it to her colleagues. She knows that at home they dress very much the same as she does, but for some reason she wants to feel older, more sophisticated than the younger types who populate almost half of the apartments and town houses in her development. The sweat shirt brings her back a few years, and she likes it.

After college I had planned to do a lot of different things—like take the Peace Corps and graduate record and law school exams—but I had taken the United States Information Service exam, and by the beginning of December before graduation I knew I had been accepted. That confused me because I didn't have time to find out what else I wanted to do, but then I decided I really wanted to do that. It was a lot of this feminism thing—I felt that I had to get out from under the pressure of the United States and get away. My friends were doing stupid things, like getting little publishing jobs in New York. None of them went on anything like a career path. But as I got closer to going away I got very scared.

That wasn't my first time traveling. Between my sophomore and junior year in college I had accompanied my grandmother on a four-month trip to the Far East—Japan, Indonesia—and back by way of Europe. That whole trip made me interested in the modern world. I began to think about what the problems of colonization were and of the colonized people. So it really was very important.

I started in USIS in June, right after I graduated. We trained in Washington, and then went to Brazil in September. It was a very interesting group of people there, very different from Harvard and Radcliffe.

I had asked for Brazil. I had seen movies like *Black Orpheus*, and after my experience at Radcliffe, I had a very strong feeling that that sort of culture would be terrific for me. It would be a rejection of Harvard–Boston values, a very direct, almost physical kind of culture, where people communicated through dancing and singing. And when I got there I followed that up a great deal. I went to all kinds of places with samba dancers, I went to voodoo ceremonies, I started going out with a wild boyfriend who was able to manipulate people to an incredible degree to get himself in and out of all kinds of situations. He was the opposite of all the people I had known at Harvard. He was a bum, but I supported him for a year, more or less.

My place was two blocks from the beach, and I used to go there every weekend. It was all a very straight set of just physical experiences, like riding along in an open jeep along the beach in very hot weather. It's funny, I saw *Black Orpheus* again after I came back and it still seemed like a true picture of the country.

I was in Brazil just after the coup that put the Castelo Branco government in power. It was a lot of fun, because they had eased up following a severe repression right after the coup. There were a great many frivolous left-wing people sitting around cafés, discussing politics by the hour. These were the people I dealt with, because my job was handing out travel grants to students and young professionals. The traditional way of doing that had been to just pick out the elected student officials of the student governments in each of the most important schools of law, economics, and medicine. I was there to figure out a better method for giving travel grants. We organized seminars, then we would have students write a paper on some subject of their choosing, then interview them, and pick them on the basis of their performance at this seminar, in the interview and on the paper. The whole thing was quite successful, and there began to be some kind of prestige attached both to being invited to the seminar and then to getting the grant. We would also program the travel in the States to correspond to the interests of the students. It was a very good beginning job—it gave me a sense of immediate accomplishment.

But after a while I found I was getting other people to speak about *their* ideas of economic development and I wasn't thinking about my own. As preparation for these seminars I had done a lot of reading on city planning and urban problems and poverty, just to find out what was going on in the United States, and I began to feel that I wanted to get involved in those things. And I was discovering that I couldn't carry out my job because it consisted of defending American policies. So I resigned from the USIS, citing the reasons in my letter as the Vietnam War and domestic problems.

A pair of red-and-white platform shoes in a store a few doors up catch Andrea Baxter's eye but she stifles the urge to go inside. She looks at her watch. Ten-thirty. A block and a half farther up Wisconsin Avenue, past a poster stand and a small head-shop, whose music and incense can be heard and smelled outside, Andrea spots a boutique that specializes in fine crystal. She goes in and walks silently among the shelves, her mind afloat on the gossamer lace upon which the glass is so delicately displayed. She is caught by the moment.

She sees a corner filled with wooden toys and closes her eyes, overcome by a fleeting exultation. Her smile reflects a modern Mona Lisa's bemusement, a cynicism still full of feminine charm, a wax-melt of independence and whimsey. She remains incredulous that her colleagues at DOT take her so seriously, but there is something about her manner and her flashing brown eyes that men find inordinately attractive. Her mouth is finely shaped, and when she smiles the corners turn up and a short pleasant laugh (occasionally mistaken for a snicker) escapes.

She moves her hands in front of her face, playing with the lavender scarf around her neck. She is as aware of her fits of fantasy as she is of her quick, nervous efforts to subdue them. She wonders if anyone notices.

Andrea leaves the crystal shop, beginning to feel hungry as she passes the Parlor, an ice cream store with a gay nineties motif and a sandwich garden in the back. Across the street is a big stone church. On Saturday afternoons hordes of gay men gather at the church, which houses the Washington Free Medical Clinic, waiting for a venereal disease center to open.

Andrea knows very little about the drug scene in Georgetown, but she guesses that the teen-agers, many of whom look as if they originated in the suburbs of Alexandria, Bethesda, Chevy Chase, and Silver Spring, probably have enough money to buy grass or acid for a long weekend.

A few doors down, sitting on a stoop and sneering at passers-by, is a scraggly young female with glassy eyes and no shoes. She looks exhausted. *Too old to be an urchin*, thinks Andrea; *if she were a dog maybe someone would help her.*

After resigning from the USIS I came back to the United States, and went to San Francisco. There I got a job working for something called the International Students' Service, which was a two-woman office affiliated with the YMCA. I think it was probably also affiliated with the CIA. I was earning $300 a month there, working with volunteers to greet foreign students on arrival in the States, and offering tours around the San Francisco area, or a weekend with an American family.

It was depressing as hell, espekially the weather. I had come to San Francisco stone cold, didn't know anybody, and I was living with a roommate in a plasticky kind of apartment. I wasn't making enough money to keep anything else. The city is very pretty, but my whole work life and social life conspired to make it very depressing. The beat generation was just about over then. I moved over to Berkeley and in December of that year the Free Speech movement started with Mario Savio. I quit my job and went to work teaching foreign students at the University of San Francisco a couple of nights a week.

I spent a lot of time at the Berkeley campus, taking a few courses there, but I just never felt at home. The place was terribly cantankerous, so radical that it's really very hard to believe. A Kennedy liberal in the East would have been a fascist pig out there. I never felt there was an opportunity to express two sides of any question—it was always one side versus the establishment. Sometimes I was on the side of the students and sometimes I wasn't. Most of the people who felt the way I did, particularly most easterners, were leaving in droves to teach at eastern universities. It got to be a terrible atmosphere—there were bombings all over the place, people getting shot, the National Guard being called out, and it went on and on and on. At first the Free Speech movement was a legitimate thing and the students won, which was great, but afterwards there were a lot of phoney issues—at least I thought they were phoney. It's hard to explain, but the Free Speech movement people got control of certain newspapers and radio stations, and whenever anything happened on campus—say a Marine showed up with a recruitment table—and somebody didn't like it, the word went out. Within an hour you'd have the radio station saying, "Okay, it's down to the Lutheran Church and everybody mobilize over on this side of campus," and everybody mobilized over there. Mass demonstrations, complete anarchy. I just wasn't a demonstrator and I was located right smack in the middle.

I remember the People's Park incident: There were a lot of people hanging around Telegraph Avenue—hippies, students, drug pushers, and everybody else. And dogs—the thing about Berkeley that distinguishes it from other places in the world is that there is more dog shit there than you can believe. Everybody has a dog and the dogs are free. Dogs went to courses at Berkeley. You could be sitting in a classroom and there'd be a St. Bernard in the chair behind you. It was really very funny. You'd be in the library and some dog would lift his leg on a table. There were a lot of things at Berkeley that got completely out of hand.

Well, Governor Reagan got it completely out of hand. This People's Park was just a university parking lot—nothing, a big mountain of mud, junk. The people who hung around Telegraph Avenue decided to clear it out, put in some playground equipment, and get some planting done. Even the merchants on Telegraph Avenue were so glad to have everybody and the dogs move a block away that they gave money for buying flowers and rakes and stuff. And they made quite a nice little park there.

But at that point the university decided that it wanted them off the property so it said, "Get out." Then the governor said, "Get out." There were all kinds of other options that were possible—the city offered to buy the land for a park and let the people continue to use it. But the university, obviously under the control of the governor, wouldn't accept that. Ultimately they called in the National Guard and for about a week there were all these guys in uniform, eight or ten of them on every single corner. There was tear gas all the time, bombs all the time. It was terrible. I developed a sort of Aw-shit, here-come-the-helicopters-again, I-gotta-get-out feeling. It's one of the worst things—the sound of the helicopters in the air all the time. You can imagine going to school in that atmosphere.

In that conflict I was for the students and the street people, who were clearly in the right. But after that came the Third World movement, the blacks, the chicanos, the Chinese, and everybody else. That was really ugly, because there was a lot of destruction on campus. Guys would come into the library and overturn the card catalog, or you'd be in a class in one of the big classrooms and suddenly you'd hear clang, clang, clang and the windows would be shattered all around. It was really unbelievable: they weren't demonstrating about anything more than that the blacks didn't want the whites in their movement.

The image of the girl on the stoop sticks with Andrea Baxter as she heads back down Wisconsin Avenue. *There but for the grace of* . . . Part of a resume races through her mind: Saint Margaret's School, Waterbury, Connecticut. Latin Prize, Cum Laude Society. Radcliffe College, B.A. in English, 1964. Creative Writing Editor, literary magazine. Travel, South America, California. 1970 to present, program analyst for the Department of Transportation, Bicycles.

She continues slowly down Wisconsin Avenue, half in a trance. The DOT is in front of her. Seventh and D, Southwest. Like many of the other new government buildings, it is identified by a simple sign—raised silver block letters on a blue background—set in a concrete block. The massive structure makes a sharply geometrical outline against the low Washington skyline, just across the street from the inverted oval of Housing and Urban Development. Andrea thinks that there is no other word but *huge* to describe these two buildings. DOT is almost 500 feet square, made of reinforced concrete, with an exterior of white marble strips that stretch from the second to the tenth floor and are separated by vertical rows of brown tinted glass. Almost 2,000 parking spaces are available in and around the Nassif Building, as it is called, and there are over a million square feet of assignable office area. A large interior courtyard contains pools, trees, shrubbery, and black marble benches where employees can sit during their lunch breaks and insulate themselves from the noise and dirt of city streets and the sterility of their offices—a temporary solitude interrupted only by the splashing of five large fountains.

There are display halls on the ground floor inside, and all the upper corridors have red plush institutional carpeting and are lined with alternating panels of blue, yellow, and orange. On the panels are enlarged color prints of superhighways, cars, trucks, country roads. The hallways are very quiet; typewriter sounds are effectively muffled by thick wooden doors. Inside each working area are a number of smaller offices, their different sizes peopled according to Civil Service grade scales. On the roof there is a room with exercise equipment and a jogging track.

At the corner of Wisconsin and P, Andrea is caught by the copper in the window of the French Kitchen, and she goes inside.

During all these demonstrations I was hanging around with a bunch of people with whom I felt comfortable but, I don't know what it was, we led an increasingly dissipated life for a period of several months. At least I thought it was dissipated—maybe I was just looking for an excuse to leave. One of these people was a successful lawyer in Oakland, but he also liked to collect skin flicks. He lived up on a lonely hill with a view of San Francisco Bay. I remember one particular Sunday—it was a beautiful, beautiful day—and six or eight of us just sat inside there and watched these flicks throughout the day. It was not a very good way to spend a beautiful Sunday.

The parties were also sort of wild. Two of these people got married, and about a month after that some of us decided to have a party for them. I love to cook so we had a lot of food and it was at my place. There was enough champagne for about a bottle per person, and we drank it all. The whole thing was not what my New England, puritanical background would have led me to do.

That was the first time I'd lived alone. It was a nice little cottage in the woods, by a stream. Raccoons used to come eat out of my hands at night. It was a very romantic place. I found it through a lady realtor who was about 85 years old. She was from Mississippi and she drove a big blue Mercedes, and she showed me this place and said, "Well, dear, I know it's more than you want to spend, but really, it's very choice."

The weather around San Francisco is usually very crummy. There's this horrible fog that settles in and it evaporates about noon and comes back about five, and I found that extremely depressing. But this summer was unusual—beautiful and brilliant and sunny. In the middle of all these parties and looking for jobs and running around and playing tennis and stuff, a bunch of us were over at the same guy's house watching the moon walk. We'd just had a party and there were some people there I didn't know. One of the guys said he was about to go to Hawaii. He was a poverty lawyer in Oakland. I said, "Gee, I've always wanted to go to Hawaii. Can I go?" He said, "Sure." So we went together. It's relatively cheap to go from California.

We went to the beach, surfing, camping, dancing, shopping. Most of the time it felt too good to be true. In the end the camping was a bit much. Half the time we pitched the tent in darkness, sometimes very late, sometimes very stoned. Once we pitched the tent and then drove out of the jungle to a place positively moonish in its lava landscape, and we couldn't find the tent when we got back. We were in a jungle high on cliffs. The stars were the brightest I've ever seen. We could have felt original there, but for the plastic and the tin cans.

But after a few days this guy was in a rush to leave. I saw no need to hurry. He became imperious: "Get in the car. Get the pack out of here. The bugs are coming. I want to watch the hula lesson." I got stubborn. His driving became dangerous. I became hostile. As it turned out, whenever we switched roles (he should always drive and navigate; I should always shop and carry food) we got mad at each other and lost things. Another time I was ordered to remove the backpack from *my* front seat because it bothered *him*. Dammit. I was sitting on the front seat for days obeying orders about guidebooks and food.

Then things smoothed over again, and we were both having a pretty good time. But you can't go on having a good time forever. You have to intersperse it with something you feel is of value to society or to yourself or your Creator. You just can't derive a feeling of satisfaction living that life.

I decided to shove it all and come back East, which I did. I applied to the Woodrow Wilson School at Princeton and two city planning schools, and I got into Woodrow Wilson. Having come constantly into contact with radical Brazilians and Americans with very different points of view, and having had to defend my own ideas, had given me a lot of confidence, but I felt I needed to go to graduate school to learn what lay behind all my thinking.

Eleven-fifteen. Andrea leaves the French Kitchen and turns down P Street, heading for the Savile Book Shop. She knows she can lose herself there for hours, but this time she is looking for something specific: a book of color photographs taken in the underground sections of Brazil. At the poetry alcove she stops to leaf through a few books. One of her own poems, a new one, pops into her head: "Advances are scheduled / on your agenda. / Our heads bang together / Instead of lips. / I parry and / Embarrass you. / My whole body / Lies lax, and alive. / Intent you apply / to obvious nodes. / I'm Gulliver, / Pinned and poked."

Twenty minutes later Andrea finds her book on Brazil, is delighted with some of the pictures of places she remembers, and buys it. She emerges from the Savile and walks straight back to Wisconsin Avenue, passing an Indian boutique, a pottery fair, and an early American furniture store featuring wall maps of "the new world."

At O Street she passes several restaurants that advertise feature singers and small bands. It is still drizzling. Two weeks ago at this spot she and Richard got into a conversation with a passing couple, from Oklahoma of all places, who asked them to recommend a restaurant. Andrea suggested a health food place not far away, and then decided to show it to Richard as well; it was one of the few places in D.C. he had not been and she had.

The Woodrow Wilson School was a very good educational experience, a complete contrast to Cambridge or Berkeley. It was a two-year program and I ended up with a Masters in Public Affairs.

I was one of 100 female graduate students out of 1,500 males. The male undergraduate body was 3,200. This situation I and my fellow female graduate students found very uncomfortable, and we started becoming more articulate about it. At one point I burst into the Dean of Students' office with some complaints about a very sexist half-time band performance at a football game (the band actually made crude and vulgar jokes about women coming to Princeton), and I spent two hours telling him how the school would have to make some big changes if it was going to be ready for coeducation. After that I got asked to speak to two alumni groups on that subject, and at the end of the year I was asked to be assistant to the provost for planning and implementing coeducation. He's now the president of the school.

To me the most important problem was the ratio; the plans they had were to get 650 girls in five years, and the work that I did proved they could get 1,200 within three years. My job was to pull all the information together and present a time-phase chart to the deans and eventually to the trustees. I also got involved in setting up a day-care center.

There was a lot of talk about the atmosphere of a dormitory. The way the Princeton dormitories were designed was for little cliques of boys; it was a very rough, impersonal atmosphere where people were treated almost like animals.

We had some really wild ideas that creative socializing takes place in bathrooms, kitchens, and laundromats, rather than in lounges, and we had this great vision of a super-duper psychedelic laundromat with Ping Pong tables, snack bars, and hot plates. But we had a rather conservative architect, and when we talked to him about building some warm and kookie bathrooms and some warm and kookie laundromats he had a fit. Architects have a very functional, abstract idea of how people live, that where you socialize is in lounges, with nice sofas and things. They have never observed that lounges are empty in most dormitories, and that an enormous amount of talk goes on in the bathrooms. That grosses them out—bathrooms are supposed to be functional, cold, and sanitary, and they're not supposed to allow space for people to sit around and chat. They did go along with the idea that people talk a good deal to each other in kitchens. We fought and fought. Architects are very hard to control.

We concluded that the universities are like the cathedrals of the Middle Ages; when you visit a place like Princeton, Yale, or Harvard, they're monuments. Of course, Princeton's changed. It was very interesting for me to observe how the power actually works, the conflict between the old and the new. Now there are coed dormitories, corridors, and suites. Once you begin to change it goes very fast. That was another thing we discovered—that if you break tradition you are catapulted to the frontier of experiment. You have nothing holding you back. Apart from working for a purpose that I really cared about, I now had access to power, the ear of the provost. I was dealing with much older people, who had been in their jobs many years.

That's been a great help in my current job, because in some way the power situation is analogous: I have relatively low rank and I'm young and I have relatively little experience in government, but I am part of the central office of the Secretary's staff and I have presented my ideas directly to the Under Secretary.

Bicycles. Andrea Baxter stares into another shoe store. In her half-reverie she picks up the reflection of two long-haired boys on bikes passing behind her, making vulgar remarks. Fey faggoted banshees, she thinks to herself, but at least they're riding bikes.

She remembers coming back to her office one crisp autumn day, four and a half years earlier, and plunging into what was to become her Great Bicycle Project, quickly jotting some notes to herself and making from them a draft memorandum for the Under Secretary:

> The following points will merit consideration in any program to promote bicycles as a transportation alternative:

Need for a reception on White House lawn on Secretary's Bicycle Day.
Cabinet officers to ride bicycles to next Cabinet meeting.
Commemorative stamp establishing some member of Administration as patron saint of bicycles.
Representation of bicycle interests in Bicentennial Commission.
Federally regulated safety standards for bicycles (first need: brake lights).
Letter from President establishing urgent need for bicycle racks at all Federal buildings (agencies, tourist spots such as Washington Monument, Smithsonian, embassies abroad).
Declaration of support from Environmental Protection Agency and President's Council on Physical Fitness.
Rubber Manufacturers' Association to put full-page ad in *New York Times* in support of bicycles.
Strategic Auto Limitations Talks (SALT) with Highway Administration, Highway Users Federation for Safety and Mobility, Big Four auto manufacturers; convene someplace neutral (not Detroit).
Washington as a demonstration city must give exclusive use of one bridge to Virginia to cyclists.
Develop Southern Strategy. Use Lester Maddox?
Next DOT legislative program must suggest a National Bicycle Administration. Should also include tax credit for cyclists as repayment for savings in precious resources.
200 D.C. cops to patrol on bicycles, effective immediately.
Alter HUD workable program concept: cities must demonstrate sound bicycle policy in order to be eligible for federal grants; equal protection to unicycles.
Post Office to begin suburban deliveries on bicycles.

It is eleven-thirty. Andrea looks longingly at a trayful of éclairs in the window of La Patisserie.

I took the Federal Service Entrance Exam because it seemed that most of the jobs for women outside of government really weren't what you'd call meaningful, with any room for advancement. I remember one insurance company where I was told, "Well, you'll get to this level and you won't go any further." I had another interview for a job doing something like library work, quite a high-paying position. I talked to the personnel man and after a while he said, "Well, do you think you'd like this?" and I said, "No, I don't think it suits my personality at all," and he said, "I don't think so either." It was good for me to learn that you didn't have to apologize for not being interested in people's jobs. I had to find something that would let me express myself. I was following my nose—not someone else's.

One of my more interesting job interviews was with an industrial design firm that had its quarters on a boat tied up at a pier in San Francisco Bay. It was unbelievable—all the girls were at least eight feet tall and had long, straight blonde hair and spoke with a European accent. All the men were about forty with salt-and-pepper hair and a sort of creased look about them. All the beautiful people. I don't know what they really did there—I think they made uniforms for elevator operators. Anyway, there was a guy there who said to me, and it's the only useful piece of information I got out of all my interviewing, "Never leave one place without getting the names of two people in other places that you can talk to about a job." That was a nice piece of helpful advice.

I'd taken my Civil Service test but didn't hear anything and I wound up in Washington, continuing to look for jobs. I was doing all kinds of things, like walking into stockbrokers' offices and asking them if they would give me their tests to be a stockbroker, or going into employment offices, the kinds of places that find secretaries jobs and then rake off half their salary the first month.

Ultimately I heard through a friend about a job in the Highway Safety Administration. The way Civil Service works, if you find somebody who wants you to take a job he then writes a position description in such a way that only a particular person is qualified. I don't know how they made my background so relevant, but I did get the position.

In my first job with the Highway Safety Bureau, I wrote testimony for hearings and papers commenting on legislation. That's a major activity that goes on in government—all these guys put bills into the hopper and you have to comment on them. I learned a lot about different things, partly because they didn't know what to do with me. I had a good deal of freedom to learn, for example, about air pollution control, so I became their air pollution expert, and then I would use that in writing testimony or commenting on legislation.

I had that job for a year. Then I went to the Office of Planning and Programming and became the agency's air pollution control expert. I wrote little information sheets on various subjects. I had a variety of different functions. And then I came to the office of the Secretary of Transportation.

It has stopped raining. A yellow-robed Hare Krishna, head shaved almost completely bald and hands beating a tambourine in time to a purposeful gait, walks past Andrea on Wisconsin. The black asphalt in the street mirrors three large puffy clouds in the sky.

She makes her way down the street, pausing in front of the Old Georgetown Coffee House. On its brick facing are painted in gold the words COPPER • PEWTER • STAINLESS • COFFEE • TEA • SPICE, and a Chamber of Commerce brochure taped to the front window has one sentence underlined: "Among all the flashy boutiques are hidden the real charms of Georgetown." To the right, just inside the entrance, sit wooden boxes of exotic candies and a large scoop. The sign above them says "enticing and enchanting." After a few minutes at the boxes Andrea fills a small bag with tropical fruit candies from Colombia, rum-flavored toffees from Switzerland, and marzipan from Austria. She looks at jars of "Tea and Coffee from the Four Corners of the Earth," a refrigerated cabinet containing whole-milk yogurt, a barrel full of fresh bread and doughnuts, and a large display of spices. She wonders what kind of people use candied coriander seed, chive-seasoned salt, or caviar-flavored creamed cheese. She tells herself to come back when she is in a more experimental mood. On her way out she pays for the candy: $4.24.

Across the street *Annie Hall* and *Sleeper* are advertised on the marquee of the Georgetown Theatre, a few doors up from Maison des Crêpes and a Little Tavern. On both sides of N Street vendors are lifting plastic rain covers from their cans of white, red, and yellow flowers. Andrea remembers when Gregory, Richard's predecessor, bought her some daisies at the sidewalk mart outside Mr. Henry's.

When people ask me what I do now I say, "I write speeches and promote bicycling." As a matter of fact they interviewed me quite a long time before I took this job. I thought it was the office of environment and urban bullshit, and I decided I wasn't going. But then I found out more, and came.

The office of the Secretary is sort of the brain trust, and it's supposed to find better ways to handle the things the Department should be doing, like better urban transportation planning. It's difficult because there are so many federal programs and each one tends to spawn its own little office at the state, local, or regional level, and each one of these spawns its own paper work. There ought to be a single form to handle a lot of these different programs. One of the problems of working in the federal government is that you don't know where to go for information.

It's very easy to criticize programs as being inadequate and poorly administered, and to think up some very bold new ones and ingenious ways of enforcing them. But the problem that you usually have to take into account in any new major structure is the political reality in Congress and those in administration. What I find interesting is thinking how to accomplish things by the development of very careful systems, even without great big splashy spectacular results.

I enjoy bureaucracy. I don't know why but I think it's because I like complex things, taking into account different points in trying to reach compromises. In any change several sources are in effect: one is pressure from the outside, which usually comes from radical groups of one kind or another, but a second source of change is figuring out how to accommodate that pressure. The people creating the pressure usually don't know how it's going to work and may not have even thought it through. If you work within a system too long, though, you can get so fascinated by the complexity that you forget the thing to be accomplished. We are in something of a dilemma now because a big and activist government has not proved to be very successful.

I guess I had first gotten interested in bureaucracy when I was in the Foreign Service. That was very bureaucratic: you have relationships between the field (in my case Brazil) and Washington. Washington would make us carry out impossible policies because they didn't understand what living and working in Brazil was like.

Down the west side of Wisconsin Avenue now, Andrea passes Swensen's Ice Cream Factory and Great Sandwiches, the Carriage House, and—tucked between Roy Rogers Family Restaurant and Sweets 'N' Things—the Key Theatre, now playing *Children of Paradise*.

The Civil Service itself is very complex. Measuring someone's performance can be extremely difficult. People find that probably the safest thing for them to do is to do relatively little, certainly nothing very bold. I think this is true of all civil servants and it's probably true at some of the largest bureaucracies in the private sector. The public relations department of General Motors probably has a similar problem because you can't measure its success very easily. So ambitious people who want big salaries see that they can hedge their bets by doing relatively little, risking almost nothing. They are more likely to have a steady procession up the hierarchy than if they go all out for a new proposal for which there is no great pressure on them outside—because if they fail, attention has been called to them. They could be stuck permanently at a low level.

Some things happened to me which illustrate this. When I was in the Highway Administration I tried to find out where to turn with a grievance. I had always been very bitter about the fact that I started as a grade 7 instead of a grade 9, where my education would have entitled me. I should have taken the mid-level Civil Service exam, but by the time I heard that I had qualified for that, I had taken this job at the grade 7 level. Well, there's something called the Witt Amendment, which says that you can't jump more than a grade in a year—this in order to prevent people from rising too quickly. But you'd think if you'd taken the wrong Civil Service test, there'd be some kind of exemption to it. It turns out in order to get an exemption from the Witt Amendment you have to get the Secretary's signature on something. But nobody was willing to do that, because I wasn't important to them.

Eventually I got promoted. But as I was walking around trying to figure out exactly what had happened to me and whether I had a grievance, I learned other things. I went to the Equal Employment Opportunity guy; I went to my personnel files. I found a piece of paper where there was a place for a man to check "Federal Service Entrance Exam scores—fair, good," and "fair" had been checked. Now, I had gotten a score of 96.5, and there's no way you can consider that fair. So I said, "Mr. Miles, why have you checked 'fair'—obviously it's 'excellent.' It's not even 'good,' it's *fantastic*." And he said, "Well, it doesn't matter—it's just a piece of paper and it did what it was designed to do—it got you from the grade 7 to the grade 9." I was mad, but I didn't know how to press my grievance. I never could figure out how to operate within the system.

I suppose it could have frustrated me, but at that time I knew I was going to be coming up here to the Office of the Secretary and I didn't have much work down there and I was just trying to figure out what had happened. I kept saying to myself, "Okay, you're making $9,000 a year—there are secretaries around here who are probably more useful to the general operation and who may work a good deal harder than you and they're not making that much money, so why complain?"

I used to be on the fifth floor, sharing an office. Now I'm on the tenth, which is supposed to be a lot of prestige because the Secretary's up here. There are certain people who are at a higher level than I am who are sharing offices, but that's not a big thing around here—people don't sweat their office space a whole lot (although when I go back to the fifth floor to see my friends down there they say, "Oh, slumming?").

At this point I'm making $24,799 a year and in a few months I expect to be promoted. I've seen the Secretary maybe two dozen times since I've been here. I've had a couple of opportunities when I could have opened up a conversation with him, but I haven't.

I'm in too much of an analytical position now, whereas my real talent is in communications—getting people to do things. My best asset is inventiveness, dreaming up things. Everything we've done on bicycles is some invention of mine. What I do is sneak something into a letter, get somebody's signature on it, then build from that. I'm a finagler, a little operator. The thing is nobody is very interested in my bicycle program, buy nobody finds fault with it either.

Andrea turns the corner at Wisconsin and M, glancing up for a moment at the stately gold dome, a Georgetown landmark, on the bank across the street. There are still more boutiques and small restaurants to the right on M Street and a large shop specializing in wooden bowls and kitchen utensils. More teenagers are congregated around a light pole straight ahead. Two months ago, when she and Richard were last in Georgetown, he bet her that the next person they would run into around the corner would be wearing blue jeans, a beard, a sloppy coat, and soft shoes or hiking boots. She sensed his conservative hackles were raised, but sure enough when they turned the corner there the creature was: a skinny, snaggle-toothed adolescent with a scraggly beard, levi's, a T-shirt beneath a red cotton jacket on which a peace sign had been painted in blue.

A small old woman wearing heavy makeup and a mink coat, her head held high, leads her poodle out of an art gallery near the Key Bridge. Andrea hears her mutter something about prices being *"just* ridiculous."* A flock of birds passes over the Rive Gauche restaurant, flying southeast toward the Potomac.

I started with bicycles in February 1971. The year before I had begun riding my bike to and from work—it was convenient and seemed like a sensible way to move. But the government's promotion really began in 1971 when Secretary Volpe mentioned bicycles a few times in a speech he made to the Washington Council of Governments. I don't know who put the word *bicycle* in that speech but I suspect it was another guy here who also rode one.

It was a good example of the way things are handled in a bureaucracy. In his speech the Secretary promised that the Department of Transportation was going to do a number of things to help Washington: develop a tracked air-cushion vehicle to Dulles Airport, do something about the highway situation, improve bus service. There were a lot of promises and then it fell to our office, Environment and Urban Assistance, to follow up on all of them. So every now and then somebody would come in here and say, "Hey, Andrea, you got to do something about bicycles." One Friday afternoon I was kind of tired, my mind just suddenly went limp, and I started writing down all those things that could be done with bicycles. That's where it began.

Lots of things come across my desk. This fellow who designs bike paths on the George Washington Parkway called me yesterday and told me a stewardess had been arrested by a cop at National Airport for riding an unlicensed vehicle—namely, a bicycle. The airport is part of the Federal Aviation Administration, which is under the Department of

Transportation: therefore, we own it, and therefore we're in a position to do something about it. I did. I called the airport manager and reminded him that National was under DOT and mentioned what the Secretary had to say about bikes. The funniest thing about that was she once got nabbed by someone at United Airlines, where she worked, for riding her bicycle while in uniform. They felt it gave a bad image to United.

I have some basic feelings about automobiles—that they take up a lot of space, that they use up a lot of fuel, that most of the time they're on the road during work trips they are waiting for traffic jams to clear up, and they are really not doing their transportation thing. I grew up in a place where I could always ride my bike to school. I'm very pleased to say I promote bicycling. I'm Miss Bicycle at the Department of Transportation.

We made a contract with the Bay Area Rapid Transit System in San Francisco for safe bicycle access to the transit stations. I managed the contract and went out there a few times to see how everything was going. We also published a bicycle pamphlet with the Department of the Interior. It's an attractive little thing which just says that the Department of the Interior and the Department of Transportation back bicycling as a means of transportation and recreation. People wrote in to the Secretary and said, "Oh, you're wonderful and we're so glad you're promoting bicycles. We think that's the most helpful thing we've seen around for years." There was an editorial in the Baltimore paper which said: "This adds up to one of the most encouraging signs of progress in American civilization that we have seen in years. If the humble bike can go on and claim its rightful place in our transportation system, the sort of place many other countries long have given it, we can hope for more and safer lanes for cyclists." That was a typical kind of reaction to the booklet.

We would get hundreds of letters sent to us by the White House— "Dear President Nixon, I love what you're doing in Vietnam, but I think you really should do more for bicycles. Would you please do something about bicycles?" I used to answer every one of them individually. I've answered an incredible amount of mail. Now we take most of them and simply send out a pamphlet. A lot of the letters are from children, a lot from bicycle organizations. I'd say one-third of them are addressed to the White House.

We're also trying to figure out which of the Department's programs can be used to provide facilities or funding for bike paths, bike racks, or anything else. We had a national symposium on bicycles at the Transportation Systems Center in Cambridge. It was an opportunity for people to talk about improving the technology of the bicycle, which is now a true nineteenth-century vehicle. For example, why should people shlep around a fifteen-pound chain to lock their bicycles up? It ought to be integrated into the bicycle design.

Paul Dudley White says bicycling is good for you. I suspect it's not very good for you when you're doing it in polluted air, or on a crowded street where you're likely to get hit by a car.

Most of what I've done has been within the Department and not with the manufacturers themselves, to get people to think positively about the bike. And I've gotten things to happen. I don't think that there are very many people in the bureaucracy you can ask, "What have you done this year?" and they can say, "Well, I've got that publication out, I'm going to have a national symposium," and so on. I don't know how much I had to do with it but it was the first time a Secretary of Transportation had anything to say about bicycles. And he said some very good things, like they're the cleanest, quietest, healthiest, friendliest mode of transportation. I wrote a speech for him called "A Better Chance for Two-Wheeled Transportation." And one of my projects was hitchhiking, which is really just another form of carpooling. I wrote a speech for the Assistant Secretary about the federal point of view on hitchhiking.

The National Transportation Safety Board issued a report on bicycling which we helped put together. Outside of this Department the Civil Aeronautics Board has developed tariffs for carrying bicycles on planes. I've gotten two agencies within the Department each to provide funds for a manual so that communities have some guidelines when they start planning for bicycles. That's a positive thing. Until now, when a community wanted to do something about bicycles, it had to begin from scratch—it had no idea where to begin.

Now the whole idea of bicycling as viable transportation has been fully accepted. There is research and there are planning documents about retrofitting bridges for bikeways; traffic engineering concepts that worked well with highways have been translated into bikeway design. The same intellectual framework is being used. A study is under way now about bike-riding in polluted air, because a lot more people are riding bicycles now.

I spend a lot of time with people. The other day there was a guy in from the Delaware Highway and Transportation Department and I spent about two hours (which my boss didn't appreciate) trying to help him out, to be encouraging. A couple of weeks before that a fellow came in from Philadelphia; they wanted to do something about bicycles there.

You have to know how to manipulate the bureaucracy. We originally suggested that the Secretary write to all the governors asking them to please do something about bicycles. Well, it turned out that wasn't the way to do it. Relationships in bureaucracies are established along particular lines. So in the end, instead of that, we had a piece of official guidance going out from the Federal Highway Administrator to all the state highway departments, saying: "Plan for bicycles and bike paths, the Secretary thinks it's a great thing, a lot of people are doing it, it's good for you, it's not a bad way to get around." We considered that a great victory, to get the Federal Highway Administration to issue that piece of guidance, because in a sense they're on the other side. But sometimes when I go down there and talk to some of the individuals, they're way ahead of me in thinking about bicycles. In the bureaucracy, there are little gnomes all over the place who have different ideas from the rest.

The sun has come out again and the sidewalks are already beginning to dry beneath a mellow breeze tickling its way along M Street.

Eleven-fifty. Swinging her umbrella, Andrea Baxter begins to hum, "I hear music and there's no one there. . . ." She is caught by the strong scent of sandalwood emanating from a rattan furniture and variety store. Inside are enormous wooden bird cages of Chinese design, inexpensive inflatable pillows and chairs, mushroom candles, hand-painted tea sets, incense holders. At the front counter a well-dressed Oriental, apparently a businessman, is explaining to the middle-aged woman behind the cash register how he acquired exclusive import rights for certain choice items from Communist China. She appears to be very interested.

Andrea once wanted to run a shop like this, before she got caught up in bureaucracy. Part of another poem she once wrote now comes to her, and she becomes momentarily rueful: "Tuesday, a day of rudeness / One died of a bureaucratic shaft / Another fired / Me blaming untimely ends on others. / As if blindfolded, whirling / Still looking for the niche / My feet on zero / While others have children, marriages / Normal passages of life / I run instead / Some witless winless circle / To prevent pain and fat."

She looks at her watch. A few minutes before noon. She leaves the store and begins walking quickly on M Street toward Twenty-ninth, where she is to meet Richard. On the way she passes a set of theaters, a Greek pizza parlor, and Canal Square, a carefully designed conglomeration of restaurants, art shops, bookstores, and clothing stores, each with an outside of antiqued brick. The rear of the square is on the bank of the C & O Canal, which is thoroughly parched now except for the recent sprinkle. An old woman sits blankly on a bench. Two squirrels scramble after one another around a nearby tree. Andrea thinks about coming back to the canal in the summer for a ride on the tourist barge.

I was very taken with Kennedy and his ideas, and I guess that's one reason government service didn't seem so bad when I was in college.

With Watergate things came to a standstill in the Department of Transportation. Even prior to Watergate you always had this tremendous sense of the closeness of the ties between the executive agencies and the White House. Every important decision was carefully cleared.

I remember a rather frightening period after Nixon got elected. He fired half the people in the Department of Labor, including the Under Secretary with whom we were working closely. He was fired by order of Charles Colson for refusing to hold off investigating the teamsters. The feeling I had was that the White House was poised to take over. We heard stories from other parts of government, where White House aides had been placed in high positions. As it turned out it never happened. I remember the feeling of relief after the Sirica decision in March of 1973. It began to look as if Nixon was not going to be able to marshal enough power to actually carry out what seemed to be a rather sinister plan to take over the agency.

I viewed Nixon's impact on the government as generally bad. I felt his understanding of how you deal with the bureaucracy and its policies was very bad. I had this feeling even before Watergate broke, because I was working for an extremely evil person—one of the worst kind of political appointees in the Department of Transportation. He was the kind of guy who would literally pick up the paper in the morning and say, "What has our President done for us today?" and then inflict that sort of mentality on us. He was Assistant Secretary for Environment, Safety and Consumer Affairs. He was such a bad guy that he had a public relations person follow him everywhere. Just seeing how we had to insert Nixon into the first paragraph of every speech gave us this overwhelming feeling that everything was being controlled by the White House—long before Watergate broke. It was really quite revolting to have to work under that kind of person. It was such a relief not to have Nixon around. It was creepy.

I have had a couple of rather unhappy experiences traveling with our Assistant Secretaries. Sometimes a trip can turn into something social. Both of these occasions happened to be in Florida. On one I had gone down there with my boss, the one with the public relations man following him around, and we all got together for drinks and I went around the pool talking with this fellow. When it was time to leave, to go back to where I was staying (which was a different place from where he was staying), the PR guy says, "Well, what's the story?" This boss was so bad that his PR guy had to ask that question. It was repulsive. On the other occasion I had to prepare a speech for somebody and he arrived very late and wanted to go over it in my room. It turned into a gigantic assault. I was completely unprepared for this and I had a lot of trouble getting away. When one of these fellows was considered for a judicial position a few years later, the FBI came to me and asked what I knew about him. I gave them a written document telling them about all this, and I said I didn't want protection under the Privacy Act—I didn't care if my name were disclosed. He didn't get the job.

But sexual favors seem to be much more a question of between people who happen to be working near each other than of job advancement. Things may be different over on the Hill. My impression from talking with people over there is that some chairmen of congressional committees are much more blatant and cold-blooded about that kind of thing. There is a lot more shuffling around in the executive offices as far as positions are concerned. As a woman, from what I understand, you have to be prepared if you are dealing with certain committees that were controlled by people whose rules of behavior were quite arbitrary. It's the kind of thing that everyone's mother warns them against anyway. It never occurred to me to think, gee, if I had had a different attitude about this I would rise in the bureaucracy. It never crossed my mind. It's the kind of thing you start coping with in college—you have to make decisions every time you get in closed rooms whether or not you want to lay yourself open for that kind of thing.

I won't be in this place forever, though. You can get stale after a while. I suppose I could stay in government and keep jumping around to different jobs. It would depend on whether I could keep myself interested or found something altogether new on the outside. I think I'd like to go into college administration or publishing.

I hope to get married some day, but if I do I'd continue working. It's really not so much marriage versus a career, it's children versus career. I've thought about having a child outside of marriage, though I know it would be incredibly difficult—emotionally, financially, and in many other ways. But I'd never get married just to have a child.

I don't think I could stand always doing nothing. Now some days I feel like going to the beach and doing nothing, but others I'm full of energy. I know how to get things done. My leisure time is spent the way I want to. I like to listen to classical music, Gershwin. I find Washington a good place for me. I jog: I run the three and three quarters miles around Haine's Point. I take ballet classes twice a week. I've sailed since I was about fifteen years old and I do a lot of that at a racing club in Annapolis. It's not idyllic and romantic—it gets competitive and tough. And I love to invite eight or ten people over for dinner and cook. I just remodeled my kitchen.

You have to think ahead if you're going to get married and have children, as to whether you can fit it in with your career and life-style. I would have qualms about putting a child in a full-time day-care center until about three, partly because I would miss him. I know two girls who work for the Labor Department who are my age; they worked full time after their children were born, until they were about eight months. Then the children got to be so interesting that both of them are now working three days a week. That might be a good way to do it because you can build up respect as a mother and as a worker during those first six months when people recognize you have this child at home. Then when you say you want to work part-time because your child is so interesting, everyone will agree and everybody smiles.

It is five after twelve. Andrea peers a block down M Street to see if Richard is waiting.

She looks in the window of a health food restaurant and glances at the menu posted on the door. No meat, but a good variety of mildly spiced vegetables, rice, cheese combinations, fruit salads, milk shakes, puddings, and natural breads. She hears soft Indian melodies from the inside. Attached to the restaurant is a small bookstore with a display of volumes of natural cookery, psychology, and yoga, together with a collection of modern posters. A young couple comes out of the store; the girl says she has just read the Forty-three Truths of Man's Existence on the ladies' room wall.

The sun comes out from behind a cloud. Andrea looks up, squinting. There are gas stations on both sides of the street here, just before a bridge over Rock Creek. Something glistening in a shaft of light hitting the muddy water turns out to be a bottle caught in a branch. Andrea taps her umbrella on the sidewalk, waiting, thinking of another poem: "Planless weekends sober me / Return the lost years / Poems, pictures, gifts / Tracking them out / Pigeons patrol outside / The refusal to settle / Unsettles me now." Finally Richard comes bounding around the corner from Twenty-ninth Street, apologizing for being late. He had trouble finding a damn parking place.

5

The Diplomat

Statesman, yet friend to truth! of soul sincere, in
action faithful, and in honor clear, who broke no
promise, served no private end, who gain'd no title,
and who lost no friend; ennobled by himself, by all
approved, praised, wept, and honored.

Alexander Pope

Diplomacy is the nearest thing to perpetual motion,
and in spite of death, disaster, subornation and
treason, the fidget wheels keep turning, the cogs
engage, the springs wind and unwind and the illusion of purpose and direction is maintained for the
comfort of the ignorant.

Morris West, The Ambassador

SOMEDAY, OF COURSE, I'd like to be an ambassador.
But it's getting tougher. There are a lot of people in the Service,
and they have been cutting back—it's a time of very bad morale
in the Department generally. Anyone who's on the diplomatic side of it
hopes he'll get to be an ambassador. But I wouldn't sell my soul to the
devil to become one. I'm not that enamored of the idea.

Jonathan Stevens is given to small mutterings (although he has
tried to correct the habit), and a murmur escapes him as he

ambles onto court number four at the Chevy Chase Indoor Tennis Club. His regular partner, Edgar Walton, walks with him; both are wearing warm-up sweaters, Stevens's half-stretched over cream-colored shorts and a recently ironed shirt.

Stevens mutters again and moves his loose, lank figure to the post at the right side of the net, where he drapes a towel over the tape and sets down his racquet cover. On the adjacent court a women's doubles match has already begun, and one of the women is shrieking at a good shot. Stevens glances at her, smiling; then he puts his hands on his hips and swivels his torso, stretching his neck from side to side, and swings his racquet with his right arm in a circular motion, first forward ten times, then reverse, exactly ten times.

From the corner of his eyes he sees Walton move to the middle of the court, in his weekly ritual to measure the height of the net. Walton stands his racquet upright against the cord, pinches the net with his left hand at the tip of the handle, then with his right turns the oval racquet face sideways above his thumb, and checks that its upper edge aligns with the top of the tape.

My father was head of the journalism department at the state university. I grew up in the Midwest and lived there from 1938, right after I was born, until I went away to college in 1956. Aside from one or two summers, I haven't been back for more than two weeks in that whole time.

Perhaps it wasn't a typical midwestern upbringing, but I certainly did all the things that people from Middle America do: growing up, going to high school, playing sports. I was interested in journalism and did local sports writing on the side.

I have one brother, three years younger. We're total opposites: I went to Princeton, he went to Yale; I did my graduate work at the University of California, Berkeley, he did his at UCLA; I live in Washington, he lives in California. This is probably one reason why we get along so well—neither of us invades the other's turf. When we were growing up playing cowboys and Indians and stuff we had this beautiful campus that is virtually all wooded, so we could run pitched battles clear across the grounds, interrupting students sitting in secluded park benches and things like that. We went to the usual number of Jesse James serials and Buck Rogers stuff on Saturday mornings.

It was a curious blend of small town and cosmopolitan. There was some consciousness perhaps of being different, in that my father was a journalist who worked with books and kept back editions of the *New York Times*. Our house was full of papers. My folks cleaned out the basement a few years back and there were four and a half *tons* of newspapers. When I was in high school and people doing historical papers would have to use the library, I just went down to the basement and dug out a stack of *Life* magazines from the 1930s. Reading books and newspapers were important activities with us. We subscribed to seven newspapers all the time I was growing up—three morning, three evening, and one weekly. There was never a dearth of material to read. I started reading the comics regularly at about age eight.

I had a tendency to do indoor things when I was very young, being slender and not developing coordination any faster than all the other tall, thin guys. About my freshman year in high school I began to get some athletic ability. At that point, being tall and in a state in which basketball players are highly prized, I became very interested in sports. I ran track and cross-country, played basketball and tennis. The cross-country team was not very good, but it followed one that had been second in the state before graduating four seniors. A year later I had gotten my letter as a sophomore and I was pretty good at track, but not so much at basketball. I only weighed 130 pounds at the time and I was as tall as I am now, about six-two. That doesn't leave much to stretch over the bones. I was a good ball player, but I played varsity only my last year, and then as a sixth man in a team. You couldn't quite say I was a regular. Our team was unusual, because the tendency was to start people in school a year before they were ready—the kids were smart. The result was that our school was forever seeing people bloom in their last year. If I had gone to more normal school systems, they would have been sophomores or juniors when they began to develop.

Because we drew from an unusual student body, which involved about half university professors' sons and daughters and half from some of the poorer areas in the country, we had a very atypical learning situation, in which the normal curve simply did not exist. There wasn't much in the middle: we had very bright people, lots of them, and people who were not so bright, and then those who had come from very poor families and backgrounds. The fact that we all got along well together is still a bit of a mystery to me.

Competition for me was more in sports than in the academic area. I enjoyed high school work—edited the school paper as a senior—but it wasn't horribly difficult. It was a bad day when I couldn't get all my homework done in the study hall. The school was a laboratory for the university, and this meant that we had a lot of student teachers. We had the runner-up in the 1952 Miss America contest as a student teacher in history, and it spoiled me. She was a beautiful lady but the funny thing was she was not by any means the best-looking teacher we ever had. There were at least two others who were knockouts.

Stevens and Walton begin to warm up. *Competitive edge*, Stevens thinks to himself, *get the competitive edge.* The two men each slap a ball into the net before one finally goes over. Stevens has known for a long time now to keep his shots toward Walton's backhand—they have been vying for close to five years. But even a fresh competitor would notice Walton's awkward foot placement and scrunched-up flailing at balls hit to his left. Perhaps it is *because* they have been playing against each other so long that Stevens never hits to Walton's left during a warmup. (*Don't let the other guy know you remember, and maybe he'll make some early mistakes.*) But Walton understands full well such scheming, just as he knows that Stevens's net game is for the birds.

Our town also had the first television station in the Midwest in 1949, and we got a television set a year later when my mother won one on a local quiz show. She did it by correctly identifying the address of a local cleaner. We were one of the few families in town at the time who had TV. There was quite a bit else to do, too. There were three movie theaters. We had an excellent cultural set-up because the university music school was probably one of the best in the country—they had a number of former Metropolitan Opera people teaching. The Met used to play there three days a year; it's one of the few concert stages in the Middle West that has been reinforced to hold elephants when they do

Aida. Music is big time there. We got to see a lot of things. But I was never really interested in music and concerts, and I went with the greatest reluctance to ballet and things like that. I did enjoy the plays, though, and participated in a radio workshop run by one of the university people, which gave us experience in acting out shows on the campus radio station.

We lived in a large stone house that was ideal. I'd like to find another one like it for my own—a one-family home, lots of space. My mother and father had each grown up in the area, and we had lots of family in the immediate vicinity. We exchanged visits at Christmas.

In high school I did the usual amount of dating and agonizing over acne and that kind of thing. In the 1950s the big craze was to go steady. Today it seems almost anachronistic. I went steady with a girl my senior year and then we broke up to go to college, dated a little bit thereafter, and then drifted apart.

Going away to college, which was something I had gradually decided I wanted to do, was probably the major change in my life from that point. Had I stayed at home I might have wound up in politics or journalism. I could have gone to the state university, but I had gotten interested in political science, history, and political economy. So in high school I began to look around for other colleges. I realized instinctively that the town was too big for both myself and my father—at the time, he was the senior department head at the university, in a very visible area, journalism and public relations—and I figured it would be better if I could get away from home. Not from any great antagonism, but simply that it would be better for me.

I had gotten very interested in the Woodrow Wilson School at Princeton. In 1955 we had taken a summer trip and visited Lafayette College (my father had taught there for a few years before working on the newspaper in Easton, where I was born); we visited Princeton, and I decided right then that if I could get in that's where I wanted to go. Well, I applied, and got in with a scholarship. This was much to my parents' astonishment, I think. They just didn't believe my record would have been good enough to get in. But my grades steadily improved all the way through high school; my last four semesters I had a straight A average. I kept getting better.

After several minutes of volleying, the only sound the hollow popping of tennis balls striking catgut, Jonathan Stevens says,

"I'm-ready-whenever-you-are." Walton asks for a few more volleys, then moves to the net, sheds his sweater, and says he is all set.

Stevens has decided to keep his sweater on for a while. He is a tall, bony man; whether moving quickly or slowly, he seems to glide with the awkward grace of a flamingo. He could be a slim Joe Palooka, a shock of sandy brown hair falling loosely over features carved from the steadfast heart of Middle America. Remnants of freckles tinge his cheeks, and a somewhat boyish grin lends a soft, deceptive sparkle to his eyes. Thin black horn-rimmed glasses complement a purposefully academic countenance.

"Ready?" asks Walton.

"First serve in?"

"Right."

Stevens always plays first service in, and invariably (for some reason he does not fully understand) puts the ball where he wants it. Setting his left foot against the baseline, he bounces a three-dot Dunlop once and tosses it above his head, a bit too high. With an exaggerated lean he lowers his left shoulder and brings the racquet up and around, striking the ball at the top of the gut, near the wood. *The Stevens Lurch*, he has thought to himself at other times. The ball flies low into the net. Stevens goes through the same foreplay on his second serve, but though the resulting shot is more accurate, it has no velocity. Walton attacks it with a roundhouse forehand of unlikely power, and the ball sails beyond the baseline. Fifteen–love.

The American academic community really got conscious of its own élite status in the late 1950s and early '60s. Faculty members for the most part were overworked and underpaid. The big increase in pay and status for university people began to come in the post-Sputnik period, well after I had gone on to college and had become interested in more intellectual things.

The president of the school was quite a dominant academic figure in the state. At the time there wasn't much problem with the budget: he just went up and laid it on the legislature and they bought it. Times have changed, of course, though we had the usual problems with academic freedom. My father was involved there. He was also very civic-minded, stemming from the fact that he had grown up in the local campus town and knew lots of the people; and being in journalism, unlike many academics, he had a very good feel for the real world. I can remember as a young child going downtown on election night and working. My dad would always set up the county coverage for the state press services, and university students would handle the legwork. He was equally at home at school and down at some of the grubby bars in town, so I learned to deal with different people, and the social distinctions in the high school were less of a problem for me than for others.

My father was strong but quiet. Reporters are not noticeably bashful, but for a guy in that field, he was rather shy. His professorial style—up until my wife went through college and sort of reduced it to a shambles—was very stern. Very good, but very stern. His former students all swear by him. Four hundred of them turned up for his retirement dinner in 1968. He is still involved in various civic things. He does a lot of consulting for newspapers that want to sort out their operations and see what they are doing. He was very active in Rotary and served as a district governor (one of the few hundreds that are selected all over the world) and on the Rotary International Magazine Committee.

Mother spent an awful lot of time with the kids when we were growing up. She worked as a newspaper reporter before she married Dad when they were both twenty-five (which in those days was pretty old—you were over the hill at twenty-three if you weren't married). She handled publicity for lots of things. She was a strong character, given to swearing at traffic policemen and things like that, but Dad ran the family. The older I get the more I appreciate how good both my parents are at dealing with people—not in the sense of manipulating, but in being sensitive to what they are thinking without being weak in their own position.

There was always a lot of give-and-take. As soon as we kids were old enough to make puns and come back with smart remarks, we got involved in it, too. Parental guidance was always exercised very subtly, so that there was not a great deal of opportunity to develop the kinds of antagonisms that you get today, like "He doesn't understand me." I can remember only one serious argument with my father that I lost, in the sense that I did not convince him that my way was right and he insisted on doing it his way. That was over the question of whether during the summers I should have to go to bed early because I got up early to deliver newspapers. The difference was over half an hour. Parents who are good enough at shaping it up so that that is the only remembered confrontation have got to be pretty good. If I had been asked when I graduated from high school how good they were, I would have given them a much lower mark.

Dad always encouraged us to go for goals. He'd say once you have decided to do something, stick to it—or readjust a goal if in the light of some obvious evidence it wasn't realistic. But neither he nor Mom ever tried to push either of us toward specific careers. In fact my Dad almost bent over backwards concerning my interest in journalism, because he was always a little bit worried that this was a reflection of parental interest and job. So all in all I have a hard time with someone who says, "I just can't talk to my parents."

Stevens mutters a passing thought about the quality of his first serve. He is by nature a cautious man, and that is why he has gone so far so fast at State, he tells himself. A better sense of discretion. Stevens bounces the ball once and hits his next serve. It is a bit easier in force than the first, and this time it is aimed for the backhand. Walton chips a good shot cross-court over the net; Stevens does not bother to chase it. The score is fifteen–all.

Again Stevens aims for the backhand, but by now Walton's feet are ready, and he runs around the ball, slicing another little drop shot, which slips toward the sideline and skims away. Fifteen–thirty. Stevens mutters, "All cuteness, as usual." He and Walton hardly talk to each other when they play, except to call out the scores.

Another shriek from the next court. Stevens bends at the knees as he launches a lob deep cross-court to Walton's backhand corner. The shot is too good, and things are even at thirty–all.

The next several points are traded. Then Walton pounces to the
net for a short shot and swipes at an overhead; the ball hits the
wood of his racquet, tips off, and goes over the tape. His advantage. Stevens would still like to win the first game, but now a
small voice sounds somewhere deep in his mind, the same voice
he has been hearing for as long as he has been playing against
Walton. This time it says, "Game, Mr. Walton." Stevens
double-faults—something he seldom does—and he hears the
voice say, "He leads, one game to love."

My first year at Princeton was the typical adjustment of a midwestern,
relatively poor student, on scholarship, working to earn money to meet
expenses, having a difficult time of it academically—and enjoying the
whole thing thoroughly. My first two years I really learned to appreciate
the so-called intellectual pursuits, but it was not entirely a happy time:
one must readjust one's self-image. As time went on, I made good
friends, and my last two years were quite happy.

I had only one problem. I ran cross-country there and was on the
freshman team. During my sophomore year the Asian flu just literally
wiped out the better part of the East Coast for about two months. I
caught it, went to bed with a high temperature and everything, was
cured, went back to running, and caught it again. The doctor said,
"Look, you are going to do real damage to your heart; lay off until
spring." I followed his advice, then went back at it my junior year. But I
had lost a little bit of the edge. So I ran varsity cross-country for only one
full season. I jarred the base of my back a little bit and had to take some
treatments—I gather it's very much like the thing Jack Kennedy had,
only a much milder case of it.

That took me out of the professional sports bracket, but it didn't spoil
my enjoyment of the campus. I began to get out and do more, generally
expanded my horizons. It was a period of tremendous personal growth.

About my sophomore year I really began to get interested in
theology—what was behind it all? Now I was brought up in the Episcopal church, carried the cross and flag, went to one of those crude
Sunday schools of the 1950s, was confirmed very early (at ten years of
age), and went to church from then on. Never having had anything

really hammered into me, I didn't have a lot of baggage to get rid of and I continued to go to church at Princeton. We had an Episcopal canon who came to the campus for a series of lectures, a very impressive guy named Canon Green, from England. He was quite good.

At Princeton for the first time I was exposed to a range of characters I didn't even know existed: some East Coast establishment types; rich, landed money from the South; as well as the really poor kids who were on scholarship. I was on scholarship and I worked. One of the guys on our hall was the son of a New Jersey dock worker. His entire tuition was being paid, but he had to put in something like 48 to 50 hours a week just to meet expenses, let along have a little left over to date with.

I was genuinely interested in journalism, but I failed to make the Press Club at Princeton. It was an elected, choice deal; they picked four out of each class and in the twenty-man competition, I was the fifth one. I therefore had to work and earn money in other ways—the Press Club people earned their own money by filing stories for the Newark, New York, and Philadelphia papers.

The need to earn money in college turned me to other odds and ends. I was in the Naval ROTC, but as a regular student, which meant I didn't get any money my first two years and fifty bucks a month thereafter—plus tuition, uniforms, and so forth. So I went to work doing a number of odd jobs, mostly light carpentry. There are some very nice houses in Princeton, and even then it was impossible to hire anyone just to do the little things. The hubbies worked in New York and got home late at night; it's an hour-and-ten-minute train ride either way. I would get baby-sitting leads from these odd jobs, which enabled me to earn a little more money, and my junior year I added to that by doing an egg route. It involved going in the truck of one of the merchants, driving over to Flemington, in the egg country, picking up the eggs, and bringing them back. In the meantime the guy who ran the business sorted eggs for the local eating clubs, and then I would deliver in Princeton. Since at that time you had no cars in Princeton except under special arrangement, because the campus is very compact, this gave me wheels once a week to get out and do things like pick up firewood from the university lot and chuck it up to the dormitory, where we could burn it in the fireplace.

In my sophomore year I went to work for the Gallup Poll one afternoon a week, as a pre-tester. I put this to use my senior year. I did a public opinion survey on the Berlin crisis of that period, which has been very helpful to me because I picked up the essence of modern public opinion techniques, from the source. I graduated with honors.

It is Walton's serve. He hits a pair of practice shots past Stevens, one in, the other out. When Walton serves he resembles a mechanical teddy bear. His delivery is too compact; there is no leverage. But for some reason his shots contain an inordinate amount of zip. Stevens has often wondered about this. Walton's game is less one of placement than Stevens's, and his winning points are more awkward and unpredictable (though he has a better forehand), but there seems to be no reason for his always being able to put up the battle he does.

The first serve hits the net. Stevens knows Walton will not let up on the second, especially this early in the set. Walton once told him about reading somewhere that a weak second service is as good as conceding the point, but whence that curious *confidence* that he can so control his body to give his second serve as much quick power as the first? Perhaps it is not confidence at all, thinks Stevens, but a mild arrogance or conceit. As it happens it is rather seldom that Walton manages to get the second serve in with power. So this time Stevens is surprised when it bounds in fair, and he cannot manage anything more than a weak return to his opponent's forehand. Walton's feet are in the wrong place, and he hits back a routine volley; Stevens, losing concentration for a second, does the same. This time Walton cranks back and shoots a sharp placement to Stevens's backhand corner. Good. Fifteen–love.

Stevens's mind wanders away to the office and to the 75-page report he promised to have ready on a new economic aid program for Zambia. Late last night, after teaching a full seminar at George Washington University, he came back to his desk at State to finish writing the proposal, and left it with instructions on his secretary's desk. Were they explicit enough?

After double-faulting the next point, Walton puts a perfect lob deep to the baseline; Stevens lopes around it and scoops a long wristy shot into the far diagonal corner. It is a lucky retrieval, but a winner, and it evens the score at thirty–all. Walton double-faults again. At thirty–forty he serves to Stevens's left. The ball is returned. Walton runs two feet forward, tucks his elbow into his hip, and pushes the ball softly across the net. This is the kind of patsy placement, thinks Stevens, that is part and parcel of Walton's game. This time Stevens is more deft than cute, and he is there to slice a forehand down the line to the right. Walton has no chance. One game apiece.

After Princeton I went into the Navy and became an operations officer on a destroyer escort off Treasure Island. When it came time to put down preference, I said I'd like to be on a small combatant in the operations department (radar communications) on the West Coast, with San Francisco for my home port. I figured that was almost too specific; but when the orders came forth, I got destroyer escort, which is small, berthed at Treasure Island, which is San Francisco to a T. And not only was it in the operations department, I was *the* operations officer. My roommate, who had wanted to be on an icebreaker out of Boston, wound up on a refrigerator ship out of Norfolk. He got the ice, but on the wrong side of the cabin door.

I was married in the Navy. I flew back home after I had been away six months. I had first met my wife the summer I got out of high school. She was at the journalism institute that my father's department ran for high school students. Things intervened and we didn't get serious for about three years. She came to the state university, majored in journalism, and my father was her advisor, so we kind of passed and touched at various points. Then it developed on through Princeton, under what then were very atypical arrangements: we both dated other people, even right up to the period after we were engaged.

I was in the Navy from '60 to '62. Afterwards, since I was already on the West Coast and wanted a slightly different university experience, I applied to Berkeley and was admitted to graduate school as a Ph.D. candidate in political science.

My last year as a graduate student was the year that Mario Savio started talking to the trees and the whole bit. It was kind of interesting. I had passed my exams in what for Berkeley was a track record, and I was doing my dissertation. When the Free Speech business started, my wife and I were head residents at the largest men's dorm on campus. I was much more conservative than my graduate school classmates. I resigned as head of the graduate Political Science Association at the point where it was voting to condemn the university president, out-of-hand, on hearsay evidence, on a speech he had given in San Diego. A number of us (not just me) felt we ought to at least wait until we got a text of the speech and heard what he had to say. Now when I say I was conservative, I'm talking about conservative in the California sense, which still puts me several degrees to the left of most others. I just happened to be a Republican. I was probably the only person who would admit to being a Republican in the graduate school at Berkeley. This was the pre-Reagan period. I had a pretty strong feeling that if the two-party system were to survive, the Republicans had to get a little stronger. This was a perfectly logical point of view to hold in the 1950s and '60s.

I'm not terribly political. I've voted about half Republican and half Democratic, pretty much for the man rather than the party. Even now I vote my conscience. Every Foreign Service officer has a right to his own convictions. The thing you don't want to do is wind up advocating them. I try to maintain the contacts with home. If you're going to be a good representative abroad, you have to know what's going on politically in the United States. The only way to do that is to keep in touch with politicians. Frankly, too few of my colleagues do that.

I went through graduate school in three years from start to finish. I was in California until 1965. I had a life to live and I wanted to get started—being married helps you to achieve this motivation. My dissertation was on the State Department's foreign policy making with the Vietnam question, 1961–1965. When I started, this was a much less exciting topic than it was later, but I had always known that I wanted to do something on the bureaucratics of policy making. I interviewed an awful lot of people here in Washington. Daniel Ellsberg wasn't one of them. You don't hear this from the Harvard professors who came down here and bled all over the Department and White House, but as for Cambodia, every objective that Nixon sought to achieve he did achieve—and nobody wanted to give him credit for it. I think the reason there was such a negative reaction on the college campuses was that by the spring of 1970 the students had just about convinced themselves the President was going to bug out of Vietnam, and Cambodia showed them something else: that at a bare minimum we were going to withdraw in good order and it wasn't going to be an uncalculated fleeing. This disturbed a lot of them who thought that we should get out right away, and they felt in some sense betrayed. I think the more intelligent ones, who were less ideologically committed to posture and position, soon began to realize that this was the plan—which explains why the campuses were relatively quiet the *next* year, when everyone thought there would be a horrible blow-up.

Jonathan Stevens takes off his sweater. One of the women on the next court lunges sloppily after a ball at the net and almost collides with her partner, who had come up herself to hit it. The two of them glare at one another, then laugh.

Stevens again lets his mind wander back to an affair of State, although he is conscious of trying not to. The wives of the president and vice president of Togo are coming into New York the next morning, and he just heard about it today. (*Typical. Less than ten hours to notify customs and immigration, to get them cleared with the appropriate diplomatic courtesy. You can bet if it doesn't all go smoothly we'll hear about it for weeks. If protocol isn't right, it becomes a political problem.*)

He moves back to the baseline for his service. Two decent backhands diminish the preoccupation with work. The score is thirty–love. But concentration and all, Stevens mis-hits the next three points, putting moderate-paced volleys into the net. He curses to himself. Walton's advantage. Stevens lashes a good shot, which twists down the line, mesmerizing him into a momentary stupor; as Walton hits it back, Stevens is still standing and watching. No excuse for that, he tells himself, and for the first time today, he flips his racquet and whispers, "Drive!" He hits his first serve long and the second into the net. He is still thinking of Togo. One–two in games.

I had been in Saigon while I was with the Navy, and this had interested me very much in international affairs. I knew I didn't want the military side as a career, and the Foreign Service, which I had been sort of oriented toward at Princeton, seemed the logical way to go. I had already taken the Foreign Service exam my first year in graduate school and passed it and gotten my security clearance. So as soon as I finished my dissertation, we hopped in the car and drove across the country and I entered the State Department. I started right in with the beginning course, orientation, language training.

In those days, you had an interview halfway through your introductory course with the counseling staff in the junior officer program, and they decided on the basis of your general interests where you'd like to go. Now the junior officers are given a list and asked to state preferences. In my case it could have been Timbuktu, which is across one of the main trade routes from North Africa to sub-Saharan Africa. There's also a choice between going to a larger or a smaller embassy. Because I was a little older than most of my entering class, I got to go to a smaller embassy, where you'd expect the chance to get your finger into more pies. I had a mild interest in Southeast Asia at the time, but I needed to develop my language proficiency, and a French-speaking post seemed indicated. I was assigned to African affairs, and in January 1966 I was sent out to the Republic of Guinea, West Africa. After Guinea came Burundi, and then in 1968 Ghana, then Zambia, and now Iran.

We arrived in Guinea in late January, two weeks before Nkrumah was overthrown as president of Ghana. Nkrumah and Guinea's president had been very close, so Sekou Touré asked him to come to Guinea and become co-president there, which was perhaps greater in honor than in fact. It was a very interesting period because of the suspicions of the government toward Americans at the time. Touré was convinced that the American government had something to do with Nkrumah's overthrow, although Nkrumah once said he knew that this was not the case.

It was a typical first tour, lots of adjustments to make. I had to learn French. We lived in temporary housing the entire time, which made life a little bit difficult. But I got adjusted to doing Foreign Service work. At that point, I was the consular officer and also the officer in charge of British interests, the British having been kicked out a couple of months earlier over the question of Rhodesian independence. I had keys to the British warehouse and was the only one seeing Guineans on a regular basis, because of my consular work. We stayed in Guinea about ten months, left in late November.

We went on our Rest and Recreation—one month's leave during a two-year tour—at a fairly early time. My wife was pregnant, and if we had not taken it then it would have come up just about the time the baby would be born. You can get regular vacations in-country, but on an R and R tour the government pays your way, your air fare, and you can have the opportunity for a real change of culture.

In the fourth game Walton delivers a sharp first service, which Stevens blocks weakly into the net. Stevens starts to mutter a compliment, to tell Walton it was a good serve, but he catches himself. He knows it wasn't *that* good, that his return was actually very bad, and he knows that he himself bridles whenever Walton insists on saying "Nice serve" immediately after fouling up the return of a mediocre service and losing the point. It is not a compliment at all, thinks Stevens; it is an excuse. In the State Department, excuses are not tolerated. If a file is left unlocked when it is not being used, the penalty can range from a slap on the wrist to a week without pay, but there *are* penalties.

Stevens comes back to win the next point, by conning Walton to his left and hitting a return volley to his right. When he does this well it is as if it had happened at Wimbledon or Forest Hills, live and in color, Rosewall conning Laver. It is precisely at moments like these, although they are relatively rare with Stevens, that the tennis bug bites.

Walton hits a very good forehand off Stevens's next service. Stevens lunges at the ball to his right, slapping nothing but air. Thirty–fifteen. Now Walton gets cute again and chips a shot just over the net, but Stevens is there to dink one back. Walton tries to put it away and misses, off to the side. On the next point Stevens is forced to come to the net when the ball caroms awkwardly off the wood of Walton's racquet. He pushes a shot. Walton lobs. Stevens retreats to his backhand, winds up, delivers a half-speed return that stops at the top of the tape and falls back into Stevens's court.

Stevens mutters to himself. He wonders whether the time he put in on his report last night was worth it. (*But what is life if not effort-and-achievement?*) Back on the court, he tries another wrist shot slanted diagonally across the court, which Walton chases but cannot reach. Stevens has forced deuce. Walton again double-faults; he grabs his right shoulder with his left hand, and there is a pained expression on his face, though no sound issues from his lips. Stevens likewise utters not a word. He has seen Walton go through this act too many times before; he will offer neither consolation nor solicitude. *I don't think I'm a bad guy*, Stevens tells himself, *I just hate excuses.* Advantage, Mr. Stevens.

Walton, suddenly cautious, powder-puffs his second serve. Stevens attacks it with an angled forehand, arched to the baseline more weakly than he expected. Walton hits it high and deep. Stevens slants back, circles around, and hits a soft three-quarter-speed overhead. It is, Stevens thinks to himself as the ball floats over the net, just too well-placed; no speed, plenty of judgment. Even Walton would concede it is a well-conceived, well-executed shot. Game to Mr. Stevens. Two–all.

Foreign intrigue is greatly overrated. First of all, although some goes on, nobody really discusses it very much. We get a general security briefing here in the Department before we go out. My own experience with this sort of stuff has been fairly pedestrian. The type of thing you do get frequently is the Russians trying to bug the embassy. That happens particularly in out-of-the-way places where they might be successful.

I've been exposed to danger, but it didn't seem so when it happened, largely because it was kind of exciting. In both Guinea and Burundi, the embassies were stoned by mobs, and in both places the cultural centers were burned. I was not in them at the time. In one case, we thought the hostile mob was triggered by Chinese influence. We spent a month under house arrest in Guinea, where you couldn't move around without an armed Guinean officer in the car. People were very friendly:

once the Peace Corps volunteers needed to go to the store and the guard couldn't let them out of the house, but he said if they would hold his gun, he would get the bread and milk for them. Touching experiences like this off and on. Coming back from the ambassador's house one evening, at the height of this period in which the Americans were under a lot of pressure, we were stopped nine times by party youth movement roadblocks. Nine times isn't that much, but it was only two and a half blocks to our house.

In Burundi, we arrived in the first plane to enter the country after the revolution of 1966. The government had chartered a plane to bring us in with the diplomatic mail, and we were flying with one of the most experienced officers, a former German air force pilot. We landed and were met by armed guards, a considerable number. The fact that my wife was seven and a half months pregnant and showing it eased a lot of the tension when we got out of the plane. And we had to stay in in the evening from then until the night before the baby was born—a dusk-to-dawn curfew in which you were supposed to be in your quarters at six o'clock and weren't allowed out until six o'clock in the morning. It turned into an ideal experience for us, a lovely thing when our first daughter was born. Added to that was the fact that now she has all the natural kind of body immunities that one acquires from growing up in a less-developed country.

The clandestineness is greatly overrated, because all you're really doing is making contacts in the country. People sometimes interpret this as a kind of spying. The classic diplomatic case is when you deal with opposition leaders in a country—the local government will assume that there is something malevolent involved. In both Guinea and Burundi we had situations in which the government was very suspicious of what all was going on; in Guinea, in fact, you could not invite Guineans to your home without getting Foreign Ministry approval, and that was normally granted only on the national day celebration for Americans. Presumably the rule went for others as well, although you're never sure these regulations are applied across the board.

When we were in Burundi, I had contact with my Soviet counterpart, who was approximately my age. Nothing ever came of it except that we appeared on programs together, he giving away books on Lenin and me giving away books on George Washington and Ben Franklin.

One afternoon we switched and he would give away *John D. Rockefeller: Biography of an American Capitalist* and I would give away *Selected Works of Stalin*, and it really threw them into confusion. When you've gone through eighty or ninety of these ceremonies, you have to do something to break the monotony.

Stevens begins the fifth game. Leaning back, he tosses the ball two feet above his head and rocks forward with the straight-down motion of a paper cutter. The ball comes off his racquet at no more than medium speed. Walton pounds his return into the net, though, then calls out half-grudgingly, "Good serve." "No, it wasn't," mutters Stevens to himself, "damning with faint praise."

The next point gets bogged down in a long pitter-pat volley, lasting five shots from each player, which Walton ends by lofting a backhand just outside the baseline. But Stevens is still having trouble with his service. On the following three points he hits short second serves, and on the returns consecutive weak backhands of his own, each sailing off toward the adjacent court on the left. Advantage, Walton.

Stevens remembers when he was younger and faster, but finds it hard to admit he has slowed down. There was a time when he could go three sets and still want more. He worries about his condition; he asks himself how much his intellectual prowess is weakened by being out of shape. He would like to get more exercise, but he does not have the time—an excuse, he knows, and one that he would regard as a lame one from others.

On the sixth point of the game Walton brings Stevens up to the net with a wooden half-lob that falls just over the cord and bounces high. Stevens gets there in time to measure it, eyeing Walton in the far backhand corner, and slices his racquet forward sharply, angling for the left-hand service box. The ball slaps the top of the net about two feet from the left post, then tips over and touches at the singles sideline.

Walton looks to Stevens. "I don't know, did you see it?"

Stevens would like to call it good but thinks it may have gone just out. "Your call, but if you didn't see it let's take it over." Walton assents, and handles the next point easily with a strong forehand down the line.

This has been the pattern of the matches between these two for a long time: each man usually finds it more difficult to win his own service. With his third turn coming up, Walton now leads, three games to two.

If I am going to make a move it better come soon, like right now. Stevens knows he is dramatizing—flipping his racquet, talking to himself—and he is also uncomfortably aware that his playacting is often superior to his play.

This time Walton comes in with two consecutive second serves that clip the edge of the service box. Stevens manages to return the second, and a corner-to-corner volley ensues that has both men scurrying back and forth from the center of the baseline. Then Walton chips a shot just over the net near the right side at the pole, and Stevens, having started from the baseline, scrambles forward desperately, a small voice urging him on. But in mid-stride the same voice tells him it is hopeless. He lunges at the ball and manages to reach it, but on the downward movement his racquet somehow knocks into his left knee; Stevens trips and falls, sprawling at the foot of the net in a swirl of green surface and mesh and white fluorescent light. The ball hits the tape and bounces back.

Walton asks Stevens if he is all right. "Yeah, I'm okay."

Thirty–love.

In the everyday life of a Foreign Service officer a lot depends on the style of the ambassador you're working for. In most embassies abroad a normal American business suit is pretty standard, although there are modest variations. For example, in the Philippines they have a dress shirt that is essentially a very fancy sport shirt, which you wear not tucked in. This is the equivalent of a business suit. In Burundi people wore what are sometimes called Nehru suits, which are slacks and sport shirt of the same color, and a jacket with a high Chinese collar. But normally the Americans in Burundi did not wear that, because there was some party symbolism associated with it. On the other hand, I know some of our people in other areas of Africa who did wear this sort of thing.

Normally, I'd wear a coat and tie when I was out of the office, but I hardly ever wore the coat inside. If you look very carefully, sometimes when they have one of these public conferences, you'll find that the State Department is probably as hairy as any organ of the federal government. Mustaches, long sideburns, all this stuff. But you don't see much of the women's-length look on your career people; you see it on some of the summer interns. Actually, if you think about service in the tropics for a while, there are some excellent reasons for short hair. There is less hang-up now than there has been in the past on what you might call the outward manifestations of conformity. In some areas of the world you do get a strong dislike for mini-skirts, so that American personnel coming there have to be cautioned to wear their dresses to the knee. In some of the Arab countries women are still second-class citizens, so there are certain rules of behavior there that are a little bit different.

The deeper you've been immersed in a foreign culture, the more you realize how little you know when you go into a place. In both Guinea and Burundi, I felt that I never really got an intimate feel for the internal dynamics of the system. Sometimes your strangeness will simply get you kicked out or make people very leery of talking to you.

The idea is to make contacts, meet people at work and at play. I have never been in a country that has had "typical" embassy parties. There are different kinds of parties, some that our embassy gives and some that you give as private individuals. In Guinea I would entertain mostly other diplomats. In Burundi, it was a lot more flexible. The American government is probably one of the cheapest around for providing its diplomats the means to have people over for dinner, to just buy a few drinks and carry on the normal amenities of life. You are not given a great deal of flexibility as to the amount of your money you spend. There are representational allowances, but they are not great, and the ambassador is under no obligation to give any of this money to the junior people. In both countries that I've served in, the ambassador made it a policy to give the junior people a share of the action. But in Guinea, for example, I got $50 a quarter. You can wipe that out in a dinner party for thirteen people if you're buying expensive food.

We accepted almost all invitations, unless there were some personal reasons we couldn't go. Even when my wife was in the last stages of pregnancy, we'd go to parties but leave relatively early. They were all pretty much standard, except that live entertainment wasn't used very often. The ambassador is the guy who usually throws the parties, and then you normally help him out by moving people around, getting them to talk to each other. In a society that's very close, this may be one of your very few really good opportunities to get to meet local people. If they come at all. I've served in countries where it wasn't uncommon if only ten percent showed—if you sent out a hundred invitations to Guinean officials, it would be lucky if ten showed up. The poor response to our parties wasn't a question of being in Africa; it's peculiar to countries which have a particularly difficult relationship with the United States at any given moment. It also depends on what kind of parties you throw. After all, the customs are entirely different there. If you invite people for eight-thirty, you'll get them coming as late as eleven o'clock—if you're planning a sit-down dinner, this can be disconcerting. So most Foreign Service officers in Guinea and Burundi and many other countries serve buffet dinners, because it's much easier to pull off extra silverware and plates if nobody shows.

In Burundi it was a little bit less expensive but that was primarily because the bulk of the embassy staff had been kicked out nine months before I got there, so one foreign officer had a representational allowance based on a staff of four people. The others had been kicked out by the Batutsi aristocrats, who thought that the Bahutu would not have rebelled if they had not been exposed to all these seditious ideas by the Americans and other Western imperialists. The catch-phrase was the "imperialist–aggressors"—no, "imperialist neo-colonists." You have to get your epithets straight here.

The pay is not all that bad, but salary isn't the only element. For example, later on, when I moved to Zambia—because it's a different climate zone—I got the maximum transfer allowance. That consisted of $175 apiece for every member of my family: a total of $525. Out of that we're supposed to replace a wardrobe and buy all the various things we need. Obviously we don't make it. The problem is that you're moving every three years. (The insurance people tell you that three moves equals one fire in damage to personal belongings.)

But there are compensations. Your housing abroad is usually paid for. You may not always like what you get, but as a rule of thumb most Foreign Service officers agree that when you go overseas you can in effect double your take-home pay. On the other hand, you'll need it to get reestablished at your next post. Our credit union does a thriving business in loans to officers. And all the expenses come at once. We've got to get virtually all new clothes, buy a car (and I can't pay for it when it's delivered—I've got to pay for it now and then wait six months for it). We've just spent $100 on electrical transformers, because in the country where we're going the voltage is 220. Now it's possible to buy an iron or a toaster than runs on 220, our record player is variable (I can flick a switch), and so's our radio. But a lot of other things aren't.

Walton tosses the ball up for his third service. It is slightly behind him and he has to twist in order to slap it across the net. Stevens pulls up to push back a half-volley return and stays rooted to the center line, about two feet from the net. Walton tries to punch the ball past him, but Stevens slides quickly to his right and slants it beyond his opponent's reach.

A winner. He smiles to himself as he walks back toward the left baseline to receive the next service. And then, *drive*! Still vaguely aware of the melodramatic seriousness about all this, which he would ridicule in others, Stevens takes pains to keep such histrionics well beneath view. Demeanor remains important to him. Public face. Cool.

Walton double-faults. Thirty–all. Stevens surrenders the next point to another sharp forehand by Walton, then manages a wristy, spinning drop shot to even the score at deuce. Walton unwinds his own teddy-bear service. Stevens has a placement in mind, and this time he executes it: a lob into the far backhand corner. Walton is caught; with a scrunched-up, effortful stroke, he pokes the ball into the net.

Advantage, Mr. Stevens. Beginning to sweat now, he thinks to himself that the greatest thing Walton lacks is style. He is not contemptuous, but he wonders whether Walton would ever bend the edge of his calling card. When leaving a Foreign Service one is supposed to pay courtesy calls on his colleagues, and if they're not in one bends the edge of his calling card to indicate that he has come by personally. Stevens himself has to go to the book of protocol for things like that. Still, he mutters, there's such a thing as style, and not everybody has it.

In Burundi, the climate was ideal—considerably better than in Washington. In Guinea, you had the rainy season and the dry season. The rainy season was oppressive, muggy all the time, over a hundred inches of rain a year (the State of New York gets 31). Guinea was also a problem with food because the economy is a bit of a mess. We ate a good deal of local foods both places, although at that time there was an American commissary in Guinea to get the necessary things like baby milk, vitamins, certain types of bread and canned goods. In Burundi we bought almost all our own food locally—in Bujumbura—and had strawberries coming from the cooler regions up north. We'd drive up about once or twice a month to the vegetable market, which was about 2,000 feet higher in elevation than the city. Bujumbura sits on Lake Tanganyika, and the Nile crest goes up on one side of the lake to 6,000 feet, and on the Congo side to 8,000 feet. It's a strikingly beautiful place to live. The beef wasn't that good in Burundi because the cattle have a social significance; they aren't killed, no matter how fat they are, so long as they can walk. You get a pretty stringy breed of beef cattle under these circumstances. The fish, on the other hand, coming out of the lake, were just excellent. Capitan, which is sort of the functional equivalent of Little Abner's Schmoo—if you fry it it tastes like chicken, if you bake it it tastes like beef—was very common. Our cook was able to carry on pretty well.

The places I've been in to date have been problem countries, where the standard American amenities are not available. For example, when we came to Burundi, the baby was actually born before her clothes and bottles and so forth arrived. Fortunately my wife was able to breast-feed her. But it's this kind of thing that makes life difficult abroad. On the other hand it is an opportunity for adventure, and both of us feel that if my job were one that kept us in the same place for more than five or six years, we'd have a real problem in making the adjustment.

Walton once again brings the sixth game to deuce, with a second serve that Stevens tips and misses. The next one he hits back, though, and after five routine forehand volleys, during which Stevens edges up to the net, he wipes away the point with a shot that catches the white line in a far corner.

"Too tough," calls Walton. Again, advantage Stevens.

Walton still has some fight left in him, and with a pensive half-volley against the sideline, he gains the third deuce of the game. But Stevens comes back to his concentration somewhere in the midst of the next volley, and finally raps a solid winner across the net. He tells himself that he's had enough of this stuff. But the next point lasts still another half-dozen pattycake shots, which Walton concludes by hitting wide—and offering in summary his expected compliment: "Good game."

The score stands at three–all.

Nowadays there is no stereotype of a diplomat in the traditional sense. We have some pictures at the Foreign Service Club that show this fellow in morning coat and vest and spats and the whole thing walking by, and two young girls in 1940s' dress looking up admiringly at him. Somewhere in every Foreign Service officer's career this stereotype probably was present, but after you have been in the Department for a while and even overseas, you realize that there are many many different diplomatic styles. My job is not noticeably different from that of a major loan officer at a bank who has to deal with the central banks of a number of other countries. Except that I'm representing the United States government. Perhaps because of the countries I've served in—which do not include any of the European capitals, where observing the social amenities is extremely important—I've always taken a very relaxed view on the grounds that if you learn what the local courtesies are you'll do pretty well, and when in doubt, do what common sense dictates. The sort of delicate, complicated protocol of an eighteenth-century monarch's court just doesn't exist there. It probably fell by the wayside when Europe did the big fade after two world wars. The Russians are not particularly protocol-conscious, in the sense of making it a big issue. They are of course sensitive to slights, and we are too; but Communist governments and the Western, democratic governments have the same basic egalitarian attitude about diplomacy and do not elevate the failure to turn a calling card the appropriate quarter-inch at the edge into a major diplomatic incident. This simply isn't done.

Even where I've been, though, you do have to keep on your toes about protocol. Once, for example, when I wasnin Conakry, Guinea, we had a new U.S. *chargé d'affaires* who showed up late at the airport for one of these ceremonies to greet some head of state. He came to the end of the line and smiled at the guy next to him and said, "How do you do. I'm so and so, United States of America." The other guy says, "*Guten Morgen*. I'm so and so, German Democratic Republic." Now since we didn't recognize East Germany at the time, the other man was agreeably surprised, and wondered if this presaged a change in American policy. It didn't; it was just a goof. But the Germans had been trying to get us to recognize them, and our man was overly friendly. Well, within thirty seconds of his return to the embassy there was a call from the *West* German First Secretary: "Since when are you guys conniving with the East Germans?" That's how closely people pay attention to those things when something counts. Obviously there had been an error—though the East German at least had been gracious enough not to push the advantage, and anyway our *chargé* had been very good at returning the sickening smile.

In this regard as a public servant there are more restrictions on your behavior and what you can do then there would be as a private citizen. But we have help. When there is a credentials presentation, all the work has been done by the Chief of Protocol's office. For example, the ambassador from Ghana will be picked up, taken to the White House, he'll present his letter to the President, and the President will give him an answer to the remarks that are written in the letter, and the speeches will be given out as if they've been delivered. Then they'll shake hands and talk about the weather and have a good time and leave. As soon as that happens, he's officially accredited as the ambassador. It's planned down to the minute. The Office of Protocol does all the work.

The worst thing that ever happened to me along the lines of protocol was kind of funny. It occurred when the prime minister of Ghana was here. We paid a call on Walter Washington in the D.C. mayor's office, and we sat down and were given coffee in the City Council room. I turned just as the mayor's aide swung around to let somebody go through, and he spilled coffee all down my suit, right into my lap. It wasn't terribly painful, just a certain feeling of extreme warmth on the anatomy. Luckily I was wearing a double-breasted black suit. Aside from sloshing for the next hour I just went right on as if nothing had happened.

Another shriek comes from court number three. The ladies are having fun. Stevens decides that it is about time he wins his service. But he hits two straight balls into the net, his second double-fault of the day, and falls behind at love–fifteen. You are pushing too hard. An old feeling of resignation sneaks through his mind. Is it worth all this? A ball rolls through an opening in the green mesh partition separating courts three and four. Walton calls for time to toss it back. Stevens thinks back again to the economic report he is writing at the office. He currently occupies a room on the fourth floor at State Department headquarters: an imposing nine-story rectangular structure, with five interior open courts, landscaped sparsely with shrubs and magnolia trees. Where one enters the building depends on one's rank and status. Visitors come by way of Twenty-first Street, along a circular driveway, arriving under a blue green cloth canopy that gives the appearance of a hotel entrance. A steady stream of cabs delivers and picks up passengers. Immediately inside there are three large State Department emblems suspended from the ceiling. Security is strict: a guard requests visitors to state name and purpose and then phones upstairs for clearance. Special badges enable visitors to proceed to their destinations. They may not wander aimlessly.

Diplomats and other Very Important Persons receive more formal, if relatively modest, receptions. Black limousines enter along another circular driveway, this one on Virginia Avenue, to deposit ambassadors and their retinues. Here the canopy is silver, and a red carpet is beneath. Inside there is another set of receptionists and guards. There is nothing posh about the decor.

The entrance at Twenty-second and C streets, however, has facilities for pomp and circumstance. Here a multicolored line of flags from 121 countries is arranged impressively above a huge world globe. In the background may be seen one of the open courts, with a large fountain of modern sculpture.

Employees at State enter and leave the building on its nondescript fourth side, and they occupy offices fed by long, very plain corridors, which appear almost out of place when compared to the lavishly furnished reception areas and dining and conference rooms located throughout the building.

From time to time Stevens himself participates in the guided tours of the diplomatic reception rooms, or in the public briefings held Tuesday and Friday mornings at nine-thirty. He enjoys public speaking, and he likes to show people around, pointing particularly to things like the plaques at the C Street entrance, which commemorate Foreign Service officers who died while on duty. ("Meddin Summers, in 1918, in Moscow. Cause of death: exhaustion.") The guided tours are somewhat different from his classes at George Washington University, where he carries the title of Assistant Professorial Lecturer. Stevens is proud of the position, although he says, "It's like a part-time job slinging hash at the local restaurant." There are not many Ph.D.'s at State. He was one of three in his entering group of two hundred.

under Johnson. The ambassadors traditionally and automatically resign *en masse* as soon as there's a new President. In fact, by the end of a President's term all the ambassadors have their resignations on file. The changeover from Democratic to Republican administrations in 1968 went relatively smoothly. Of course, the Secretary and Under Secretary (now called Deputy Secretary) changed immediately. The regional assistant secretaries were changed, but for the most part in favor of career people, and over a period of about a year. Not all of the top-level ambassadorial jobs—London, Paris, Rome—were changed right away. They made an initial decision not to move for the sake of pure movement, but to try to get people in to do the jobs they had to do. Carter has done about the same thing.

This was in contrast to the take-over when the Kennedy administration came in. I was not here then, but I've read enough about it. The major nominees were made known early in the game and nearly the whole staff was ready to go and in place by January 20th. When Kennedy was inaugurated, the rest were confirmed and sworn in almost immediately, and within a month you had maybe twenty or twenty-five new people in key places.

Foreign Service officers are prohibited by the Hatch Act from taking an active part in politics. To that extent they are under the Civil Service. Over the last twenty years or so the Secretaries of State and the Deputy Secretaries have stayed out of most of the regular political in-fighting. Kissinger was probably the exception, especially in 1976. Now everyone knows that when the Secretary gives a speech it is a political event, but there hasn't been much extreme partisan identification. When there is it might be called "statesmanlike politics."

Stevens feels well in control now. Walton has not uttered a word for ten minutes, and, tennis being a game of emotion and psychology whether in a club match or at Wimbledon, his silence is a signal. With Stevens, confidence soars and ebbs, although his self-assurance is much more constant during intellectual exercises. He does his crossword puzzles in ink.

The four ladies on court number three leave, walking through the mesh partition at the back. One of them reminds Stevens of

Alison Palmer, at State, who several years ago lodged a highly publicized complaint that she was being discriminated against in promotion and assignment. The Department is now making an effort to attract, besides women, minority groups like Blacks, Chicanos, and Indians, for a better balance in the Foreign Service. Most of the officers, though, even many of the women, think that Alison Palmer pushed her case too far.

Stevens stares at Walton, then hits another serve.

Most junior officers don't get to see the Secretary very much. But when I was in Washington I worked for Rodgers's chief lieutenant for a year and a half and saw the Secretary, at least to say hello once or twice a week. As a desk officer I had little contact with him directly, except when the chiefs of state visited. On the other hand, I used to do an awful lot of paper work that required the Secretary's attention, and a lot of it was pretty much taken up and used verbatim. I was abroad during most of Kissinger's reign.

One who compares bosses and ex-bosses in public doesn't survive long, but frankly I'm not really in a position anyway to say much about Cyrus Vance. I've never met the man, haven't seen him work. I haven't been in Washington since Vance took over, but he seems to be using the organization more than Kissinger did.

We do tend to run in different social circles, too. The big men are tremendously busy and go to parties more or less under intense pressures and scheduling difficulties. When the Secretary's staff people leave, he sometimes has short parties or little get-togethers. Our primary contacts are in meetings or briefing sessions. If you manage to handle most of your problems at the lower levels you may hardly see the Secretary or Deputy Secretary. But Dean Rusk once said that desk officers in the Department are now making the same kinds of decisions that the Secretaries of State were making thirty years ago.

In 1974 and 1975 I took Persian language training in Washington prior to going to Iran, where since mid-1976 I've been deputy head of the political section. My concerns are basically domestic politics, plus the general stuff connected with running a six-man section. By the time the new ambassador, William Sullivan, arrived, I had been acting section chief for six months. It was very interesting. Our family has also enjoyed big, overcrowded Tehran after six years in Africa—despite the traffic. And for two years I've been captain of the embassy tennis team. We've beaten the British each time, and last year we cleaned out the Foreign Ministry, in what for them was a real shocker, to win the Golden Samovar.

I personally don't think Watergate directly affected the Foreign Service very much. Perhaps we're used to that sort of behavior abroad and so it's easier for us to understand when it happens. And many Foreign Service officers have seen enough of similar activities in other administrations, close up, not to be wholly shocked by what happened, even if we may have been somewhat surprised at its scope and stupidity. I think it confirmed some views that the Nixon White House crew was awfully dumb, but not much more.

Walton returns Stevens's service, then scurries to the far corner of his forehand court to retrieve a high, almost unnecessary lob, which he returns down the line. Stevens chases and reaches it just in time to angle his racquet upward for another chipped lob; this one Walton returns to Stevens's feet. Stevens short-hops the ball, scooping it over the net, and retreats once again to his baseline, in the center. But Walton's attempt at a cross-court is wide. The score stands at forty–love, Stevens.

Logic is one thing; ambassadorships are another. When you get to the ambassadorial level, you are a personal representative of the President. Now, if the President is interested in a change or a new view in a situation, he may not want someone who has been identified. We have people who have served most of their careers in Europe and Africa who wound up in Latin America in a tough situation, precisely because the Secretary or the President wanted a new view in, a new focus. Someday I could conceivably end up in Canada. It's conceivable, but unlikely. I don't have the resources—private resources—that would enable me to support the embassy in Canada. Most career officers couldn't afford to go to Ottawa, Rome, Paris, Bonn, London. The road to London may be the road to the poorhouse for Kingman Brewster.

Usually between 65 and 70 percent of ambassadors are career officers, and between 30 and 35 percent are political appointees, brought in from the outside. This varies from administration to administration. There is a standard set of ranks. Ambassadors get paid the same, straight across the board. There is no difference between a political ambassador and a career ambassador in this regard—just a difference between being an ambassador in London and being an ambassador somewhere else, like Timbuktu.

Foreign Service officers are paid the same kinds of salaries as domestic civil servants, although our scale goes in descending order—so an FSO 1 is similar to a GS 18. In an expanding service, promotions come fairly regularly, but the last few years the promotion list has been abysmally small. Some good people have already left. We realize that there is no way the system can be perfect, but a lot of us feel that certain things have been done which don't make any sense. Unless there are changes, over the next few years the Department will systematically disembowel its best people and encourage them to go elsewhere.

My whole thesis, and one which I have put out *ad nauseam* around here, is that the difference between the private and the public sectors isn't very great. Even in a private company there are going to be promotion and morale problems. Nixon may have done well in substantive policy—seeking an era of negotiation as opposed to an era of confrontation. But I think he made a mistake in shrinking back the State Department. It has meant in effect that the era of negotiation is coming upon us when we are least prepared to tackle it.

But there are a good many people besides the recent Presidents who have felt that the State Department is too big. The Foreign Service people get into these little brouhahas among themselves that put Congress at a loss as to what to do. Over the years we have not, by and large, been very suave in administering ourselves. For a group that is supposed to be sophisticated politically, we have been awfully poor at lobbying with Congress. That's changed over the last four years (and we have at least one senior official in this building who's growing gray not very gracefully because of it). If certain hard decisions had been made throughout the '60s, we would not be in the position we are now. But who knows whether it was a political problem in previous administrations or whether it was just people who weren't farsighted?

Stevens bends down to tie his shoes. Walton looks impatient.

The State Department is probably the most masochistic, self-flagellating organization in existence. My former boss used to be amazed that Foreign Service officers whom he met and found superior to any other civil servants in the federal government were always downgrading themselves and their problems. Another factor in all this has been the disquiet over Vietnam, and the question where American foreign policies are going generally. It's hard to say whether we lost a significant number of people over that (the personnel office is horribly defensive). But I suspect that at times Vietnam or Vietnam-related resignations constituted perhaps as high as 20 percent of the junior and lower-middle-grade-officer corps. There are much deeper questions here, about how the Department's involvement in Vietnam has affected its ability to be an essentially nonpolitical advisor to the President. There are very differing views on this. The real test is when administrations change and the same Foreign Service officers who were loyally carrying out the policies of one President are asked to carry out those of another. In periods of maximum consensus in foreign affairs, this doesn't create serious problems. But if Senator McGovern had won the presidency in 1972, one could have expected more major changes in the top hierarchy of the Department than if, say, Senator Humphrey had won. President Carter, of course, has called back into the State Department several of those who resigned earlier and blended them with some career officers and some other new faces.

I've only been back to Washington for one year since 1972, but my thoughts all along about Vietnam and southern Africa seem to have run true. The State Department will have some big problems with Vietnam in the years to come—those who supported it versus those who didn't. You can see that, I'm told, in some of the infighting surrounding Richard Holbrooke (the East Asian Assistant Secretary) and W. Anthony Lake (of the Policy Planning staff), both Carter appointees.

The Department had been planning for years for this period when we've begun to move on China. I'm quite certain we could staff an embassy in Peking tomorrow, with Chinese-language speakers, four or five consulates, and all the rest, if the need came through. We've done the same thing with the Soviet Union. There's a major language training program, which is one of the strengths of the Service, to keep people in some of the more difficult and harder languages. In that sense we are ahead of the game. But after all, that's what we are paid to do. The people who have carried out the old policies and have developed emotional and intellectual attachments to them, if they have real difficulties, either resign from the Service or request reassignment elsewhere.

Actually the ferment inside the Department is much greater than outsiders realize. This is one of the little myths people have, that bureaucracy is monolithic. If the *Pentagon Papers* told us anything, it was that the basic infighting and arguments within the Department were much more sophisticated than the crap that went on on the college campuses in the mid-60s. It should be reassuring that this kind of internal debate goes on. This is true with regard to African questions as well.

Of course we occasionally run at cross-purposes with other groups. The most difficult people used to be those who would argue that the Peace Corps is an integral part of the American diplomatic team. That isn't the Peace Corps' intention or image at all. On the other side were those officials and some volunteers who argued that the Peace Corps should have absolutely no contact with or guidance from the chief of mission. But three different Presidents successively reaffirmed the ambassador's role as director of *all* American activities in the host country. This includes Peace Corps, AID, USIS, the whole range. It doesn't do the Peace Corps any good to operate in isolation.

There is much greater consensus now than there was ten years ago on what the proper relationships are for Peace Corps volunteers and for the embassy people. For instance, no diplomat who really knows anything would consider Peace Corps volunteers as a source of information to be cultivated. If you happen to know Peace Corps volunteers who are very close to the people up-country, you can sometimes get a very good idea of the life there. But you would not seek them out to do this. In several countries in Africa, most notably Uganda, there has been concern that the volunteers are introducing the native youth to things that are not good for them. And so you get edicts in places like Uganda banning the wearing of mini-skirts and restricting the size of motorcycles. In this connection all international volunteers are somehow thought of as Americans: being the first to start a Peace Corps, we get inflicted with the sins of the others.

The embassy people try to get the volunteers to recognize these things. But Peace Corps people often go their own happy ways in ignorance. And there is nothing sadder than to see a guy in his hippie clothes, who thinks he's the cat's meow, suddenly put on the airplane by the minister of education as a subversive influence. All because the poor kid—he's not a poor little kid, he's just a dumb ass, frankly—hasn't made any attempt to understand local cultural sensitivities.

Stevens tosses the ball high in the air, and reaches back to slam it forward as hard as he can while still maintaining a brief measure of control. The ball goes into the net.

His second service, as usual, is soft—but Walton, resigned, hits a wild forehand. Stevens watches it sail into the green mesh at the back of the court. He feels a surge of relief, and a quiet satisfaction.

Game and set.

6

The Procurer

Gold alone will not procure good soldiers, but good
soldiers will always procure gold.

Machiavelli

A DAZZLING SUN shines past the lone cloud in the sky. For James Reddy, squinting up at the blue and glad he is retired from the Department of Defense, it is an unusually clear day to idle his small boat along the shore line downriver from Seneca Falls toward Great Falls, about fourteen miles outside Washington. He wants to take full advantage of his free time.

Not many people know the variety of fish that can be drawn from the Potomac, but Reddy has been around the capital long enough to fathom the spawning patterns of perch and bluegills and the locations of relatively unpolluted pools of water. *Potomack* in fact is an Indian word meaning "plenty of fish"; pike and carp abound here, as well as sunfish, channel catfish, mud catfish, blue catfish, largemouth and smallmouth bass, goggle-eyed bass, suckers, and crappies. When Captain John Smith first explored the river in 1608 he was struck by the multitude of water life, "lying so thick with their backs above water—for want of nets, we attempted to catch them with a frying pan, but we found it a bad instrument to catch fish with; neither better fish, more plenty, nor variety, had any of us seen in any stream." Reddy tugs at his rod. Seven o'clock on a morning in May, and he has until noon to pick up his grandchildren. He basks in his liberty.

James Reddy believes in the good old days and remembers them with passion. Though more articulate and sensitive than the Archie Bunker countenance he sometimes presents, he nevertheless respects the same values: flags are for saluting, armies for joining, wars for winning. Rules are there to be obeyed. What is life without loyalty? He is confused by young people, because he recalls favorably when children were disciplined, with a strap if necessary, and everybody in the family pitched in to put food on the table, help around the house, and take vacations together. Something in the back of his mind longs for the simplicity of the past. It is a sad kind of longing, and it comes to the fore most often in the midst of simple pleasures, today mingling rudely with the water lapping at his line.

I think kids have a perfect right to demonstrate, so long as they don't destroy public property, or deface the flag of the United States and wipe their tail on it and everything like that. I have high respect for my government and my country. I fought for it. They haven't. I believe in it and I defend it.

Patriotism today by the young people is dead. They don't even know what it means, my own kids included. I have an older son who was drafted and got out of the Army after two years. It changed him completely from what he learned in college. When he went into the armed forces he totally hated it, but when he came out he had a certain healthy respect. Fortunately he never served in Vietnam; he did his two years of duty in the Pentagon.

Kids today are spoiled. In the first place they don't have the discipline we had. Their moral values have changed. They have on the campuses what they call "moral convictions and moral rights." On dope, it's the same thing. My son said he smoked marijuana at college but that it gave him such a headache the morning after he hasn't tried it since; he'd rather drink beer now and then. But he said, "If they want to take dope, they have a moral right to. They are only ruining themselves." I said, "No, they are ruining too many other people. How about their parents, how about their community? If they end up addicts, it's going to be your tax money and mine and everybody else's that's going to have to take care of them."

I'm all for Women's Liberation. If they can cut the mustard to do the job, that's their own personal conviction. If a girl chooses to get married and doesn't want to have any kids and wants to take pills and everything else, that's between her and the man upstairs. I can't question her motives and I don't intend to.

I blame myself and every other parent my age for the different values of kids today. We didn't use the same discipline factors that my parents gave me. I think we have spoiled them. They have too much freedom. When I was a kid all the time I lived in the house I was subject to my mother's and father's house rules, regardless of whether I was 16, 18, 21, or 24.

By today's standards I have good kids, but if I judge by the standards of the '30s and '40s, no. My oldest son's got a small beard, he wears mod clothes. But he's not a hippie—there are no beads on him. He's got a good job over in the Census Bureau. Maybe in another twenty years my children will be saying about me what I'm saying about my parents, and about their kids what I'm saying about them. That's life. Let's face it, your values change over the years.

Reddy is relaxed, half-sitting and half-squatting in the creaky wooden rowboat, as the sun weaves supple shadows against his beige knit shirt. Brown Farah slacks, tightened at the waist by a narrow alligator belt, are hitched up above his brown canvas shoes. He props his rod in a corner of the boat, folds his arms across his chest, and tips his head back to catch the bright morning rays.

Even though most of his working years were spent behind a desk he has a ruddy, lean face, with prominent wrinkles lining his cheeks and forehead and small crowsfeet around his calm, self-assured eyes. His hair is solid brown on top, white at the sideburns, and all of it is cropped short. He prides himself on his physique. Although not muscular, he is in fine trim for a man of 65; just a hint of paunch pulls the alligator belt slightly askew. His hands, too—rough, hard, calloused, and gnarled like the knots on a hickory stick—belie the fact that he has been an indoorsman. He puts a cheroot in his mouth and flicks open a flame from a World War II Zippo lighter. His breast pocket is stuffed with three more cheroots, a small pipe, a pouch of tobacco, a comb, two Bic pens, and a notepad.

He puffs and smiles. So far he has been able to savor retirement, not at all given to the neuroses born of working overtime. He put in his hours, took home his paycheck, and looked forward to these free days for too long to rue inactivity. At least that is what he tells himself now, barely a year away from the job.

Besides, he always did love the water. He grew up among the narrow rivers of Maryland and Virginia. Even as a young boy he was comfortable with them. He remembers many a spring and summer day spent alone or with one or two friends, fishing from the shore or a small rowboat with a simple rod and line. For bait he used plump, squirming earthworms dug up from the dewy sod early in the morning, and the waters were always generous with their perch and catfish. It was nothing but sheer irony that his many years with the Navy Department served more to keep him away from the sea than to lead him to it.

My father was born and raised in the Swiss Alps, near the crest of the Bierse Zierdel. He came over here in 1898. The way he tells it, he went through Ellis Island and then took the ferry to New York, to the Battery, and was walking down Wall Street when a recruiting sergeant from the Marine Corps got hold of him. He showed him his papers and the sergeant drew up an enlistment form from them. My father signed, not knowing what he was signing. That night he found himself in a recruiting station and the next day they took this group of about 35 immigrants down to the Philadelphia Navy Yard, where they were all inducted into the Marine Corps. He spent four years there. He must have been no more than eighteen. About 1902 he came to the Washington Navy Yard, worked there until about 1917, then went to Dayton, Ohio, as a boilermaker. The next year he came back to the Navy Yard, where he stayed until he retired in 1940. He died at 91.

I was the oldest of three brothers and four sisters. We were a very close family and still are today, even though we are scattered.

When I was young anybody who owned an automobile was a millionaire. But we got around, took picnics, like to Great Falls by train, or we took the streetcar to Glen Echo. We moved back to Washington during World War I, when I was about four. We lived in southeast D.C. My father would walk about two miles to work every day. I went from eighth grade into public high school. My father couldn't afford to continue me in Catholic High School because by then there were seven children in the family.

My oldest sister's been in a convent 35 years, in the Holy Cross Order. She got her Ph.D. in education, taught college at Dunbarton, and she's been principal of a number of grade schools.

My next sister graduated from Georgetown University Hospital, became a registered nurse, was married, and had three boys. Both she and her husband are now dead. They had turned alcoholic; that's what killed them. A very brilliant girl. Her husband just happened to be one of those types who started drinking during Prohibition. There are no alcoholics in my family whatsoever and there never have been, and the only way I can see it, she just joined him later on.

My third sister is a graduate of the old Emergency Hospital School of Nursing and was the first girl drafted into the United States Army in World War II. She was commissioned a second lieutenant, in October 1940. Her name was pulled and she had dinner that evening with President Roosevelt and his wife. Then she went to Camp Wheeler, then to Guadalcanal, Australia, and New Guinea, then to Hawaii with a station hospital. She was a forward surgical nurse all through the war into the Philippines, until the surrender. She came back to the United States and was at Valley Forge Hospital for a while, then Germany. She met a colonel in the Army who was shot down during the Berlin airlift and lost an eye. After thirteen years in the Army, she gave up her commission (she was a major) to get married. They are now living in California.

Then I have a brother six years younger. For the last 30 years he has been a manager of a tavern out near Walter Reed Hospital; it's sort of a nightclub where they serve drinks, liquor, and pizza, and all that. At one time they had a big trade from medical people at Walter Reed. They're getting ready to close now because it integrated.

My next brother went into the Navy when he was 17, put 22 years in, and retired as chief of damage control. He's married and living in Virginia Beach.

And the youngest sister is married to an officer who just retired after 30 years in the Air Force. They live in Tampa, Florida.

During the Depression years, you couldn't get a job anywhere. I delivered newspapers and with the proceeds I usually bought all my own clothes. We kids were brought up that way. My parents didn't take all the money away from us, but they used to put most of it into a kitty and that's what they used to buy our clothes and whatever we needed. My father always provided, though, and my mother could stretch hamburger with rice and make a meal for everybody.

High school was different than grade school. I took the business course—bookkeeping, typewriting, business English, woodwork. I thought I was getting a diploma after four years, but to my horror many years later I found that I hadn't graduated from high school at all—I hadn't completed the number of hours required by the District of Columbia. All I got was a certificate. When I started taking college courses I had to go back and take an equivalent examination.

Education then was compulsory to sixteen years old and hookey was rarely heard of. Kids went to school because it was close enough that if you weren't in school the teacher would call home—that was her duty. Your father was waiting for you. It was rare that you ever heard of a parent who didn't discipline a kid if he knew he was caught playing hookey. He couldn't talk his way out of it. And they used the leather, the belt, and the stick in those days.

I was catcher for the Eastern High School championship baseball team in 1932. Got all my fingers broken. We belonged to the Boy Scouts and you could get into Griffith Stadium then for twenty cents and sit in the bleachers. I went out there a lot. In fact I saw Babe Ruth play in Washington, and Walter Johnson pitch out there—he'd goggle them very good—and Sam Rice, Joe Cronin, Bucky Harris when he managed the Boy Wonder.

Reddy casts his line in a long arc away from the boat, sits down, and pulls a newspaper from beneath the wood plank behind him. He is content to troll; the sun cuts through the morning breeze and warms his face and shoulders. He squints at the paper.

In the mid-forties, just after returning from the war, he would fish in the Potomac close by the Capitol, sometimes even during his lunch hour. Before long though the river became too polluted around Washington, and with a growing family and house to look after he would find fewer and fewer afternoons for fishing. So he regulated hook and line to weekends and vacations, and took to walking in his spare time. After a while he became something of an amateur historian of Washington landmarks, and would spend the noon hour wandering through Arlington National Cemetery or among the monuments and parks that cluster around the Potomac on the District side. And it came to pass that Reddy abandoned eating lunch altogether: only extreme cold weather could interfere with his routine. Even in the rain he could be seen, a solitary figure in flowing poncho, common, glorious, making his way around the Reflecting Pool or ascending the steps to the Lincoln Memorial. After his retirement fishing once again became his primary recreation, and the walks were less frequent, but Reddy still thinks of them as the best way to keep in touch with American history.

A lone white cloud sits high in the early morning sky. For the next hour and a half Reddy lolls. A half-dozen fresh casts land him a bass and two small catfish, but beyond that there is nary a nibble.

I used to think my Dad was the dumbest damn immigrant you'd ever seen, with some of his ideas: I thought he was perfectly ignorant. But by the time I got to be 21 I realized how brilliant he was. He instilled a very patriotic instinct in us kids. Everyone in my family, all the boys anyway, went into military service.

My father and mother demanded that we major in American history. My father knew American history from one end to another. It was something he always studied because he believed this was the greatest country on earth. He used to tell us about the monarchies in Europe and what had happened with them, and how this was the land of opportunity. "You children, it's there for your taking, the opportunity. You have to work with other people. You've got to be at peace with yourself." This was instilled in us by our parents. "Help your brothers and sisters, help your neighbors when you can, and don't look for the almighty dollar every time you go to do something. That isn't right. You live by the precepts of your religion and you respect everybody else's religion. Just because you're Catholic doesn't mean you have a lock on heaven."

My parents spoke German and when we lived in Dayton we lived in the German section. At that time the city was broken into Polish, Hungarian, and German ethnic groups. When my mother went to school, they taught German as a language. If you were from the Polish section, you learned Polish in school. If you were Hungarian, you spoke Hungarian and English in school. They taught both languages coming up.

My mother and father were practicing Catholics. They demanded that you go to church every Sunday, and go to Catholic school. They would have sacrificed anything to send the children to Catholic school, although tuition was only ten dollars a year, I think. Nuns ran the school and discipline was high.

We had examinations in June at school and we'd get out early and sneak down to the river, which was about half a mile away. You'd go skinny-dipping, and you learned how to swim. Sometimes we'd go out and pick blackberries and take buckets of them home. Got full of chiggers, too.

It was altogether different in those days before the electronic age. Our family still had a crystal set radio with head phones, and baseball was about the biggest thing. You ran barefoot and there were lots of open fields behind you and you could always start playing baseball with a group of kids. You didn't have all of the area swimming pools then or anything like that. The Tidal Basin was open down here to go swimming if your mother would let you. We were forbidden to go in the Anacostia River, but that was the place I learned how to swim. Of course, it wasn't polluted then.

We had a happy childhood. We were well-knit, different from today. Values have changed an awful lot with the innovations and inventions and everything we have now. I imagine today children spend at least a thousand hours a year watching television. In those days we didn't have it; if you got a pair of roller skates for Christmas, that was a rarity. We interreacted more with brothers and sisters. And I read every Zane Gray book that came out. I read *All Quiet on the Western Front, Twenty Thousand Leagues Under the Sea.* I used to have a lot of favorite authors.

College education is highly overrated. There's indiscrimination in giving degrees to supposedly graduate electronic engineers, mechanical engineers, aerospace engineers that didn't know their ass from a hole in the ground. I had 90 days to get rid of some unqualified kids from Howard University and I hated like hell to do it, but I did. What is happening is that you're using integration to try to bring percentage levels up without qualification. There's your problem.

We all had chores to do at home. We burned coal for heat and it was my job to sift the ashes out every day and sweep the floor. I'd take care of the trash and the garbage, too. We didn't have refrigerators, so in the summertime every day I had to go to the ice company, which was about six or eight blocks away, and buy a block of ice. I'd bring it home in my wagon and put it into the ice box. Chores were different then. My kids didn't have to do the things I was forced to do as a child.

My parents were some of the most honest people you'd want to see. Those values have changed today. If a child was incorrigible, one of the worst things he could be told—the thing that always brought him around—was "I'll put you in reform school." I don't know where they sent the girls; maybe they threatened to put them in the convent.

As I look back, there wasn't any one of the seven children that wouldn't do anything in the world for my mother and father. My brothers and sisters were always over there; for years they took Dad to the store when he couldn't drive any longer. We cut their grass and we kept their home. You don't see that today. I have a daughter fourteen years old who won't wash a dish—my wife does it all. I have no problem that way—they're good kids—but as they get further in life, they are probably going to wish they had more discipline when they were younger.

At eight-thirty, still without another bite, Reddy decides to give the boat one more hour, then go ashore. He wants to leave enough time to follow his old walking route around Arlington Cemetery before meeting his grandchildren at the Washington Monument.

I graduated in 1932, or at least got my certificate, and for a year and a half I lived at home and did all the chores around the house. College was absolutely out of the question for me at that time. We didn't have the money. We had sold the house in Southeast by then and moved to the suburbs. Today Southeast is a very nice, fashionable part of town. But then it was right in the middle of the Depression, and my father saw an opportunity and got a good price. He had a row house with three bedrooms upstairs and a bathroom, a living room, dining room, a big kitchen, and a big area in the basement. When we moved he bought a great big, brick masonry house. It was built for $8,000. I sold it a few years ago to some executive for $32,000.

Washington was different in those days. For one thing, we never had a racial problem where I lived in Southeast. There were maybe seven or eight blocks of colored and we played baseball together. But they had their own places they went and we had our own and they were respected. They went to all the stores—everything was integrated that way—but they had their own movie theaters. We played together and we got along together. You never heard of any fights. You'd go into any colored neighborhood, like the one within two blocks of where I was raised, and you never found it trashed up. You might have found gaudy colors, like yellow, purple, and what have you that weren't conventional then among the typical whites, but relations were very, very good.

Welfare is a sore subject with me. I believe in welfare where a person who's destitute cannot get a job, or is prevented from doing it through sickness. He should be helped to live in dignity. And I don't think that in doing so it should even be said that he's on welfare or anything like that—that's beneath his dignity. But by God I hate like hell to see all these people that are on welfare just to draw that check. It won't work. I think there's a job available for everyone who wants one. Roosevelt made them, didn't he, and I did it for a dollar a day.

I do remember that a colored child had no chance whatsoever, and he knew it, of getting to the artisan rank of bricklayers, carpenters, and so on. Although the colored children were educated the same as I was, they could only look as far as being a laborer or a helper. That didn't change until the fifties, after World War II.

I had plenty of friends who were colored, but it was forbidden to do anything together socially. They knew it and we knew it. Schools were absolutely separate, but they had schools as good as we did back then. In the rich sections of Washington, out Embassy Row and Sixteenth Street, way out Michigan Avenue, the school systems were far superior to what we saw in Southeast.

I have good memories of those days. Right after the First World War, around 1918, I can remember all the soldiers coming back and camping in Southeast Washington. I guess it was the whole Second Division. I remember going over there where they were cooking, and they would give me candy and things like that. My dad had about three officers sleeping at our house. They were there about three weeks until they all got assembled, then they had this big victory parade that lasted all day long, going down Pennsylvania Avenue, past the grandstands at the White House. I went to see that.

And Fourth of July around here was really something. You could buy fireworks anywhere and the place literally exploded. You'd see who had the biggest display on the block. On Memorial Day we hung out a flag and they had speakers at all the cemeteries. I remember going over to Congressional Cemetery year after year where they'd have part of a Marine Band playing. Afterward, they'd put up a big stand and you'd have speakers, and always the Gettysburg Address—I can still recite the whole thing.

Times were happier then. We didn't have the tension we have today. My dad used to take me out along the Potomac River with a couple of fishing poles, pay ten cents to go over a chain bridge. We'd go fishing all day Sunday, after church. Sometimes on Saturday we'd go to the B & O Canal and see canal boats with mules pulling them coming from Cumberland, loaded down with grain and brooms. I still recall those.

By nine-thirty Reddy has drifted downstream, to just outside Great Falls on the Potomac, a nicely appointed recreation area with picnic grounds and hiking trails. He has hauled in a lone perch to add to the bass and catfish—a modest morning's catch, but he is satisfied. He maneuvers the boat over to a tiny wharf nestled among the pine trees near a small concrete bridge, and leaves it with an old black man. Then he walks to the parking lot, puts the fish in a plastic bag in the trunk of his car, and drives east toward Washington.

Forty minutes later he is passing through the golden-statued entrance to Arlington Memorial Bridge. In 1921 a traffic jam marred the Memorial Day ceremonies at the Tomb of the Unknown Soldier, and the government's response was to build a lavish span: 90 feet wide, a full one-third of it given over to pedestrian walkways. Nine stately arches lend an appearance of elegance, but the middle one is actually a steel drawbridge. In the summer, when concerts by the Marine Band are held on a bank near the Lincoln Memorial, the bridge looks almost majestic beneath the stars and the planes flying into National Airport.

Arlington itself is huge and impersonal, but its monumental quality is also its greatest virtue. While other burial grounds crowd the mind with memories of death, Arlington is somewhat transcendent, rich with the dignity of men who died in noble causes. At least for James Reddy, its endless rows of symmetrical graves suggest more the persistence of the spirit of liberty than the grim price of war. Green and white shine in the sun. The grounds are expansive, the long lines of headstones interrupted only by larger monuments commemorating the dead of several wars.

Another contrast sometimes strikes Reddy, that between Arlington Cemetery and the Pentagon, a few minutes away. There, too, the scale is monumental, but Reddy feels that rather than dignifying the history and sacrifice of men fighting for a cause, the military hides behind a facade both undistinguished and impregnable, cemented by a ponderous bureaucracy that has forgotten the very lessons of honor that Arlington perpetuates.

Reddy crosses the bridge and turns left, thinking back to the time when every few days he would spend a quiet hour among the dead. Sometimes he would walk briskly around the southeast quadrant, making a full circuit before returning to his office via the Jefferson Davis Highway. At other times he would linger at one of the monuments or among a particular group of graves, occasionally seeking out some landmark he had read about or coming back to photograph the view from its site. He is well acquainted with all the major monuments and most of the landscaping. Even the relatively few trees at the cemetery take him back into the past: the huge elms and oaks that once abounded there were felled after the Civil War broke out, when General McClellan used these fields to drill recruits for the Army of the Potomac.

My first job was washing pots in Childs Restaurant. I got ten dollars a week and two meals, and I worked from nine o'clock in the morning until nine at night. That included peeling potatoes and picking eyes out of them, running the dishwasher when the regular man was out, bringing in all the supplies, and mopping the kitchen.

But the owner was losing money; he couldn't afford to pay me the ten dollars a week, so after about three months he let me go and had the second cook do most of my work. I was just walking the streets. There weren't any jobs to be found. Then in July of 1933 I joined the Civilian Conservation Corps, which Roosevelt had started. They paid $30 a month, of which $25 was sent home and you got five. I was there over a year, in Wolf Gap, West Virginia. Came out in August 1934.

I had taken a Civil Service examination for an apprenticeship in the Navy Yard, near the Washington Naval Gun factory. But they were on a Hoover economy pay-cut at the time and there was a moratorium against hiring. They had the famous Section 213 in effect—a man and wife couldn't work in the government together, but they would allow two persons living in the same house, like a father and son, or a father and daughter, or a brother and sister, to work. Roosevelt finally lifted this moratorium on hiring sometime during 1935. When I came out of the Civilian Conservation Corps, I got called for a job in the Washington Navy Yard. That's when I began my government career. It was about the end of June 1935.

I started as an apprentice toolmaker, $11.11 a week for 40 hours' work, of which I went to the apprentice school sixteen hours a week and worked three eight-hour days. It was very good work, enjoyable, and I was learning. They taught algebra, geometry, physics, mechanics, orthographical projection, isometric projection, mechanical drafting, blueprints, and so forth. It continued for four years and then every year you take an examination and if you pass it, you get an increase in pay. My first raise was to $18.52. I graduated in September 1939.

In the meantime I did three years with the District of Columbia National Guard. When I finally got out of the school I was getting about $36 a week. Then I became a journeyman; I was third-class toolmaker. I graduated first in my shop and third in the entire class in the Navy Yard. The master mechanic called me in the office and gave me a special rating as a shop planner and estimator, which was a pretty good honor and carried six cents an hour more. That was an office position; I didn't have to work out in the shop. By April of 1940, I was advanced up to first class and getting $42 a week on an hourly wage rate.

I had a nice position, I was making good money. I had no problem with my folks. I had no reason to want to leave. I don't know what happened, but soon I was just tired of being there. In August of 1940 I wrote three letters requesting a transfer—one to Coco Solo, Panama, one to Pearl Harbor Navy Yard, and one to Cavite Navy Yard in the Philippines. They were all identical (except that I changed the headings in each), and they all requested a transfer as a toolmaker first class. I would pay my own transportation (which you had to in those days). The one from Panama came back and said there was no position open, but the one in Pearl Harbor offered me a job. I sent a yes answer. Two weeks later a better offer came in from Cavite, but I had already accepted the one from Pearl Harbor. (As it turned out, later on I missed being a prisoner of war by about two weeks.)

Approaching the cemetery from the south gate, the entrance closest to the Pentagon, Reddy passes near the graves of William Jennings Bryan and Rear Admiral Peary. The Coast Guard Memorial is modest, a bronze sea gull poised upon a coast carved in stone. Reddy drives slowly, continuing in a northerly direction until he reaches Fort McPherson. This is itself a sort of monument, he thinks, since it has never been manned. It was built at the end of the Civil War, one of 127 forts that encircle Washington, and the years have softened its bellicosity. Now it is little more than a reminder of the Union's nineteenth-century crisis, an undesignated monument to *semper paratus*.

It is less awesome here than at the grander, marble-laden places in the cemetery, and Reddy feels relaxed with the fort's more genteel history. He looks at his watch—ten-forty-five— pulls over to a shady spot, takes a small sandwich bag from the seat beside him and a can of Metrecal from the glove compartment, gets out of the car, and sits down under a large oak tree. Elsewhere in the cemetery he would feel out of place eating, but it is quiet here, and no one is within sight.

In October of 1940 I registered for the draft, but two weeks later I went to the board and said I was leaving to accept employment in the Pearl Harbor Naval Yard, and I got permission.

I took a choo-choo train out of Union Station in Washington, changed in Chicago, and got to Los Angeles in five days. It cost $40.75 for one way. By the time I got out there I was as black as coal because in those days they had nothing but coal-burning trains. But when I reached the West Coast I found I couldn't get a ticket without buying a round-trip, and I didn't have enough money. I didn't know what to do—I had about $60.00 in my pocket and they wanted $125.00 for a round-trip ticket. What the heck is the use of buying a round-trip ticket when I've got a job over there and I'm going to stay? I was in this little hotel and I met some sailors in a bar and we got to talking. One of them was a yeoman and he told me to meet him the next day at the 12th Naval District. We finagled something with my orders, and he got me passage to Pearl Harbor on an oil tanker called the U.S.S. *Brazos*. It only cost me a dollar a day. The trip to Hawaii took ten days because this tanker was loaded with oil. You couldn't see the bridge from the stern, and I was always back in the stern. I was one of six passengers. Then the captain wanted to know if there was any passenger who could play bridge—it was auction bridge in those days—and I was the only one of us who could, so I got in real good with him. After that, I was always up in the wardroom playing bridge. I was the captain's partner. The chief engineer and the first mate always let us win.

Early in the morning after ten days, I got my first view of Hawaii. It was beautiful. The ship maneuvered all around there and didn't land in Pearl Harbor until nine o'clock at night, when it was dark. In Honolulu in those days, when the tourists came in they brought out the Royal Hawaiian Band and the Chamber of Commerce had the girls go up there and put flower leis on everybody when they got off the boat. But Pearl Harbor is a Naval Base: you pick up your baggage, tool box and everything, leave the gangway, go ashore, and you're right there. No leis, no reception.

Life was beautiful there. That first year before the war started was the best of my life. Sometimes you feel like you don't even want to do anything there in the islands. You wake up in the morning, say "What's the use of working today?"—and you don't. Every ten days a new batch of tourists would come in. I paid $30 a month for a room right on Waikiki Beach, about three blocks from the Royal Hawaiian Hotel and a block off Waikiki Avenue. With overtime I was making about $65 a week. We were preparing Pearl Harbor to be a Naval Repair Yard—the Gibraltar of the Pacific.

His mid-morning lunch concluded, Reddy rises from the shadow of Fort McPherson and begins walking northward through Arlington Cemetery. He ponders for a moment the regularity of his habits. Although now that he has retired and his time is his own, he realizes that so many years of the same daily regimen have tuned his inner clock to a rigid pace. Here, now, to wander again through the network of paths at Arlington, he has left himself nothing more or less than his habitual hour: the old walks were seldom longer or shorter than that.

The sun is bright, and a warm breeze gently moves the patches of roses and peonies from side to side. Farther on, tufts of grass surround several memorials to those who died in the Spanish-American War, and other tombstones—cast on a more modest, human scale—commemorate the dead of Teddy Roosevelt's Rough Riders and even the nurses of the Army and Navy. This is one of Reddy's favorite spots, though he is more likely to take in the landscape here than the monuments. For the most part they are unremarkable—perhaps with the exception of the U.S.S. *Maine*. The mast of the sunken battleship, raised from Havana harbor in 1912 with its conning tower and shrouds still intact, is set imposingly in a marble base near the graves of the war's fallen sailors.

Reddy wanders along the rows of headstones, feeling the strange intimacy of older conflicts. He remembers his father's tales of American bravery and valor in an earlier age, before the First World War introduced the terrible new machines of destruction and misery. He lingers in front of the Rough Riders regiment, imagining Teddy Roosevelt at the head of his troops. He has always admired the great deeds of the warrior president. Weren't they grander, and in a way simpler than Eisenhower's?

It is an abrupt reminder of those long years in the Civil Service. Reddy turns away from the Rough Riders' memorial and heads westward in a slow semicircle that leads him through a section of ground once set aside for black soldiers. Burying blacks in a separate area never struck him as especially strange: he grew up in a time and place where segregation was a way of life. To him it never implied oppression. By the 1950s he had long since joined the rest of Washington's middle-class and middle-level bureaucracy in its flight from the city to the predominantly white, single-family-home communities that surround it.

On Saturday, December 6, 1941, there was a formal, white-glove inspection of the fleet at Pearl Harbor by Admiral Kimmel and Admiral Richardson. Everything was wide open. No ammunition aboard. On Monday the whole fleet was heading back to the West Coast for the Christmas holidays. I was supposed to work that day from eight o'clock until four-thirty, but they told the day shift to come in later on at midnight instead, to finish up all the work there, and they would close the yard down at eight that Sunday morning.

I worked with two other mainland fellows, both from Detroit—one from General Motors and the other from Ford. In fact Fritz, Johnson, and I were the only three white machinists in the whole machine shop, the others all being local types—Portuguese, Japanese, Chinese, what have you. The three of us went to work together all the time, and we went in at midnight, as ordered. The *Pennsylvania*, a battleship, was in dry dock and I was working on a big shaft in the machine shop. There were also two destroyers in dry dock, the *Cassin* and the *Downs*. We worked all night. At quarter of eight in the morning they cut the power down, and we washed and changed clothes and came outside about ten minutes to eight.

We were waiting for eight o'clock to punch the time clock and take off. The sun was up and it was a beautiful morning, about 75 degrees. I said, "After church, we'll meet at ten o'clock at Waikiki Tavern and eat, and maybe we'll go over to the other side of the island. We'll take some beer over there and go swimming."

Just then Fritz said, "Hey, Jimmy, look what's happening over at Hickam Field. There's some gigantic explosions going on over there." Now Sunday morning is no time for war games, and they had already had the inspection the day before. We were standing outside the machine shop, and alongside of us was a row of ships docked all up and down. No more than 25 feet in front of us was a large cruiser, the *Helena*, and outboard of that was a mine layer, the *Ogalala*. They were getting ready to have church services on the fan tail of the *Ogalala* and there was a band warming up there—a tuba, a trumpet or two, et cetera. All of a sudden, three planes peeled off right in front of us. As they dropped down we saw—uh-uh—big red balls on the wings! You knew darn well right then they weren't American—we've got blue with a white star there. And we knew that our planes had retractable landing gear. These didn't. Wheels hanging down, they dropped torpedoes. Not even a minute later, all three of them had gone under the *Ogalala* and hit the *Helena*. All hell broke loose. At the same time they were firing guns; one got me right in the arm. I didn't know what had happened. There was fire, steel flying everywhere. The three of us took off.

There weren't too many people running around. There was only a skeleton crew working there at night, and probably at least a third of the sailors were asleep, since it was the morning after the inspection. The Pearl Harbor Navy Yard is a big sprawling place. Between the main gate and the repair basin where the ships were is possibly two miles. Between the main gate and the bachelor officers' quarters was a nine-hole golf course, the last hole of which was just across the street from the ship printer's shop. We ran to that ninth hole and dug a hole in the sand trap. About ten minutes later, the sand fleas ran us out. We went back to the shop and changed clothes. I had messed my pants by that time.

There were very few fires in the shops, and what few civilians were around there attempted to put them out. They weren't wasting ammunition on shops, civilians, or anything like that. At one end of the shipyard complex was what we called the tank farm. With all these tanks holding gasoline and diesel fuel and oil, if the Japanese had hit them they could have burned the whole thing down. But they didn't. I'll never know why, but their only idea was to hit the ships and sink them.

By this time all the power was off, so we went back out. There was a slight lull in the noise of the exploding magazines and ammunition, and we started up toward the dry dock. Just then we heard the planes buzzing around again. They dropped just one bomb on the *Pennsylvania*, which had an armored deck, then they hit the *Cassin* and the *Downs* right alongside. They hit those big 250-foot destroyers and turned them off their blocks. The fuel oil came gushing out and they started burning. There was shrapnel and all kinds of stuff flying around, the ships were blowing apart, the noise was deafening. We were trying to get some of the people off the *Cassin* and the *Downs*. There were some sailors in there and they were trying to wake some more up and bring them out. Then some officer down in the blockhouse went and flooded the dry dock with water—the fuel oil was burning on the bottom and he probably thought the water would put the fire out. Instead, when the water hit, it just brought the burning oil up to the surface. They probably lost quite a few men at that point. They couldn't get them off any more.

I can recall there were five battleships no more than a hundred yards from us at Ford Island in the middle of the harbor, right over at 1010 dock. After the Japanese hit the dry dock and got another destroyer over at the Marine Railway, they concentrated completely on those battleships in battleship row and hit them with every high-level thing they had. There was no interference. They had already taken out all the planes lined up at Hickam Field—those were the explosions we had heard in the beginning. There wasn't one of our planes that got off the ground. Not a shot was fired at the Japanese.

It had all started about five minutes to eight and it came in waves and bounces. You'd see some high-level bombers, some low-level ones, then you wouldn't see or hear anything except all the fires and explosions. Then you'd see some more coming up. Until about eleven o'clock, when the last wave came over. There were none after that.

Reddy walks eastward, past the amphitheater at the Tomb of the Unknown Soldier. The question occurs to him now, as it has in the past, whether the single boy honored here, chosen for his anonymity, might not by chance be black, like the soldiers in the field through which he just passed. The honor guard, whose sentries pace silently and singly, back and forth on their one-hour shifts, are almost always white, and the ambiance of the tomb itself bespeaks a pomp ordinarily denied the humble. It is no ordinary monument, though; perhaps a black man does lie here, buried beneath the mass of marble. On the other hand the Unknown Soldier is, must be, colorless. Would it be justice anyway, thus to memorialize a nameless black man for his sacrifice, so close by those others whose color made their labors thankless and whose graves often went unmarked and uncared for, in war or in peace? Reddy does not think in precisely those terms, nor does it occur to him that during the First World War black men were still segregated into "colored regiments," and that General Pershing would most likely have known the race of his otherwise anonymous soldier merely from where he had fallen in battle.

Away from the tomb now, Reddy walks slowly down the white granite steps to the wide lawn that slopes gently down from the terrace, past clumps of boxwood, through a group of cedar trees. Then he turns to look back at the tomb. From this perspective it is almost as fine a sight as it was from the terrace, perhaps even more so: set off by the Memorial Amphitheatre, which rises directly behind it, the stark composition of marble and sentry against the sharp blue sky is striking. A moment's further reflection, and Reddy starts walking again, this time northward toward the Custis–Lee Mansion and the Kennedy grave, away from the few visitors now milling around or sitting on the lawn.

When the attack at Pearl Harbor was over, I went to have my arm sewed up at a place they set up to treat civilians and sailors. If it was too bad they stretchered them out and took them to Alela Hospital—if they could get them up there. They were doing their best to take care of everybody. I waited in line about fifteen or twenty minutes. Then they picked a bullet out of my arm. It wasn't deep. They put some iodine on it (they had no tetanus shots) and clamped it because they had no string to sew it up. A corpsman did that. No doctor. Then he bandaged it up and I went back to the shop.

About three o'clock in the afternoon they asked for some volunteers. At the end of battleship row was a battleship called the *Oklahoma*. They had hit it with four torpedoes and the thing went completely around, 270 degrees. A big sixteen-inch turret was jammed down into the mud, and the keel was hanging out on an angle. There she was, lying there. The hull was sticking out of the water; the rest of it was down in the mud. Some boat had gone past and said there were some people in there; they heard them knocking. They wanted volunteers to see what they could do. Fritz, Johnson, and myself went over. The water's possibly 20 to 25 feet deep at that point, the turret's down in the mud and there's eight or nine hundred tons of metal slipping down there holding it down. Sure enough we heard some tapping—I was the only one who could understand Morse Code—some SOS's and tapping that there were 23 guys inside in an air pocket. So we went back to the shop and got all the 1-inch, 1½, and 1⅜ drills we could get our hands on, put them in a box, and toted them right out to the boat at the end of the dock.

In the meantime, the oil was burning on the harbor and they were organizing parties to try to foam it down right around where we were. We got ahold of some air drills, some hose, and some tarpaulin. Because lights were absolutely forbidden, we got some flashlights and we put some blue and red paper over them, what we could find, and we worked until about five, six o'clock at night. We took the boat over and prepared to stay there all night. Then we went back to Ford Island and found what we figured we'd find, an air compressor, and took that down. We found some old oil drums and we got all the gasoline and diesel fuel we could get out of them and started this air compressor up there with the tanks. We dragged a line a hundred yards off the shore to the hull of this boat and we knocked the barnacles off the area we decided was under the tapping. From there on we took turns. We had a tarpaulin tent over there and using air drills (we couldn't use a torch on it on account of gas) we drilled a 23-inch hole through 2½ inches of bottom metal, right on through and we chipped that damn thing right out of there. We got to them about ten, eleven o'clock the next morning.

They were in a big air pocket in there. Now this was a 33,000-ton battleship, and it's about 450-feet long and it's completely turned over. After we drilled through the bottom 2½ inches, then we had to go back and drill through that double bottom. That's when the air pressure broke and she settled down about another foot. We went and drilled that other one out, then we sent some soup down there but it got cold, and we sent some water down at the end of the hose. They were in there Sunday morning to Monday night. They were in water up to their waists.

We got 23 out and wrapped them in blankets. The last two we pulled out were unconscious, and we ripped them apart. The blanket slipped off of one of them and ripped him up, just like that. It was a horrible-looking scene. We only had a hole about that big around and it was all jagged. But he was unconscious before we took him out. Dead. They think he may have had a heart attack. The other one died I guess an hour and a half later. Someone said they could feel heartbeats, but I couldn't. I was too damn tired.

The three of us went back to the shop and I lay down on a ball of rags and went to sleep. The next morning I got up and had my arm taken care of again. I had torn out all the clamps on the wound. I got a civilian citation out of this. It's on my record, signed by Forrestal—he was Assistant Secretary of the Navy then.

When it was all over everybody went through an initial shock phase. I didn't feel any personal anger toward the Japs. This was something different. You see people dead and everything and you feel a certain animosity towards that nation and the people in it and the ones that did it, but you don't feel a personal anger. If you got that feeling, you'd go berserk. A few hours later, you start reflecting back and you think, "Man, I'm alive," and then you try to sort out what happened.

Reddy glances at the Custis–Lee Mansion. It and the Kennedy grave are to him the most poignant features at Arlington. The mansion was formerly called Arlington House, built by George Washington Parke Custis, Martha Washington's grandson, some time after the War of 1812. Lafayette visited it during his last trip to America in 1824. Seven years later Robert E. Lee married Custis's daughter, and the family lived at Arlington until the outbreak of the Civil War. It was from there that Lee wrote to the Secretary of War declining command of the Union forces about to invade Virginia, and resigning his commission in the United States Army. Shortly afterward he left to join the Confederate Army, and his family fled with him. Union soldiers took Arlington after crossing the Potomac, soon after the war broke out, and they occupied the estate continuously from that time.

The Union did not acquire legal title to Arlington until 1874; by that time, however, the land was already being used as a soldiers' cemetery. The mansion was neglected except for one wing in which the cemetery's offices were housed. Finally, in 1925, Congress voted funds for its restoration, and now it contains some of the original furnishings lost in the confusion of war and the years of disrepair that followed.

Reddy does not go inside today. He prefers to admire the building's sunlit architecture and the view from the portico. The house itself is an early example of Greek Revival construction, with eight stocky Doric columns of stuccoed brick modeled after the Temple of Poseidon. Though somewhat heavy and graceless, they are solid, and perhaps even inspiring when viewed at a distance, as from the sloping hill that was once the front lawn of the mansion and is now the site of the Kennedy grave. Perhaps the finest feature of the mansion is its unparalleled vista of Washington, more striking now than a century ago. This day it is a magnificent marble city, clear and bright, like a postcard.

After the attack at Pearl, we started reorganizing, looking toward the defense of the place, which was of course horribly inadequate up till then. They were clearing up Hickam Field so they could take on B-17s and B-19s, the Flying Fortresses. They didn't know if the place was going to be attacked or if so whether they could hold it. We didn't attempt to raise any ships because we didn't have the manpower. We only had 1,700 men working there—it was just a little repair yard out in the middle of the ocean.

But after the famous battle at Midway, although we lost the *Yorktown* and a few other ships, the Japs couldn't land—we turned them back. Although they had Guam, we (or the powers that be) realized that Hawaii was going to hold. By the next June the influx started at Pearl Harbor, civilian workmen pouring in there. Incidentally, during that battle of Midway there were three Jap planes that got through, and unbeknownst to anybody they dropped some bombs on Honolulu. They hit the University of Hawaii and a few other places. But it never was made public. Even after the war I never saw anything about it, although I had examined the craters myself.

As the work at Pearl Harbor started expanding I put in for a promotion and was accepted, even though I didn't yet have the ten years of experience required. I was awarded a job as senior ordnance planner and estimator, which was a very high position at the time, and I held that until I left in July 1945. From then on there wasn't a battleship carrier coming into that Navy Yard that I didn't write all the job orders for repair, battle damage, overhaul—the complete services of the whole Navy Yard.

Reddy squints out over the Kennedy grave to the Memorial Gate and the grand sweep of the Arlington Bridge, on past to the Lincoln Memorial, all the way to the Washington Monument and the Capitol. He bends down for a moment to tie his shoes.

My folks didn't know anything about what happened to me at Pearl until about a month after the attack, when I got a cable through. Later, in 1942, I was able to call Washington on a censored phone from Hawaii. That's how I got engaged. I had known this girl in D.C.—she went to school with my younger sister and had been around our house quite a few times. I had taken her out a couple times before I left for Hawaii, but I went with a lot of girls then—we weren't engaged at the time. But I just got lonesome. I was 29 years old and I decided maybe it's time I got married. I didn't know how long I was going to be there. So I called her up one night from Hawaii and I told her if we're going to get married, you're going to have to come over here—otherwise, the deal's off. She could have said no, I don't want to, and I would have said, fine, thank you. It was a spontaneous thing.

As it turned out, she liked the idea. I called her at ten at night Hawaiian time, three A.M. in Washington. She was really surprised. So she came over in September of '43. The only way the government could get her over there for me was if they offered her a job, which they did. According to Hawaiian law, I had three days to get married. She came over on a Wednesday and Saturday we got married, at Waikiki Beach, at St. Augustine's Church, at nine o'clock in the morning. I'm still married to her.

All the officers in the Navy Yard fixed me up a beautiful honeymoon. I got a priority on Hawaiian Air Lines for the next morning, Sunday. In fact, the admiral did it. He threw two people off the plane, and we went from there to Hilo, the big island of Hawaii. They had already arranged for rooms at the Nan-a-Loi Hotel and at the Volcano House, and they gave me ten days off and priority back.

We had a real nice furnished apartment on Waikiki Beach for $55 a month. I stayed in Hawaii until 1945 working as a planner and estimator, and my wife was secretary to the security officer. She had a two-year contract, but after eight months she had to break it because of an act of God. My oldest daughter was born over there in Queens Hospital.

As it turned out my wife was very unhappy with the island. There were wartime conditions and a million and a half men there, and many wives had been sent back to the States. She wasn't working while she was pregnant. She went to a Chinese doctor—couldn't find an American. He was real good, but he didn't believe in holding weight down or anything. She went from 119 pounds to about 190; all I'm doing is bringing candy and anything I can think of home from Pearl Harbor, because that's all she wants, candy and cakes and everything. Later on, though it was really tough, she finally lost all that weight.

When she was pregnant all the sailors used to whistle at her. Then she'd push the baby buggy down the street and she got angry when a coconut almost fell in the baby buggy. She missed her mother and all this stuff. So finally I had enough of it and I put in for a transfer to the Washington Navy Yard. I knew the war was over—we had already dropped the first A-bomb. So I transferred back as a planner and estimator at the Washington Navy Yard.

Now peering across the Potomac from the Custis–Lee Mansion, James Reddy thinks back to the times when he would walk here for a breath of fresh air, away from the stultifying bureaucracy of government.

Oh, but it's good to be retired! He wonders how Gordon Rule is doing. Like Reddy before him, Rule had long been an outspoken critic of the Navy Department's indulgent attitude toward cost overruns and bonuses for large corporate suppliers. But Rule made the front pages with some scathing testimony before a Senate subcommittee; the Navy was miffed, and shortly afterward he was demoted from his position as overseer of naval procurement programs. Reddy was not surprised. After seventeen years as a naval procurement officer himself, he was well acquainted with the cynicism that greeted anything more than a cursory concern about quality or an effort toward elementary efficiency. But he was heartened when the conflict surfaced, when Rule refused to resign after being requested to, and when public pressure forced reinstatement to his old job three months after his demotion. True, the Navy bureaucracy never showed the slightest sign of contrition (the official explanation was that the minor task to which Rule had been assigned was concluded) but at least in this case it had made restitution.

Reddy admired Rule's tough-mindedness as he is proud of his own, but he wonders now whether anything can really be done about the Navy's prodigal procurement practices. Can the system really be changed, or are governmental waste and corruption inevitable by-products of the free-enterprise society? Besides, the public is probably resigned to official squandering, to the extent that it is aware of what goes on. Reddy has mellowed, though he still feels a certain sadness, not because he may be missing the excitement of a modest wave of bureaucratic reform, but because he now regrets having kept his own discontent to himself so long. What would have happened, he asks himself, if he had been more vocal in his criticisms, if he had spoken out more to his colleagues or to his congressman or to the press, instead of just to an occasional superior—and a military superior at that? He knew a number of people besides Rule with similar feelings about the Department's diminishing concern for efficiency, but none of them ever raised their voices. Reddy believes that their inaction is due partly to a desire for security, but even more to the sense of futility that overcomes many civil servants after only a short time in government.

I came back to Washington and I had 30 calendar days' leave with pay due me. I reported to the Navy Yard and told them I wanted my 30 days' leave. I had to find a place to live. I couldn't stay with my mother and father; we all agreed that married kids should not live at home. The Navy said, if we find you a place to live that's acceptable, and the price is right, will you give up your leave in the interest of the war? I told that dumb lieutenant he didn't know what the war effort really was. Two days later they called up and said they had a house for me. It was one of these defense housing units they had put up, a nice little place over on East Capitol Street and Greenway, $35 a month. I took it right away and went and bought some furniture real quick, till the crib and everything came back from Hawaii.

I went to work, but in two weeks they called me in and said, "We hired you back as a planner and estimator, but we don't need you as that—we were forced to do it by the Navy Department." So they put me back to first-class machinist.

When the war was over, since I didn't have veteran's preference, I was laid off. That was January of 1946. I started hunting for another job and I finally found one at the General Accounting Office at about half my former pay. I worked as a special claims searcher there from April 1946 until February 1947. Then I went back to work in the Navy Yard as a tool engineer, designing jigs and fixtures for ordnance material. I was there until 1949, when again there was a big layoff under Secretary of Defense Johnson. He cut defense spending way back, to practically nothing.

Then I took a job in cryptography here in Washington, at the Naval Signalling Laboratory. I took an oath that I'd never reveal what I did. I was in charge of a model shop of about fifteen people. It was all top-secret work. I had a good job there, made good money, put in a lot overtime, loved my work. I guess I was knocking down $12,000 a year, which was darn good. I worked there a little over a year. Then all of a sudden Congress or someone decided to move this place to Fort Knox, underground. Since I had just bought a new home, and moved into it, I decided I'd have to leave this good job and go back to work at the Navy Yard, which I did, as a tool equipment specialist, GS-9.

I wasn't there eight or nine months when the appropriations ran out, and they were going to fire me again. So I went back and took this professional rate, P-3, as a tool designer. It paid about five or six thousand a year. (They did away with these professional rates when they went into the new GS rating system.) And the money ran out on *this* job somewhere in '51, right before the Korean War. They laid me off again.

Everytime I got laid off it was because I didn't have veteran's prefer-ence. So I said the hell with it. I was in the Naval Reserve, and with a little finagling I finally got them to enlist me for four years in a construc-tion batallion. I took the oath of office and went in one day before my layoff was effective, which meant that I would get my job back when I came back four years later. I was 39 years old, had two children, was financing a home, and my wife was pregnant. My wife got an allotment of $300–$325 a month and that's what she lived on. I only kept $20 a month. As an enlisted man, I got a first-class mechanic rating, diesel and gas engines, in a construction batallion. I enlisted over in Anacostia, and they sent me up to Rhode Island.

I was at the Greenland Icecap for one whole winter. When I came back, I went to college for a semester at the University of Rhode Island. That fall they sent me to North Africa on a secret deal there, one of these SAC bombing places where they have one-third of their bombers up in the air all the time. I can't reveal what that was but the civilians all left and they sent the Sea Bees in to complete it. We finished that, and I returned to the University of Rhode Island for about five months. Because of my background I was always picked for confidential areas. This time I was down on Grand Turk, 1,100 miles out of Miami. For two years I was down there as engineering officer on a base for underwater oceanographic survey.

Grand Turk was a little island six miles by three-quarters of a mile. In fact, the Grand Turk channel was where the astronauts were supposed to land. We put up a landing strip and a guided-missile base on one end of the island. Then on the other end we put up a tremendous base. The terminal building has all top-secret stuff in there.

When I got out of the Navy, I went back to work in the Navy Yard. Besides a GS-9 tool equipment specialist I was also technical advisor on a rehabilitation of all the tools and test equipment in the Navy Yard. I only put in about a year, '55 until '56. In the meantime I continued going to school. In 1956 I passed an examination down in the Navy Department. They gave me a raise as a production engineer in electronics. I went to work there in September 1957 and stayed until I retired.

I had worked all the way up to a GS-14. My title was General Business Industrial Specialist Supervisor. I was always in guided missiles, surface-to-air missiles. The people under me and I wrote the procurement contracts—all the technical aspects, all that we were to buy, all the quality-control requirements. I had to get into contracts when I became a production engineer. At one time I had three supervisors under me, and about 23 people altogether. Then I decided I'd had enough. When you put in so many years and when your take-home pay and the retirement benefits you're going to get are within a hundred dollars of each other, you might as well retire. There comes a point in life when you have to look for some enjoyment. I wasn't married to the job. They paid me well and I figured I'd given them everything I could. I ended as a GS-14, making good money, almost $25,000 a year.

Reddy leaves the Custis–Lee portico and walks down the slope toward the Kennedy grave. He wonders if there was any conflict between civilian personnel and military men as far back as the Civil War.

Several years ago a special committee appointed by the Navy to look into deteriorating morale among its civilian employees developed "a package of initial recommendations," among them one to change the requirements for appointment to decision-making positions, which was now almost exclusively military. The committee did not hedge:

> The Contracting Officer is no longer allowed to really utilize his broadscale procurement expertise. Instead, he has been relegated to the role of a glorified clerk who is charged with only the very limited and narrow responsibility of negotiating contract prices. The authority and responsibility of the Contracting Officer is no longer clearly defined nor clearly understood. . . . The real question at issue is who is responsible for determining how something is to be procured?

The validity of numerous other civilian grievances was also recognized, from sloppy filing habits to misguided racial quotas ("the word 'qualified' seems to lose its meaning in the case of some minority races and instead, it appears a quota system is used which places little emphasis on ability or qualifications").

Over a period of years, from 1960 to 1970, there was a planned take-over by the military of all supervisory positions. In the Naval Ordnance Systems Command, you only had to look at the Department of Defense phone book to find out that practically 80 percent of all division directors and branch heads are military. They are supervisory, all the way down. Before 1966 I myself used to function as a civilian branch head, but then a lieutenant was placed over me as a military branch head—with full authority over my decisions. I had signature authority, but he could overrule that. He was a limited-duty officer in electrical engineering, and was absolutely and horribly inadequate in production contracts and in their technical administration. Consequently he was always listening to the contractors and initialing waivers and deviations—always over my technical advice not to do so. As a result, missiles were delivered with inadequate quality control, and in some cases the government had to fund additional money to fix them. The records of the types of ammunition delivered between 1940 and 1960 and the degree of quality control that was observed will bear me out.

Ninety-nine percent of the time the Navy military man is a graduate of Annapolis and holds a degree in ordnance engineering only. He is brought up in the military, esteemed by the military, and depending on the particular branch of the Navy he's in, he's either a very good fly-boy, a very good ship commander, or a very good ordnance officer. As such he knows how to command men, to put the ship where it's supposed to be, and in certain areas he's a communications expert—he knows how to direct his search radar, his weapons radar. At that point his responsibility ends. He's subject only to the Code of Military Justice.

Now take a civilian. A civilian supervisor got his position by virtue of the fact that he passed a competitive examination under Civil Service, codified by laws of Congress. He has a position description he has to fulfill, and he knows his duties. It all follows a prescribed set of rules and regulations set down by the Civil Service Commission. He knows what can happen to him if he should happen to stray from those principles set down in that position description. There is a wide gulf between him and his military counterpart. The military man has no constraint whatsoever; if a military supervisor pulls off something that is wrong and costs the government a lot of money, he is rarely held responsible. Instead, he is usually transferred to another command in another place. Then the next military supervisor takes over, and when he is confronted with the mess that his predecessor left him he can always say, "It didn't happen on my watch. I only got two to four years to stay here and I'll do as I please in that two to four years."

Not all military are like that. There are some real good dedicated people that try to work with civilians, and Watergate has changed things. But I know the cases of three captains who were transferred out because in the procurement of missiles they tried to hold contractors responsible, to play the game the way Congress actually set it down to be played. I know of one captain who had to retire, another who lost his command in the Naval Ordnance Systems Command and is today filling out his time as head of a recruiting station in Cleveland, and another who retired two years after he was transferred. They were four-stripers, and two of them were Annapolis graduates.

Reddy hitches up his khaki pants and strolls slowly toward the Kennedy grave.

You also have a caste system in the Navy. It starts with the admiral and works down. An officer usually takes his orders from the next higher up. He always goes to the register real quick to find out who his superior is and when did he graduate from Annapolis, to find out where he fits, because he knows his superiors are going to fill out his fitness report, which affects whether he advances in grade at some later time. He plays ball with the ones higher up regardless of what it costs him underneath, in order to attain promotion. I think this is what happened all through the government, and what made Watergate inevitable.

Now once a man has put in his retirement or his resignation papers, he is supposed to be dropped immediately from any list of promotions. Yet under the buddy system things are a little different. There was a captain in Naval Ordnance System Command who was second in command, and he had been passed over four times for admiral, and he made many statements that he was retiring. It was a known fact within the command that he had put in his retirement papers—he had even put notices on the bulletin board for woodworking machinery which he wanted to buy second hand, as that was going to be his hobby. But he was a friend of Admiral Zumwalt, who somehow put him on a promotion list. His name was the last one added to the list and Congress passed it. Today he is a rear admiral, retired.

They also have this thing called "double dipping," where an officer will retire from the armed services and then go immediately into a high-level Civil Service position, stay there for 20 years while he's getting his military pension, then collect a pension based on 40 years' government service. But Carter's putting a stop to that, I think.

The military take-over started in 1960 when they merged the old

Bureau of Ordnance and the Bureau of Aeronautics into the Bureau of Naval Weapons. Now the Bureau of Ordnance had been one of the oldest agencies in the Navy Department, probably 135 to 140 years old. The Bureau of Naval Weapons was a comedy of horrors and in 1966 they changed it back to the way it was before. A naval officer outside of the commandant used to be merely advisory to a civilian top supervisor. It was his place to see that the arms and ammunitions that went to the fleet were of the best type, called it to the attention of the civilians if they were not, and noted if there was anything going wrong and if they arrived at the various weapons stations and ships on time. That used to be his role. But now they are trying to get the military sole control over the acquisitions of all naval ordnance systems themselves. Today captains and admirals sit in the top commands of all surface missile systems, torpedoes, and whatever else the Navy is buying. There is always a captain or an admiral that commands and directs the civilians, telling what they want done and how. You can't use your own independent judgment anymore. You're in a corner.

My conviction is that a man going into procurement as a commissioned officer, subject only to the Uniform Code of Military Justice, should have no place of command in acquisition or procurement, because he does not have any background, he has no schooling, he has no education in these matters. He knows how to run ships. This is his role and his place. Could you put him aboard ship if all he knows is procurement, or if all he knows is electronic engineering? What good is he to fight a war then?

Reddy moves on. Until now his walk has been relatively undisturbed by other visitors, but at the Kennedy grave there is actually a small crowd. In less then a decade, it has become the most frequently visited spot in Arlington Cemetery. Reddy comes here less often than he goes to the other monuments, not so much because of the crowds, which on weekdays are not generally large, but because the death of the young President still disturbs him, and he is also discomforted by the simple, impersonal design of the monument.

He ambles now to the brink of the rectangular marble terrace,

stares briefly at the eternal flame and the three slate markers
bearing the names of John F. Kennedy and his two dead children, and stands for a long moment gazing past the grave, to the
bridge and Washington in the distance. Then he turns and begins
to walk slowly southward toward his car.

History is one of the most fascinating subjects that you can study. I
think Truman made a beautiful decision. He'll go down as a better
President than Roosevelt. And I'm not a military man, I'm just looking
at what was happening over there. I saw Roosevelt in Hawaii in 1944
and he looked horrible. He was running for President again, his third
term, but he had what was known as a brain trust behind him and he
was just voicing opinions. I don't think he had full control of all his
mental faculties.

Personally I would rather have seen Taft as President after that.
Eisenhower? I can't even say he was a military hero. He was a tactician,
an obscure colonel made a general for one purpose, and that was for the
invasion of Europe. Eisenhower didn't do any more than carry out the
brain trusts of President Roosevelt and his group of advisors. They
picked him because he was a good, sensible man and would carry out
anything that the President of the United States, as Commander in
Chief, told him to do. I would think that Patton as a fighter on the field
was far superior to Eisenhower, but Eisenhower was the best man they
could have gotten to get the logistics together, to get everything there
and in the numbers needed. He and his staff didn't have the benefit of
computers at that time—it was nothing more or less than judgment. But
when the American people were called upon they supplied him with
more of anything that he ever needed when he started.

As a President, though, Eisenhower was a Republican and mediocre.
He didn't rock the boat, and he didn't run any grave deficits. The
country was in a period of resurgence. We suffered from no depressions,
there was almost full employment. He just happened to be in at that
period of time when everything was fine and dandy. What major decisions did he make? I can't recall any.

I'm neither Democrat or Republican, but an independent. I voted for
Kennedy because I thought he was a good man. He was trying for the
same kind of resurgence of the country that Roosevelt was seeking in

1932, trying to pull everybody together. And I think that if he hadn't been assassinated and had been given a good chance, he would have done it. He had youth on his side, and that was what he needed. That's what we need today. He inherited the Bay of Pigs invasion from Eisenhower. It was completely and independently financed by the CIA and done with Cubans; if you study history you'll find that out. It never had a chance to succeed for the simple reason that Castro knew about it and was waiting for them. They were just murdered on the beaches. I don't think it was Kennedy's fault. He had some bad information coming from a previous Republican administration. Maybe they were trying to embarrass him. I don't know.

One thing that sticks out is the way that he stood up to Russia, with the whole resources of the United States behind him. He did not back down when he confronted Khrushchev. He said you're not going to put defensive missiles on Cuba, and by God if you want to go to war over it, nuclear or otherwise, we'll do it. He made the Russians back down, and that in my estimation is going to make Kennedy a great man.

Kennedy did not escalate Vietnam. He just sent in a few more advisors and a lot of supplies. He did not send large numbers of military people, maybe eight or ten or twelve thousand but not hundreds of thousands. On the other hand, to his damnation, he also had this fellow Diem murdered because I guess he didn't like the way he was handling the country. At least, Kennedy knew all about it and didn't try to stop it.

I voted for Johnson. I can't say he was great by any stretch of the imagination, nor can I say he was a total flop either. There's a few things that stick out about him. When you get to Vietnam and his escalation and his Tonkin Gulf proclamation, he had everybody in the United States behind him. I believe he could have wound that war up if he had given explicit orders to the military, "Get it over right now." But he tried to run the war with his advisors in the White House, having McNamara as Secretary of Defense, naming what targets to try to pull out. They didn't have any bombing accuracy whatsoever. Then he stopped the bombing, and thought he was going to get a peace out of it. He just hadn't studied that type of history over that side of the world, or the Oriental mind.

I voted for Nixon over Humphrey, who was too liberal for me, and again over McGovern, who was so far out the only other choice I had was not to vote at all. I thought Nixon would make a very good President, but he prevaricated; he used his office illegally even though he thought it was for the good of the country. I thought Agnew was a very good man, but he committed the same error that all politicians do, used his high office for kickbacks.

Personally, in all my time in government, I have never accepted gratuities from any contractor in any way, shape, or form. And I was offered plenty. I even had a color television set delivered to my home for a Christmas present by Sylvania, which was a big government contractor, and I turned it back. Now this was back in the early sixties, when color TV cost an awful lot of money. My wife called me up and said they delivered a color TV set and I told her to tell them to get that thing the hell out of there. "Take it away. I don't want it and don't want to hear any more about it." I have two sets now, but I bought them with my own money.

Ford did a tremendous job in trying to clean up after Watergate. I voted for him, although I still think Carter is a very great man.

Driving back across the Arlington Memorial Bridge toward Washington, Reddy glances out the window in the direction of the Pentagon. For a moment its cavernous image fills his head. The adjectives often used to describe the place—*huge, immense, monstrous, massive*—all seem to miss its real meaning, although it is indeed a Brobdingnagian fortress: each of the five exterior wings is as long as three football fields, enclosing an area of more than 6½ million square feet. There are five interior wings, each with five floors, a mezzanine, and a basement, separated by three open courts and a roadway. The world's largest food-serving operation is carried on in its four cafeterias, where up to 6,000 soldiers and civilians are fed together daily. There are parking spaces for 9,300 people. Reddy still regards the Pentagon as a monument to deceptive efficiency, something he attributes to the fact that two-thirds of its employees are military.

After the war ended and Reddy had been discharged, he often walked from his office in the old Navy Department Building to the cemetery or along the Mall and back during his lunch hour.

He had come to a Washington in which the various services were an integral part of the scheme of things in government; the military's administrative offices were cheek-by-jowl with those occupied by senators, congressmen, and the staffs of the executive departments. Monuments and museums were everyone's neighbors. The Navy Department Building had been erected in 1917 as a "temporary structure," but the Navy stayed until 1968, when the building was demolished and new headquarters were set up in Crystal City. And the services, though not immune to internecine squabbles and petty jealousies, lived on relatively amicable terms with the rest of the bureaucracy. The military–industrial complex had not yet been identified. Reddy came to know the Navy as an almost romantic carryover from an earlier era. He would think back to his job at the Washington Naval Gun Factory, when the Department itself still manufactured its own firearms. Of course, even then there were shufflers of paper and papers aplenty to shuffle, but the lowliest bureaucrat was never more than a short ride by trolley car from the machinery that turned more or less in harmony with his own forms and figures.

Then things began to change, and somewhere along the line it dawned on Reddy that, while he had begun his career as a turner of machines, he was going to end it as a shuffler of paper. For a few years he thought that the standards of an earlier time would of necessity be restored, and he never conceived the day when machine work and paper work would be so remote from one another, when he would have so little control, that his own job would be virtually meaningless. Yet by the time he was finished, that is what had happened.

The money for defense is apportioned properly, it's just the inefficiency in the way it's *spent* that gets me. I would say that you could reduce the defense budget from 15 to 25 percent and still get the same amount of weapons—maybe even better ones. Now in the Navy this means about 15 to 25 percent of $12 to $15 billion—that's the annual appropriation. I know of many a case where they ask for something they already have and they take everything off the shelves and deep-six it, without any type of audit.

I've worked with government procurement contracts for fifteen years, and practically every directed contract resulted in a cost overrun. Over a period of years a way of life has developed between industry and the Department of Defense. There has been a marriage between top military directors and industry to the point where there is hardly a change from year to year in the procurement of weapons. Competitive procurement only exists on small, large-quantity individual items—for instance, stock materials such as nuts and bolts and issues of clothing. Because these items are highly competitive the government gets a good break. But when you get to sophisticated weapons like aircraft, ships, and all types of ordnance equipment, it is rare that large multimillion- or billion-dollar contracts are done competitively. These are usually ordered on what is known as directed procurement.

As a technical supervisor over surface-to-air missiles for more than ten years, I had to deal with a couple of billion dollars worth of procurement. That's *billion*, not million. From the office of Admiral (Chief of Naval Operations), the directive usually comes down: "You will procure from . . ." and then they'll name a company like General Dynamics or Bendix. In aircraft it's Boeing; submarine missiles, Lockheed. These are marriages of convenience that are peculiar to our form of government, where you get annual appropriations. It's hard to go out and secure competition with year-to-year procurement methods. If we were on multi-year procurements, where we knew Congress would continue to appropriate the funds and pick it up say for four or five years, we could get a tremendous break for the taxpayer by going competitive.

With directed procurement, where the technical and the contract and the legal people sit down—once it has been decided by the military to direct a buy to one of these corporations—it's a known fact between this corporation and the government that they are going to get the contract. So the only limitations on cost are, what is the appropriation and how much is going to be directed? And the contractor will always come in with an estimate that will be millions above the annual appropriation. But he'll always know beforehand, through the military and through his program managers, how much is in this budget. He knows that better than we do.

The contract is often no more than 30 days old when the contractor will come in with about fifteen changes, and say it is impossible to build to specifications without some changes going in. There are usually provisions in contracts for necessary changes. But then a large controversy often exists between the technical group (like the one I was supervising) and the contractor himself, where we are trying to hold these costs down. Usually the contractor has us over a barrel; he says, this being the case, we cannot deliver the weapons you want without these changes going in. Nine times out of ten he gets his way, and there's a contract overrun from the very start, in the form of changes, that will run into millions.

In 1960, for instance, there was a directed procurement contract with Bendix for 220 Talos missiles. The appropriations for it were about $22 million. At the end, it ran something like *seven million dollars over* the original procurement that we had intended to pay. Practically all of the overrun could have been avoided with more effective procedures.

In that specific contract, which was the first procurement of the Talos missile, the first missiles that came off that line were test-fired at sea, and the first ten of them proved terribly inadequate. They never got to the target area, they caught fire, the combuster burned through, and all of them went into the ocean. I immediately stopped production on the combuster. After something like eighteen months we found out that the Bendix Corporation engineering was horrible. There was a difference in altitude of 6,000 feet between the White Sands Proving Ground, where the test results they gave us came from, and the sea level of the ocean. Because of this difference in atmospheric pressure, the missiles would burn through the combuster area. We lost them all. We had to put immense changes in there.

Then we got into the next two-year contracts. The situation was very desperate because at the time, under the Kennedy regime, we were in the Berlin crisis. We added more missiles to the contract and we were delivering them onto loaded ships, putting missiles in the magazines with big signs on them saying, DO NOT FIRE—DO NOT USE. They were just to make a show of force in the Mediterranean. These missiles all had to come back, at a tremendous cost, and be retrofitted—all the combusters pulled out. I remember negotiating those changes in the first three contracts, amounting to a $7,600,000 overrun just to fix the combusters up, to make them so they would perform according to the original contract.

Although into each contract we put specifications that they meet quality-control provisions which are hard to circumvent, and we also put a quality-assurance evaluation test in, the contractor always finds means and ways of getting around these requirements. Consequently the missiles as delivered constantly have to be repaired. And the military is fully aware that they are being delivered this way, because the files are full of memoranda and technical analysis of what has transpired.

I think it's a way of life with the manufacturer: in order to get a contract he will come in low and figure he'll recover many, many more dollars, running into millions, in cost overruns and changes, in order to get a higher profit margin.

There's a feeling that because it's for defense, the money will always be found somewhere no matter what the cost. They will rob Peter to pay Paul. I've had wide experience in defense budgeting; in fact, on three missiles I alone wrote all the budget analysis and the backup that ultimately went to Congress. But when the others got finished with it, it was always inflated another 20 to 25 percent before it went to the appropriations committee. They knew that the committee may cut off a little bit of it, but they would always come out 20 to 25 percent more than I had thought was needed.

Reddy circles the Lincoln Memorial and turns right onto Constitution Avenue, heading east toward the Washington Monument.

He was always a devoted father, and now that he is retired he can spend more time with his grandchildren. One of the things he enjoys most is taking them into Washington for trips to the National Zoo or on a tour of the monuments and parks he has come to know so well. When they are a bit older he wants to show them the museums of the Smithsonian Institution, and maybe even visit some of the old Civil War battlefields. He has been to all of them himself.

He parks his car along Constitution Avenue near Fifteenth Street and takes the fish he caught this morning out of the trunk. His daughter is waiting at the northwest base of the Washington Monument, where they had arranged to meet; she smiles at Reddy and says she has to run. Sean, ten, and Karen, eight, are excited to be with their grandfather and eager to get moving. Reddy gives the fish to his daughter, takes his grandchildren's hands, and walks around the flag poles at the foot of the monument. He is very ordered with his tour, pointing out the government buildings in the distance and reciting the names of the four drives that run the length of the Mall: Madison, Washington, Adams, Jefferson.

But Sean and Karen are overwhelmed by the soaring monument and the kites flying high above the expansive grounds surrounding it, and pay little attention. Reddy lets them run free for a while. History can wait for a few minutes, he tells himself, while the kids enjoy themselves. They will not climb the monument today; there will be enough walking as it is. He sits down on a bench with the children's jackets and the picnic lunch their mother has packed for them.

I believe in the adequate defense of the country but I don't believe that it should be over-defended. I'm not a hawk in the sense that we should be armed to the teeth, flaunt it all over the world. We don't need that.

Prior to President Roosevelt, under the Arms Limitation Treaty in 1921 and the Briand-Kellogg Peace Pact of the Harding administration, we were woefully unarmed. But it didn't make any difference because there was no other nation in the world in any better shape. I guess we were trying then to do with peaceful coexistence. This would be good if it were the case all over the world; we would need no more than a police force for internal problems. In World War I we had an isolation problem. They even stopped President Wilson from joining the League of Nations. We scrapped all our battleships but four, and made aircraft carriers out of them. We made a few treaty cruisers, but we couldn't have any more than two turrets on these cruisers. (We put three turrets on them by putting ballast tanks on some cruisers such as the old *Trenton*, the old *Honolulu*, and a few other ones; by pumping up the ballast tanks they could raise the bow of the ship and get longer range out of them.) This was up until Roosevelt.

Kids were trying to get in the Navy and they couldn't take them because they were held down to 125,000 men. We had very few ships except for some of World War I vintage and earlier, battleships from the Great White Fleet. Then there was a resurrection of military might in Germany and Italy. We were still suffering from isolation then during the Spanish conflict, when our government kept hands off both sides—which I agreed with. We had recognized Communist Russia under Roosevelt. When Germany re-armed and started going into Poland, Roosevelt was stuck with all the laws on the books and tried to find ways to circumvent them. One circumvention was Lend-Lease. He also started to build up his army. He went into the draft, for which we were woefully inadequately prepared. Some of the citizen army they had drafted didn't get uniforms for as much as six months, and they didn't even have any training weapons. You can look in the papers back in that period and find what they called the broomstick or stovepipe army. We had lots of plans on the books, though.

Then when December 7th hit, all industry jumped in and gave us a citizens' army that was second to none. They gave us a Navy where when we asked for two ships, they gave us three. We asked for five tanks, they gave us seven. When Ford started building planes, Liberator bombers, they were coming off one an hour. The American people as a whole jumped into that thing and you've never seen anything like it in all your life. I sincerely believe that the United States practically single-handedly won that war on both sides. Surely Britain was down and out and there was nothing left but the United States, and she had to take on Japan and Germany both.

In my estimation, after studying the old agreement and everything, we made a bad deal when we divided Europe down the middle at the Oder River. Roosevelt agreed to it, and if you study Winston Churchill's memoirs you'll find out Winston did not. We're still in that division today. We had to stop Patton from going over into Czecho-slovakia, because he was confronting the Russian Army by going beyond that line of demarcation that he wasn't supposed to. Whether that was good or bad I don't know. Certainly when we were to make Germany a pastoral state under the Morgenthau Plan, Truman saw through it and stopped all the heavy equipment going into Russia and immediately they instituted the Marshall Plan to start rebuilding Germany.

I thought bombing Hiroshima was a damn expedient way to end the war a year sooner and to save a bunch of people's lives. What do you think it would have cost the Americans in the invasion of that island? They were entrenched in there and they knew darn well that no matter how much they bombed it out, just like they bombed North and South Vietnam, you can't get in there and root them out. You are going to have to land, like we did at Iwo Jima and like we did at Quajung. I saw some of them Marines cut up in bits coming in from those places.

Your values are different when you're fighting a war for survival. If my sisters and brothers and my children are in it, I think of their safety. I don't give a damn if I'm going to bomb two million civilians out. If it's going to stop it right then, do it. If it's going to take the military installation out along with it, do it. They should have let MacArthur go and stop that Korean War way, way back.

In a few minutes the children, a bit winded but nonetheless exhilarated by their romp among the kite flyers on the monument grounds, return to their grandfather. They want to climb the monument; Reddy says no, not today, and the three of them set off toward the Tidal Basin.

Early in the century the area that is now East and West Potomac Park was swampland, and the Tidal Basin was formed in order to flush the harbor that had been created in the reclamation process. When he worked at the Navy Department, Reddy would often walk through Potomac Park. The river here is now badly polluted, but the park continues to be one of the loveliest sections in the capital—its chief adornments thousands of cherry trees, a gift from the city of Tokyo to the city of Washington, which line the borders of the basin and continue southeast along Ohio

Drive. In April the cherry blossoms burst into a panoply of dappled pastel.

Sean and Karen run among the trees. Reddy is sad, in a way, that they do not realize what has happened to the harbor, where he often used to fish before the Second World War. Nothing lives here now save the trees.

Reddy takes the children for a paddleboat ride in the Tidal Basin. Then he heads back to the Reflecting Pool facing the Lincoln Memorial. Passing the monument dedicated to John Paul Jones, he mentions the commodore's famous battle against the British in 1779. They have never heard "I have not yet begun to fight." He cautions them not to fall in as they run along the edge of the pool, laughing, sometimes stopping to look at their images in the water.

I had some inside dope on Vietnam that probably people don't know but they should. My son-in-law was a sergeant, enlisted man, and he was over there as a Green Beret three times and in Indonesia once; he helped train that whole Indonesian Army, until the Sukarno take-over came. Had he been captured there he would not have had the United States government behind him—he volunteered for it. He was a gung-ho guy. He served in Laos eight months. At one time he and his group of no more than 24 officers ran a 15,000-man mercenary army of Cambodians and Laotians into Vietnam itself, and they ruptured the Ho Chi Minh Trail, cut the pipe lines, fifteen times. He was wounded three or four times. One time he dropped 300 feet from a helicopter that was shot down and landed in a tree. The other two guys got killed.

My son-in-law told me many things. For a period of about 75 or 80 years, South Vietnam—around Saigon all the way into Cambodia—has been honeycombed with tunnels and underground defenses that you have never heard of. They have thousands of tons of supplies and ammunition under there. They had factories where they could dig out an undetonated American bomb and take it apart and make land mines out of it. They even had plants under there that could outfit recruits from South Vietnam. He saw them. Well, his group smoked them all out. They closed that tunnel system there, and the last sanctuary they had were all these underground bases in Cambodia. To Nixon's credit and against everything the American people thought, he did go in there and root them all out. He also stopped the supplies coming in from the gulf down below.

If you're going to fight a war, fight it with everything you've got to its conclusion and stop the damn thing. Don't prolong it for years and years for your munitions makers back here. This is what I believe and why I didn't believe in Johnson. Under Johnson, the missiles we had weren't worth a damn. The bombs we were dropping weren't worth a damn. No accuracy. Nothing was working, quality control was horrible. I'd say maybe 25 percent of what we were dropping were duds and didn't even go off.

Prior to August 1969, when the Paris peace talks started, we spent maybe $22 million with the Bendix Corporation to take the Talos and make an armed missile out of it. I took part in taking the terminal guidance sections out of 68 missiles and giving them to the engineering group who fitted them all out with new guidance systems. They spent a few million dollars more getting three cruisers fixed up to fire them and see what the heck was going to happen. Now this money was not ever actually appropriated by Congress. It was borrowed out of various over-run funds. They tried it out at White Sands. I looked over the reports and found out that the damn thing was not operating right. Now the Russians and the Vietnamese are not dumb by any stretch of the imagination; they'd use search radars at about three or four different places to search the plane out, get the course, the target bearing, and everything else, and they'd avoid being hit. We launched maybe about 20 to 25 of these damn Talos things over North Vietnam. They didn't hit the first damn target yet. The missile got out there and indiscriminately went down in the rice paddies. Some of them hit towns. These Talos missiles are great big tremendous things—30-something feet long and 30 inches in diameter. When they landed, that warhead went off. First thing you know we get an order from the President of the United States saying to quit indiscriminately using whatever you're using over there, 'cause they threatened to cut off the whole Paris peace talks. This is the military for you.

That ended the Talos arms deal. We still got some of them in the stockpile. They are on the books as ready for issue, but they'll never use the damn things because they're no good.

McNamara didn't want to prosecute the war the way Johnson did.

You could see it in all his directions to us coming down the line. He did give service to the President, but he did not want to prosecute the war in any way, shape, or form. If he did, the two of them together could have probably closed it in nine months from the landing at Da Nang, or brought it to a conclusion way back in '68 or '69. All they had to do was get about five divisions of mad Marines, put them on an island, train them for six months, no liberty, not anything, and send them in. Cut it in half, so when you get over to the Laos side, it's ended. But they never cut it off. It was inevitable that the Communists would eventually take over.

The children grow quieter as they approach the end of the Reflecting Pool, and Reddy decides to have them rest before going up the steps and inside the Lincoln Memorial. Briefly he tells them about Lincoln and the emancipation of the slaves, quoting from some of the nineteen books he has about the Civil War, and this time both children listen attentively. They have heard something of Lincoln in school.

In the early twenties there was a protracted debate in Congress about the location for the memorial. The place finally chosen was a swamp near the Potomac full of quail, frogs, and insects, but most people agreed with Lincoln's secretary and biographer, John Hay, who said that the shrine "should stand alone, remote from the common habitations of man, apart from the business and turmoil of the city—isolated, distinguished and serene." Now some two million visitors a year come there. After the Capitol itself, it is the most popular attraction in Washington.

A few minutes later Reddy and his two grandchildren climb the steps of the Lincoln Memorial. Before going inside Reddy turns them around to look back at the Washington Monument, now striking and austere in the bright noon sun, and then points to the left, showing them where the Navy Department used to be before it moved to the Pentagon. Then they turn and enter the gleaming white marble temple, passing between two of the 36 fluted columns at its entrance, which represent the states in the

Union at the time of Lincoln's assassination. On the parapet are 48 festoons: there were that many states when the memorial was completed.

Inside, the gigantic figure of a brooding Lincoln looms at the rear of the hall. Carved into the wall above him are the words

IN THIS TEMPLE
AS IN THE HEARTS OF THE PEOPLE
FOR WHOM HE SAVED THE UNION
THE MEMORY OF ABRAHAM LINCOLN
IS ENSHRINED FOREVER

When the building was dedicated in May 1922, sculptor Daniel French stood against a column watching the people approach the huge statue. When he saw the humble, clumsy, and poor shuffle self-consciously toward Lincoln, and then quietly pull off their hats and bow their heads, he was moved to tears.

Today even the students who clatter noisily from tourist buses every spring instinctively lower their voices when they enter the building and stand beneath the great seated figure. It has become more than a statue.

The papers that Ellsberg put out were policy and didn't reveal any top secrets, but there's such a thing as ethics. Ellsberg should be sent up for life for what he did. This country was built on ethics and there was a lot of dirt going on, like in Grant's administration, and in Lincoln's, and so forth through the years if you want to study American history. If everybody thought the way Ellsberg did, you wouldn't have a country.

There's a great deal that the military and the civilians in DOD know that the public doesn't. I think it should be made public, but I don't think it should be ferreted out and done the way Ellsberg did it. If somebody makes a wrong decision, it shouldn't be covered up. If I make one, damn it, I should stand up and be counted on it. I think anything that doesn't reveal a military secret should be declassified by law. That should have happened a long time ago. In fact, orders have gone out to declassify all World War II stuff. That hasn't been done, and it hasn't been done on Vietnam. There should be some laws passed by the Congress of the United States independent of the President. The President happens to be part of some of these deals, along with his Secretary of Defense. When top decisions are made on policy, not military but policy, then after they have served their usefulness—say, 30, 60, 90 days, even give them a year—they should be made public in the Archives of the United States. If this were the law, Ellsberg would be in the clear on practically everything he put out.

But when a man enters government service, he takes a sacred oath that he will not reveal secrets. He has accepted a sacred trust. Regardless of whether he in his own mind thinks they are top-secret or not, he does not have the right to disclose those. The government itself is supposed to do that.

Now there is a way of life that when the government wants to leak something out—the State Department, the military, and all of them— it's prearranged. They'll call a press conference over at the Department of State or at the Pentagon. They'll say now I'm going to give you a piece of material and you can publish it but don't use my name. That's the way press releases go.

When I left the government, I didn't take anything marked CONFIDENTIAL with me, and I wouldn't. I took an oath and I then had a responsibility to God and my country not to divulge it. Ellsberg did not have the right to do it either. He could have come out and said, "I know of certain things," and he could have written congressmen and certain committees to let them know it and suggest that these things ought to be made public, here they are and this is where they're at. I have myself written such letters to 42 congressmen. If they are declassified and given to the general public, they could become a political football. I once threatened to go to the press, when I testified before Congress about cost overruns. But the chief counsel of the committee told me it would be very detrimental to my country; he told me the material in there was confidential, of a secret nature. I believed him. I figured they were going to take care of it (which they never did). But I believe in these moral principles. I always did and I always will, until I die.

Reddy leads the children into the halls on the right and left sides of the memorial, where Lincoln's second inaugural speech and the Gettysburg Address are inscribed in the marble. Soon they return to the outside and descend the steps. Reddy takes a few photographs of his grandchildren with Sean's Instamatic, posing them in front of the memorial and alongside the Reflecting Pool. Then they go to a shaded spot in the park along Constitution Avenue and sit down on the grass for their picnic lunch.

Reddy glances once again at the park where the old Navy Department Building used to be, and his last days with the Navy flash through his mind. Barely a month after he had retired, he sent a carefully documented letter to Congressman F. Edward Hébert, then chairman of the House Committee on Armed Forces. Copies were mailed to the other committee members, as well as to Reddy's own congressman. The letter was ten pages long and set forth a detailed list of grievances about "the deteriorating, deleterious, demoralizing condition" that existed in the Naval Ordnance Systems Command.

> I have witnessed and have taken part in three reorganizations that have left this Command a demoralized, fragmented shell of the former Bureau of Ordnance that was the acme of technological ordnance advancement. . . .I would like to emphatically state that if the erosion of the image of naval management continues in the Congress, and in its employees, the time is close when it will be difficult and perhaps impossible for those of us who will be desperately pressing to provide for the security of this country to get the electorate and funding support necessary.

He charged that "when military types are given absolute authority . . . over both business and technical aspects they are under absolutely no obligation to carry out the procurement laws, regulations and policies of the Congress, DOD and Navy," but that they are governed only by the constraints of the Uniform Code of Military Justice.

Specifically, Reddy pointed to abuses of direct procurement by which program managers for the American surface-to-air missiles (Terrier, Tartar, and Talos) then in use could circumvent the requirement for competitive bidding in cases where complex alteration, repairs, or overhauls were necessary. The abuses, wrote Reddy, led to misrepresentation, or "fabricated justification of intent."

He said he found it difficult to understand the military rationale behind favoring the Bendix Corporation, a company with "a questionable record of deliveries," with hundreds of millions of dollars in procurement of guided missiles and accessories. For the two decades Bendix had been the sole source of engineering, production, and repair for the Talos missiles, according to Reddy, its record was "full of waivers, deviation and changes." At one point, he wrote, Bendix delivered 470 missiles (approximately sixteen months late) "the first 55 of which had a deficient combuster coating that would result in catastrophic failure in flight." Forty-five were repaired at government expense, costing $378,000. Later all 470 missiles were found to have defective nitrogen tanks. Bendix took them back, then presented a claim for $245,000 to cover the repair work. Yet the Navy's official legal counsel "has yet to find any claim, changes, waivers or deviations submitted by contractors to issue a determination in favor of the Government." Instead, claimed Reddy, the lawyers consistently counseled against "costly" litigation.

He concluded that, although he had just retired and "the Navy has treated me very good," he had always taken pride in seeking to obtain the best possible ordnance material for the fleet, and, in addition, he felt obliged to call to the committee's attention "the state of disheartened demoralized conditions that have become such a reality."

When the children finish eating Reddy leads them by the hand down Constitution Avenue, toward the car. At Eighteenth Street he stops to buy popsicles from a street vendor. Two girls of college age, dressed in levi's and tight-fitting sweat shirts, pass by on the sidewalks. At the Ellipse, Sean takes a picture of his sister and grandfather, and when they reach the Alexander Hamilton Monument, not far from the car, Karen asks for one more photograph. Reddy hoists her up onto a ledge, positions Sean at the foot of the statue, steps back twenty paces, and aims the camera.

Congressman Hébert acknowledged receipt of Reddy's letter and said that the matter "would be taken under advisement." Some weeks later Reddy appeared before the committee's investigative staff, and everything he charged was duly documented and verified. At the end of the meeting, though, he was left "with the distinct impression that the overcosts I cited were being written off as money down the drain. It was an election year."

He wrote other letters to other legislators and received similar responses. The chief of the Naval Ordnance Systems Command himself, an admiral, reported to his superiors that Reddy's allegations were "at best in some cases half truths without giving all the facts." But somewhere along the line, while he was asking himself if his own purpose was not really to assuage a guilt for failing to speak out sooner, or to reassert his own sense of righteousness, the scandal died aborning, and Reddy even gave up his efforts to demand an apology. Not long afterward he retired.

The light changes at Fifteenth Street. Reddy notices that traffic is not as heavy as usual today, at two-thirty in the afternoon. Taking his grandchildren's hands, he crosses Constitution Avenue and points to the car. They pull away from him and race each other to it.

I've got so much stuff to do in my spare time, I don't know where to start. I study electronics, trying to keep up with lasers, the latest in solid-state. For nine years I was merit badge counsellor with the Boy Scouts; I was treasurer of a Boy Scout council; I'd go to camp with them. Even after my son was finished with them and I figured the Boy Scouts were used as a baby-sitter, where other poppas wouldn't even join us when we needed them, I loaded my car with kids and took them to Camp Sheridan. I couldn't see personally injuring the poor kids because their fathers wouldn't come around. I've got out and sold doughnuts, three and four hundred dozen on a Saturday, in order that we could buy a bus for the troops. One time I engineered a whole deal with them and took a whole busload to the World's Fair in New York.

I don't read any fiction, but I do look at *Time* and I enjoy *National Geographic*—I read that from cover to cover. I'm usually glued to football during the season. And I'm a supervisor usher at RFK Stadium and get to go to every Redskin game free. Been doing that about ten years.

I like to fish, but right now I have to go way up to get away from the pollution. I've been going fishing ever since my dad showed me how when I was a kid. If I catch a couple of good fish to eat I'll take them, but if I get too many I'll put them back in the water again. I have my own motor at home and I rent a boat. I used to fish on the Chesapeake a lot, from way back; I knew the bay like a rockfish.

The children are waiting at the car. Sean has finished his popsicle, but Karen is out of breath from running and gives the rest of hers to Reddy. He buckles them in and, sucking orange ice, heads out New York Avenue toward home, as the children fall asleep in the back seat, all of them dreaming of past and future days in the sun.